Coevolutionary Pragmatism

The China-Africa economic tie has experienced lasting rapid growth since the 2000s, attracting lots of discussion on its nature and effects. A key question is whether Chinese engagements provide an alternative paradigm to existing mainstream models, such as Washington Consensus, for developing countries. However, theories on state–market dichotomy can hardly explain the strong momentum of bilateral cooperation. By examining a broad range of practices with solid field research, including trade, infrastructure, agriculture, manufacturing, industrial zones, labor, and socioenvironmental preservation, this book proposes a new angle of nonlinear circular causality to understand Chinese approaches to work with Africa. Guided by the pursuit for sustainable growth rather than by specific models, Chinese actors are able to experiment diverse methods to foster structural transformation in Africa. In particular, the author carefully records mutual influences between Chinese and African stakeholders at all levels, from grassroots to policymaking, to illustrate the effects of coevolving industrialization.

XIAOYANG TANG is an associate professor in the Department of International Relations at Tsinghua University and deputy director at the Carnegie-Tsinghua Center for Global Policy. His research interests include political philosophy, China's engagement in Africa, and the modernization process of the developing countries. He is the author of *China-Africa Economic Diplomacy* (2014 in Chinese) and has published extensively on Asia-Africa relations. He completed his PhD in the philosophy department at the New School for Social Research in New York. He also worked for the World Bank, USAID, IFPRI, and various research institutes and consulting companies.

Coevolutionary Pragmatism

Approaches and Impacts of China-Africa Economic Cooperation

XIAOYANG TANG
Tsinghua University, Beijing

CAMBRIDGE
UNIVERSITY PRESS

University Printing House, Cambridge CB2 8BS, United Kingdom

One Liberty Plaza, 20th Floor, New York, NY 10006, USA

477 Williamstown Road, Port Melbourne, VIC 3207, Australia

314-321, 3rd Floor, Plot 3, Splendor Forum, Jasola District Centre, New Delhi - 110025, India

103 Penang Road, #05-06/07, Visioncrest Commercial, Singapore 238467

Cambridge University Press is part of the University of Cambridge.

It furthers the University's mission by disseminating knowledge in the pursuit of education, learning and research at the highest international levels of excellence.

www.cambridge.org
Information on this title: www.cambridge.org/9781009257831
DOI: 10.1017/9781108233118

First published 2020
First paperback edition 2022

A catalogue record for this publication is available from the British Library

Library of Congress Cataloging in Publication data
Names: Tang, Xiaoyang, author.
Title: Coevolutionary pragmatism : approaches and impacts of China-Africa economic cooperation / Xiaoyang Tang, Tsinghua University, Beijing.
Description: Cambridge, United Kingdom ; New York, NY : Cambridge University Press, 2020. | Includes bibliographical references and index.
Identifiers: LCCN 2020026280 (print) | LCCN 2020026281 (ebook) | ISBN 9781108415293 (hardback) | ISBN 9781108233118 (ebook)
Subjects: LCSH: China – Foreign economic relations – Africa. | Africa – Foreign economic relations – China. | China – Commerce – Africa. | Africa – Commerce – China. | Economic development – Africa. | Economic development – China.
Classification: LCC HF1604.Z4 A3578 2020 (print) | LCC HF1604.Z4 (ebook) | DDC 337.5106–dc23
LC record available at https://lccn.loc.gov/2020026280
LC ebook record available at https://lccn.loc.gov/2020026281

ISBN 978-1-108-41529-3 Hardback
ISBN 978-1-009-25783-1 Paperback

For my parents

Contents

Figures

Tables

Preface

This book does not merely record China and Africa's economic cooperation, but also presents reflections on the dynamism of global development. These reflections are closely related to my personal experience of growth.

When I arrived in Africa for the first time in 2007, the continent reminded me of my childhood in Shanghai. Born in the mid-1970s, I witnessed the difficult times at the beginning of China's reform. We were a family of three squeezed in a room of less than eight square meters. There was no toilet, and no kitchen, either. We had to go downstairs to use the public toilet and families lit up smoke-filled coal stoves in the street. In the hot summer, my parents took turns fanning me and catching mosquitoes all night, just to let me have a good sleep. When it rained, large areas of the city were flooded and students would walk in the water to go to school, trousers rolled up to the thighs. Old-styled cars manufactured decades before and worn-out combo taxis were running on the roads. Hundreds of people lined around the bus stations during rush hours, anxiously waiting hours long for a bus to come, which, when it did, was always overloaded with passengers without even one inch to move. Children's clothes were changed only once a week, if not longer, and possessing no toys, they kicked stones or played around the sand piles. ...

All of these memories are reflected in today's Lagos, Nairobi, or Dar es Salaam! I often wonder whether foreign visitors in the early 1980s thought about China as we think about Africa now: poor, backward, dirty, bureaucratic, lazy, and so on. Compared with societies in advanced economies, they look like two different planets; the gap seems difficult to bridge over centuries. Just as the *Economist* magazine called Africa a "hopeless" continent at the beginning of this century, there were numerous people, both foreigners and Chinese, who just several decades ago considered China to have no hope.

This comparison between Africa's present and China's past underlies my research on China-Africa during these years. Why and how did China achieve its dramatic transformation, whereas Africa's economy stagnated for decades? Furthermore, how can Chinese engagements contribute to Africa's growth? These are common questions of researchers working on the China-Africa relationship. To answer these questions, I started to draft a book on Chinese and African economic diplomacy in Chinese as early as 2012, when I was still working in Washington, DC. However, during this process, I realized that these questions should be studied from broader perspectives.

First, development is a comprehensive sociocultural rather than an economic issue. The biggest challenge for development lies in divergence of values and goals of life. Africans do not understand why Chinese people are so pushy and obsessed with efficiency, a divergence popular views and some researchers attribute to cultural differences. However, I recall similar culturalist views in China in the 1980s and '90s, but the evaluation for the Chinese was exactly the opposite. At that time, Chinese people were depicted as unambitious, self-content, nepotistic, conservative, narrow-minded, idling around, and obsessed with ideology; by contrast, Westerners were regarded as pragmatic, efficient, disciplined, and hardworking. Countless media articles and social debates within China reflected on such sociocultural divergence and called for more pragmatism. Radical changes of thinking accompanied the economic development at the early stage of China's market reform. Unfortunately, the transition of intangible cultural values can be easily overshadowed by the demonstration of material gains. Moreover, the triumphing new values tend to consider traditional views as wrong or unreasonable, negating their values completely and burying them into oblivion. However, living through this transition, I clearly remember the rapid changes of zeitgeist in the socioeconomic transformation. Similar interchanges of cultural values can as well be seen in the ongoing China-Africa engagements.

Second, development consists of diverse practices and lives of ordinary people, not just clear-cut policymaking. Witnessing the whole process of China's market-oriented reform, I remember the turbulence and mundaneness of the changing period. There was much uncertainty and many disputes over every decision made. Back and forth movements were common, accompanied by pro- and counterarguments from various parts of Chinese society. Development is to move the entire society forward despite the numerous divergences. Every step is small, but full of sweat and thoughts. It's through the concrete efforts and interactions in everyday life that the country accumulates momentous transformation. Having experienced the details of this history, I don't see any miracle in China's development story, because each activity and exploration is so real and concrete. It is only when people neglect the innumerable tiny changes in life that they may be surprised by the accumulative achievement and call it a miracle. The daily activities and thinking are critical for people to understand how transformation really happens and functions. Hence, my research carefully chooses case studies and depicts details to illustrate concrete challenges and efforts in Africa's transformation and China-Africa interactions.

Finally, the key concern for development of a modern economy and industrialization is sustainability, which refers to continuous productivity growth, financial health, as well as social and environmental balance. The effects of sustainable growth must be examined in an extended time period, at least decades long. Therefore, the book does not aim to offer conclusive findings on this question; instead, I focus on shedding light on how Chinese and African stakeholders think about the sustainability issues and how they try to tackle the problems. In a history that is still ongoing, it is more helpful to understand what different people are deliberating and doing rather than to rush to make judgments on them. The researchers, readers, and practitioners are all parts of the living history of the world, facing the challenge of sustainable development as the biggest global challenge in our time. I hope that this book does not only represent an alternative view, but also serves as a bridge for various parts of the world to understand each other so that their efforts can converge toward the common goals.

In this context, I would like to thank the thousands of government officials, entrepreneurs, and professionals in both China and Africa who have been interviewed by me over the past decade. My interviews were additional work for them, but they often volunteered to provide help despite their busy schedules. In a few cases, interviewees answered my questions while handling their daily business. However, such conversations for several hours or even just several minutes were incredibly enlightening, from which I was able to learn about their experience and gain wisdom from their years or decades of practice. These interviews opened my eyes and were crucial to my research. It can be said that these practitioners are my real teachers for studying China-Africa ties.

Additionally, I would like to thank Professor Deborah Brautigam, whose rigorous research and fact-based findings on China-Africa relations have laid solid foundation for future research on this topic. Doing research with her has completely reshaped my academic career and, consequently, my life. Her insights and methodology helped me transform from a philosophy PhD to a researcher in development studies. I also sincerely appreciate her willingness to write the foreword for this book.

Discussions with other colleagues during the writing process of the book were also extremely valuable. I am especially grateful to the anonymous reviewers on the book proposal and manuscript. Their suggestions and comments greatly helped me refine my arguments and improve the structure. I also would like to thank Dr. Chris Harrison and Joe Ng from Cambridge University Press for supporting and encouraging me to complete this book.

Several sections in this book are taken from my book 中非经济外交及其对全球产业链的启示[*China-Africa Economic Diplomacy and Its Implication to Global Value Chain*], which was published in Beijing 2014. Cheryl Mei-ting Schmitz translated these sections from Chinese to English. Irene Sun Yuan, Janet Eom, Addison Yang, Victor Perez Garcia, Saeger Godson， Gloria Enrico, Hu Xiwen, Jack Jia Zetong, Xiong Xinghan, Tang Xiyuan, Xiao Qijia, and Yu Han helped me with related research work during the writing of this book. I would like to extend my gratitude to all of them.

Funding for related field research trips has been provided by German Boell Foundation, the Center for Economic Policy Research (CEPR) Private Enterprise Development in Low Income Countries (PEDL), the DFID-ESRC Growth Research Programme (DEGRP), China-Africa Joint Research Program, and Ministry of Education. The publication of this book is financed by Oxfam Hong Kong, but the views of this publication are mine and do not necessarily represent those of Oxfam Hong Kong.

Foreword

Deborah Brautigam
Bernard L. Schwartz Professor of International Political Economy and Director, China Africa Research Initiative, Johns Hopkins University, School of Advanced International Studies

China's recent engagement in Africa remains controversial, and much misunderstood. One partner is a large, densely populated country with an unprecedented recent experience of rapid agricultural and industrial development. The other, with its fifty-four countries ranging from the tiny to the immense, is a region where unprocessed raw material exports still dominate most economies. Yet these two vastly different areas were not so very different when the first post-Mao Chinese arrived to seek business opportunities in Africa, as China's doors to the world began to reopen in the early 1980s.

Structural transformation accelerated in modern China after 1978, when Chinese leaders forged an alchemy that mixed a developmental state in Beijing, an entrepreneurial population, and the power of markets. And then they began to experiment, carefully but steadily, "crossing the river by feeling the stones," as Deng Xiaoping famously said. Chinese leaders have cautioned for decades that African countries should not try to copy China's development experience but rather feel their way across their own rivers on their own stones. At best, China's structural transformation can provide opportunities and ideas for African journeys.

The Chinese government began financing projects in Africa in 1960. The first Chinese construction firms began competing for African contracts in 1979. Chinese firms started equity investments in the 1980s, just as I was beginning my own research on Chinese aid and investment in Africa. Finance, investment, and research have all accelerated over the past two decades.

In this remarkable, thought-provoking book, Tang Xiaoyang draws on academic training in business management and philosophy and more than a decade of field research in Africa and China. I first met Tang Xiaoyang at an April 2007 China-Africa conference in Washington, DC. He had traveled down from the New School in New York, where he was studying for a PhD. In English tinged with a slight German accent from his time at the University of Freiburg, he told me he was planning to do two months of fieldwork in Angola and the Democratic Republic of the Congo to study Chinese companies.

The field of China-Africa research was tiny at that time. Only a handful of scholars with Chinese language skills had done field research in Africa. We soon began collaborating on research. Over the next decade, Tang Xiaoyang and I traveled to China and to Africa on eight field visits and wrote a number of papers together. Separately, his own fieldwork has taken him to at least fifteen African countries, many for multiple visits. I learned a great deal from him and grew to trust him as a talented researcher and a friend. His research is both wide and deep, immersive, almost anthropological. He knows the challenges as well as opportunities Africans face with the acceleration of Chinese interest in their continent.

This book covers Chinese engagement across a number of sectors, from trade, to infrastructure, to special economic zones. It is replete with examples from the field that ground the analysis and make clear how China's development approach works in practice. Living in Beijing, active as a scholar and adviser, Tang Xiaoyang has an insider's knowledge of Chinese policymaking and the sometimes daunting trials Chinese firms face in Africa.

His book brings into focus just how different is the Chinese approach from that adopted by much of the West. Whereas the dominant Western view is confident that good governance (democracy, transparency) leads to sustainable economic growth, and indeed, may be a necessary prerequisite, the Chinese see development as structural transformation, with the modernization of agriculture and industry as the foundation. Whereas the West devises recipes and rules for how Africa should change, the Chinese tend to accept African countries, whether well- or ill-governed, as they are, and adapt their approach according to the local conditions. China's approach in Africa is governed by flexible pragmatism.

Tang Xiaoyang's book shows us how China-in-Africa is a learning process. There is no blueprint. A Chinese foreign-aided agricultural demonstration center in Malawi combines company business with aid to experiment with paths to financial sustainability. The company will train farmers, but also develop seeds and grow vegetables that can earn income for the center. A manufacturer who invested on the invitation of an Ethiopian prime minister ends up advising her host government on the practical policy changes that need to be taken to make her industrial investment profitable. A Ghanaian entrepreneur learns plastic recycling from a local Chinese factory, and then buys machinery from them to set up his own plastic recycling operation.

These stories and many more form the solid foundation of Tang Xiaoyang's argument. This book is destined to be a classic. It is thoughtful, thorough, and grounded in more than a decade's accumulation of evidence. We still have very much to learn about the realities of China's engagement, but there could be no better guide to these realities than Tang Xiaoyang.

Abbreviations

AGOA	African Growth and Opportunity Act
AQSIQ	China General Administration of Quality Supervision, Inspection and Quarantine
ATDCs	agricultural technology demonstration centers
BOT	build–operate–transfer
BRI	Belt and Road Initiative
CAADP	Comprehensive African Agricultural Development Program
CAC	China-Africa Cotton
CADF	China-Africa Development Fund
CCECC	China Civil Engineering Construction Corporation
CCP	Chinese Communist Party
CCTV	China Central Television
CEO	chief executive officer
CIFOR	Center for International Forest Research
CJIC	China Jiangxi International Economic and Technical Cooperation Co
CLETC	China Light Industrial Corporation for Foreign Economic and Technical Cooperation
CNMC	China Nonferrous Metal Mining Co.
CNPC	China National Petroleum Corporation
CSFAC	China State Farm Agribusiness Corporation
CSR	China South Railway/Corporate Social Responsibility
DFID	Department for International Development (UK)
DRC	Democratic Republic of Congo
EGP	Egyptian pound
EIA	environmental impact assessment
ENR	*Engineering-News Record*
EPC	engineering, procurement, and construction
EPZ	export processing zone

ETCZ	economic and trade cooperation zone
EU	European Union
EVA	ethylene vinyl acetate
FDA	Fundo Desenvolvemento Agricole
FDI	foreign direct investment
FOCAC	Forum on China-Africa Cooperation
FRELIMO	Frente de Libertação de Moçambique (Mozambique Liberation Front)
FTZ	free trade zone
GDP	gross domestic product
GMP	Good Manufacturing Practices
IDEA	Institute of Development and Education for Africa
IEA	International Energy Agency
IMF	International Monetary Fund
IPDC	Ethiopian Industrial Parks Development Corporation
LFTZ	Lekki Free Trade Zone
LIDI	Leather Industry Development Institute
MEP	Chinese Ministry of Environmental Protection
MFA	Multifiber Arrangement
MFEZ	Multifacility Economic Zone
MOFCOM	Chinese Ministry of Commerce
NEPZA	Nigeria Export Processing Zones Authority
NFCA	NFC Africa Mining Plc
NGOs	nongovernmental organizations
OECD	Organisation for Economic Co-operation and Development
PRC	People's Republic of China
RENAMO	Resistência Nacional Moçambicana (Mozambican National Resistance)
RMB	renminbi
SASAC	State-owned Assets Supervision and Administration Commission of the State Council
SEAs	social and environmental evaluations
SEZ	special economic zone
SFA	Chinese State Forestry Administration
SITEX	Benin Industrial and Textile Company
SME	small and medium enterprise
SOE	state-owned enterprises
TAZARA	Tanzania-Zambia Railway Authority

TEDA	Tianjin Economic and Technological Development Area
TICAD	Tokyo International Conference on African Development
Tsh	Tanzanian shilling
TUICO	Tanzania Union of Industrial and Commercial Workers
UNCTAD	United Nations Conference on Trade and Development
USD	US dollars
WC	Washington Consensus

1 A "Model" with No Model

1.1 The Driving Forces Behind China-Africa Engagement

Since the early 2000s Chinese engagement in Africa has attracted an increasing amount of global attention. In November 2006, representatives from 48 African countries, consisting of more than 1,500 businesspeople and 41 heads of state, attended the Forum on China-Africa Cooperation (FOCAC) Summit. For the first time, China demonstrated its impressive political influence over the entire continent.

In 2009, China surpassed the United States to become Africa's largest bilateral trading partner. Despite recent drops in the volume of Sino-African trade that followed the 2014 peak of $210 billion, China has remained the leading partner in Africa. Sino-African trade in 2018, for example, amounting to $204.19 billion, was worth more than Africa's trade with the United States, Japan, France, and the United Kingdom combined.[1] The strength of Sino-African trade is not an anomaly but rather the product of long-term trends. Between 2000 and 2014, Sino-African trade increased twentyfold. During the same period, China's outward foreign direct investment (FDI) stock in Africa also grew from a paltry $491.2 million in 2003 to approximately $43.30 billion in 2017.[2] These startling figures are only the conservative estimates. FDI that is channeled through offshore centers, for example, is not accounted for in these estimates, nor are African assets that are acquired by foreign-based Chinese firms.[3]

With Beijing's support, Chinese investment in Africa is only poised to grow. In his speech at the headquarters of the African Union in 2014,

[1] United Nations, Commodity Trade Statistics Database, 2017. https://comtrade.un.org/db/ (accessed October 28, 2019).

[2] National Bureau of Statistics of China, Annual Data, 2017. http://data.stats.gov.cn/ (accessed October 28, 2019).

[3] Mayer Brown, Playing the Long Game: China's Investment in Africa, *The Economist Intelligence Unit* (2014), p. 5. For example, Sinopec Group bought Swiss firm Addax Petroleum in 2009 and acquired Addax's assets in Africa.

for example, Chinese Premier Li Keqiang outlined Beijing's ambitions to expand Sino-African bilateral trade to $400 billion and Chinese FDI stock in Africa to $100 billion by the end of 2020. At the China-Africa Johannesburg Summit of 2015 and Beijing Summit of 2018, President Xi Jinping announced in total $120 billion in funding for the period 2016–2021 to support African development. Data from the *Engineering News-Record* (ENR), which analyzes the top 250 international contractors, show that Chinese contractors held a whopping 59.8 percent share of Africa's entire construction market in 2017.[4] From infrastructure construction to trade and investment, China is a prominent player across a multitude of sectors in Africa.

The strong momentum of Sino-African relationships eclipses the influence of other global powers in Africa. In response to these strengthening ties, the US Congress held two hearings, in 2011 and 2012, to evaluate the shifting power dynamics in Africa. Senators expressed strong concerns over China's rising economic and diplomatic profile in the region.[5] At his nomination hearing for secretary of state in 2013, John Kerry plainly articulated the root of American concerns: "China is all over Africa – I mean, all over Africa. And they're buying up long-term contracts on minerals, on ... you name it ..."[6] The American media has also become attuned to Washington's concerns over China's growing presence in Africa. CNN national security analyst Peter Bergan opened his remarks on President Obama's 2013 tour of Africa by saying, "There is a one-word subtext to President Obama's trip to Africa: China."[7] Likewise, during Japanese Prime Minister Shinzo Abe's week-long visit to Africa in 2014, a senior Japanese official was quoted stating: "Wherever he goes, Prime Minister Abe is asked if he is there to

4 Gary J. Tulacz and Peter Reina, The Top 250 International Contractors, *Engineering-News Record* (August 2018), 20.27, 42.

5 Hearing before the Subcommittee on Africa, Global Health, and Human Rights of the Committee on Foreign Affairs House of Representatives One Hundred Twelfth Congress, First Session, November 1, 2011, p. 3. Second Session, March 29, 2012 (Serial No. 112–138), p. 32.

6 UPI, Kerry: Relations with China critical, January 24, 2013. www.upi.com/Top_News/US/2013/01/24/Kerry-Relations-with-China-critical/66861359058003/ (accessed July 10, 2020).

7 Peter Bergen, Obama's goal in Africa: Counter China, June 26, 2013, edition.cnn.com/2013/06/26/opinion/bergen-obama-china-trip/ (accessed July 10, 2020).

compete against China."[8] The Trump administration's Africa strategy, released in December 2018, did not name the major African countries, such as Nigeria, Egypt, Ethiopia, or South Africa, at all, but mentioned China seventeen times, taking it as a primary rival to compete in the continent.

Many African leaders also expressed their appreciation of cooperation with China. Rwandan President Paul Kagame, for example, pointed to the unique strengths of Chinese engagements. He argued that while neither European nor American aid delivers sustainable development, Chinese assistance mainly promotes trade and investment, "bring[ing] greater opportunity for wealth creation in Africa."[9] Senegal's former president Abdoulaye Wade described Beijing's involvement in Africa as follows:

> [A]s I tell my friends in the West, China is doing a much better job than western capitalists of responding to market demands in Africa . . . . China's approach to our needs is simply better adapted than the slow and sometimes patronising post-colonial approach of European investors, donor organisations and non-governmental organisations. In fact, the Chinese model for stimulating rapid economic development has much to teach Africa . . . the Chinese are ready to take up the task, more rapidly and at less cost.[10]

His successor, President Macky Sall, had a similar view: "The cooperation with China is much more direct and faster than the cooperation we have with Western countries – the United States, European countries, and other bilateral donors. There are a lot of criteria on governance, on this and that, and a lot of procedures. That's one of the obstacles to effective cooperation: too many procedures . . . I'm not saying that what China is doing is better, but at least it's faster."[11]

The speed of growth of the Sino-African economic and diplomatic ties is indeed even more impressive than the scale of bilateral

[8] BBC News, Japan PM Shinzo Abe to pledge $14bn to Africa, January 9, 2014, www.bbc.com/news/world-africa-25668503 (accessed July 10, 2020).

[9] Paul Kagame, Why Africa Welcomes the Chinese, November 2, 2009. www.theguardian.com/commentisfree/2009/nov/02/aid-trade-rwanda-china-west (accessed July 10, 2020).

[10] Time for the West to Practise What It Preaches, *Financial Times*, January 23, 2008. www.ft.com/intl/cms/s/0/5d347f88-c897-11dc-94a6-0000779fd2ac.html#axzz45pKxcciP (accessed July 10, 2020).

[11] Macky Sall, Africa's Turn, *Foreign Affairs*, September/October 2013. www.foreignaffairs.com/discussions/interviews/africas-turn?page=show (accessed July 10, 2020).

cooperation. FOCAC received little African attention initially. Only four African presidents attended the inaugural FOCAC in 2000. At the time, Beijing was competing with established cooperation programs such as the Tokyo International Conference on African Development (TICAD), which was founded in 1993. Chinese firms held only 8 percent of the African construction market share in 2001 – one-third of French and one-fourth of US companies' holdings at that time; however, Chinese companies' market share became larger than all others combined fifteen years later.[12] How did China manage to achieve so much in such a short period of time? What does the development of this relationship mean for the African continent and the world?

Some researchers argue that Africa welcomes China as a business partner because it offers an alternative to the Western approach. Barry Sautman and Yan Hairong report: "For many Africans, then, there exists a 'Chinese model,' now often labeled the 'Beijing Consensus' . . . It is an image of a developing state that does not fully implement WC (Washington Consensus) prescriptions, does not impose onerous conditions on African states' policies, and is more active than the West in promoting industrialism in the global South."[13] Deborah Brautigam also argues that China is applying the successful experiences of its own development to Africa. This new approach helps China get results that differ from those achieved through Western initiatives.[14]

However, researchers have diverging views on what the exact nature of China's model is. The Chinese development model is often dubbed the Beijing Consensus, a term coined by Joshua Cooper Ramo in 2004, suggesting an alternative model vis-à-vis the Washington Consensus, which was summarized by economist John Williamson in 1989. Williamson listed ten policy reforms for economic development that had been agreed upon by neoliberal-minded policymakers in Washington. Among other measures the list included fiscal discipline; reordered public expenditure priorities; tax reform; privatization; as well as the liberalization of interest rates, exchange rates, trade, and

[12] Chuan Chen, Pi-Chu Chiu, Ryan J. Orr, and Andrea Goldstein, An Empirical Analysis of Chinese Construction Firms' Entry into Africa, in *The CRIOCM2007 International Symposium on Advancement of Construction Management and Real Estate*, Sydney, Australia, August 8–13, 2007.

[13] Barry Sautman and Yan Hairong, Friends and Interests: China's Distinctive Links with Africa, *African Studies Review* (2007) 50, 81.

[14] Deborah Brautigam, *The Dragon's Gift: The Real Story of China in Africa* (Oxford University Press, Oxford, 2009), pp. 311–312.

FDI. The Washington Consensus stresses the role of market forces, limits the government's intervention, and promotes economic liberalization.[15] Contrary to the market–government model central to the Washington Consensus, the Chinese state is an autonomous power that can intervene directly in the economic sphere.

These two sets of sociopolitical conditions have emerged as a central topic of debate between advocates of the Washington Consensus and those of the Chinese approach. In his book *The End of the Free Market*, US political scientist Ian Bremmer describes Chinese capitalism as an authoritarian tool utilized to control the country's economy: as the title of his book suggests, Bremmer considers the system that the Chinese government supports a threat to free market economies.

A number of authors echo this view. David Brooks compares democratic capitalism in the West with state capitalism in China and other emerging countries. Brooks argues that the former is a better system in political, social, and economic terms, whereas the latter only serves the interests of the ruling class and is characterized by cronyism. To Brooks, the state capitalism model's existence is justified only because societies in which it flourishes display low levels of trust, implying that state capitalism is an immature system relative to its open market counterpart.[16] By comparison, Western democratic capitalism is characterized by freedom, political equality, pluralistic democracy, and rule of law.[17]

Many criticize the Beijing Consensus and its sociopolitical effects on other countries. Pointing out China's support for authoritarian African governments, for example, Denis Tull writes, "China's economic impact may prove to be a mixed blessing, whereas the political consequences of its return are likely to prove deleterious."[18] Human Rights Watch likewise alleges that "China's policies have not only

15 John Williamson, A Short History of Washington Consensus, Paper commissioned by Fundación CIDOB (Centro de Pensamiento Global) for a Washington Consensus conference, p. 6.

16 David Brooks, The Larger Struggle, *New York Times* Op-Ed, June 15, 2010, A29. www.nytimes.com/2010/06/15/opinion/15brooks.html?_r=0 (accessed July 10, 2020).

17 Edward Younkins, The Conceptual Foundations of Democratic Capitalism, *The Social Critic*, Winter 1998. www.quebecoislibre.org/younkins16.htm (accessed July 10, 2020).

18 D. Tull, China's Engagement in Africa: Scope, Significance and Consequences, *Journal of Modern African Studies* (2006) 44, 460.

propped up some of the continent's worst human rights abusers, but also weakened the leverage of others trying to promote greater respect for human rights."[19] The Council on Foreign Relations finds that "most disturbing to U.S. political objectives is China's willingness … to protect some of Africa's most egregious regimes from international sanction," and goes on to say, "China's aid and investments … are attractive to Africans precisely because they come with no conditionality related to governance, fiscal probity, or the other concerns of Western donors."[20]

In turn, supporters of the Chinese model counter by accusing practitioners and proponents of the Washington Consensus of political dogmatism. Joshua Ramo calls the Washington Consensus "an economic theory made famous … for its prescriptive, Washington-knows-best approach to telling other nations how to run themselves," labeling it "a hallmark of end-of-history arrogance."[21] Justin Yifu Lin, former World Bank senior vice president and chief economist, points out that policies advocated under the Washington Consensus often fail to consider "the structural differences between developed and developing countries."[22] Mao Zengyu criticizes the Washington Consensus for "barbarian-like privatization," instead preferring the Beijing Consensus, which in contrast fosters market economies with gradualism and an emphasis on local knowledge.[23] Sharing this view, Chinese officials believe that political conditionality indeed affects economic development in other countries. China's deputy foreign minister Zhou Wenzhong has clearly articulated this view in past interviews, stating: "Business is business. [China tries]to separate politics from business … . [whereas the West tries] to impose … market economy[ies] and multiparty democracy[ies]

[19] Human Rights Watch, China-Africa Summit: Focus on Human Rights, Not Just Trade, November 2, 2006. www.hrw.org/news/2006/11/02/china-africa-summit-focus-human-rights-not-just-trade (accessed July 10, 2020).

[20] Council on Foreign Relations, More Than Humanitarianism: A Strategic U.S. Approach Toward Africa, Washington, DC, January 2006.

[21] Joshua Ramo, *Beijing Consensus* (London: Foreign Policy Centre, 2004), p. 4.

[22] Justin Yifu Lin, *New Structural Economics: A Framework for Rethinking Development and Policy* (Washington, DC: World Bank, 2012), p. 38.

[23] Mao Zengyu, *Stiglitz and Counter Economics – From Washington Consensus to Post-Washington Consensus to Beijing Consensus* (*Sidigelizi yu zhuangui jingjixue: cong Huashengdun gongshi dao hou Huashengdun gongsi zaidao Beijing gongshi*斯蒂格利茨与专柜经济学 – – 从华盛顿共识到后华盛顿共识再到北京共识) (Beijing: Economic Press China, 2005), p. 242.

on ... countries which are not ready for it. [China is] also against embargos, which you [the West] have tried to use against us."[24]

Chinese officials' and researchers' comments indicate that the antagonism between the proponents of the Washington Consensus and those of the Beijing Consensus is very different from the kinds of antagonism prevalent in the Cold War era. China and the West no longer disagree on the value of capitalist markets. To some extent, China attaches even more value to commerce and economic growth than Western countries do today. Obsessed with growth and development, China is often seen as a mainstay of developmentalism.[25] Therefore, China does not differ from the West in its goal of developing a market economy but rather in its approach to reaching that goal. The Washington Consensus and structural adjustment programs assign developing countries with restructuring of their sociopolitical systems. However, the diverse and complex sociopolitical conditions particular to each country render implementation of all the given prescriptions nearly impossible. By contrast, China was able to develop by promoting market economy and international trade while maintaining a sociopolitical system different from that of the West. China proves that a market economy can flourish without following the Washington model.

1.2 Lack of the Beijing Consensus

However, the tenets of the Beijing Consensus or Chinese model are contested; namely what kinds of alternative sociopolitical conditions are conducive to the development of a market economy? Joshua Ramo formulated three theorems to describe the Beijing Consensus: (1) commitment to innovation and constant experimentation; (2) stress on sustainability, equality, and chaos management; and (3) self-determination in financial and military affairs. He argues that these ideas are appealing to other developing countries that have been disappointed by the development models taught by developed countries.[26] Highly optimistic, Ramo's characterization has been criticized as idealistic and partial. Arif Dirlik calls Ramo's conception of the China

[24] Howard W. French, China in Africa: All Trade and No Political Baggage, *New York Times*, August 8, 2004.

[25] Arif Dirlik, Developmentalism, *Interventions: International Journal of Postcolonial Studies* (2014) 16.1, 32.

[26] Ramo, Beijing Consensus, pp. 11–12.

model "a 'Silicon Valley Model of Development' that has little to do with the national situations to which he would like to speak."[27] The process of development in China has involved substantial low-cost labor, pollution, social inequality, and foreign investment. Ramo's theorems appear to be utopian constructions that do not reflect realities on the ground.

Some scholars tend to consider the Beijing Consensus or Chinese Model as a new variety of the "developmental state," a model of industrialization defined and led by a strong and pro-development state. This model is closely related to the success of Japan, South Korea, Singapore, and Taiwan's systems. Because markets often fail in the late-developing countries, developmental states provide public goods to enterprises and citizens and incentivize growth in and protect certain industries and economic sectors.[28] The Chinese government has explicitly adopted some of the policies of its neighbors. Yet, remarkable divergences can be seen both between China and these countries and within China itself.

Scott Kennedy points out that the most competitive economic segment in China, the coastal private sector, actually grew out of a more liberal market system, with little governmental protection and interference. By contrast, sectors in which the Chinese government strives to form cartels or provide preferential policies, such as China's steel, telecom, and solar panel industries, either remain uncompetitive or have overcapacity problems. In general, China has been more open to FDI and imports than Japan and South Korea.[29] In addition, the role of the Chinese government has changed during different stages of China's development. During the early years of market reform, Chinese officials used informal and individualized channels to contact businessmen, often lacking the knowledge and capacity to regulate the economy effectively. Modern bureaucracies similar to those in China's East Asian neighbors did not develop in Chinese provinces until the 2010s and only then in economically advanced areas. However, bureaucratic

[27] Arif Dirlik, Beijing Consensus, Who Recognizes Whom and to What End? 2011, p. 2. www.chinaelections.org/uploadfile/200909/20090918025246335.pdf (accessed July 10, 2020).

[28] See Robert Wade, *Governing the Market: Economic Theory and the Role of Government in East Asian Industrialization* (Princeton, NJ: Princeton University Press, 1990), pp. 30–32.

[29] Scott Kennedy, The Myth of the Beijing Consensus, *Journal of Contemporary China* (2010), 19.65, 471.

improvements appear to be the result instead of the source of economic growth. Today, governments in China's so-called "backward" regions still struggle to appropriately manage their market activities and investment projects.[30]

Unlike the Chinese government's strong control and maintenance over the nation's political and social spheres, control over the economic sector is neither geographically homogeneous nor consistent. Similarly, Sino-African economic engagements also have a good mixture of state-led projects such as the large infrastructure deals and purely market-driven activities such as trade and manufacturing investment. In the purely market-driven sectors, the Chinese government often appears inept in influencing and managing projects. Therefore, the developmental state model cannot explain a large part of China's development success and its growing ties with Africa.

Another perspective to analyze the China Model lays emphasis on the meritocracy of selecting competent and entrepreneur-like technocrats to run the government. Daniel Bell and Eric Li both argue that because Chinese officials are evaluated according to their ability to promote economic growth, they can more effectively lead the country to achieve prosperity than those who are elected, as in Western democracies.[31] However, a growing number of scholars, including Nobel laureate Paul Krugman, criticize Chinese leaders for being incompetent in managing the economic downturn and financial turbulence of recent years.[32] Yuen Yuen Ang further points out that the same personnel system has quite divergent outcomes in different regions throughout China's reform period. While some localities, concentrated on the coast, grew rich and have good governance, others remained

30 Scott Kennedy, The Myth of the Beijing Consensus; Yuen Yuen Ang, *How China Escaped the Poverty Trap* (Ithaca, NY: Cornell University Press, 2016), pp. 8–14, 33–34.

31 Daniel A. Bell, *The China Model: Political Meritocracy and the Limits of Democracy* (Princeton, NJ: Princeton University Press, 2015); Eric Li, The Life of the Party: The Post-Democratic Future Begins in China, *Foreign Affairs* (2013) 92.1, 34–46.

32 Paul Krugman, China's Naked Emperors, *New York Times*, July 31, 2015. www.nytimes.com/2015/07/31/opinion/paul-krugman-chinas-naked-emperors.html (accessed January 17, 2019); Minxin Pei, Behind China's Woes, Myth of Competent Autocrats, *Nikkei Asian Review* (February 1, 2016). http://asia.nikkei.com/Viewpoints/Viewpoints/Behind-China-s-woes-myth-of-competent-autocrats (accessed January 15, 2019).

poor and predatory.[33] Consequently, personnel management can hardly explain China's success story.

A set of literature considers China's success story to be the result of the second-best strategy. Instead of completely following the recipes of the Washington Consensus and implementing shock therapy, the Chinese government adopted a gradualist reform strategy. First, Beijing encouraged farmers to produce market-oriented goods. Then, the Chinese Communist Party began allowing township-and-village enterprises, private enterprises, and joint ventures to expand their business territories. All the while, the government maintained dual-track pricing and hybrid property rights systems to avoid drastic socioeconomic disruption.[34] Scholars argue that incremental reform can use "second-best" institutions to stimulate markets in the beginning and eventually forge a mature market with best practice.[35]

However, this view implies that pragmatic reform is only a "transitional" step toward the ultimate destination of liberal market institutions. Reform has brought about tremendous pro-market changes in China. Not only has the private sector grown rapidly, but China has also joined the World Trade Organization and adopted numerous international standard business practices. Nonetheless, despite becoming the second largest economy in the world, China is still fundamentally different from the West regarding its economic system and engagement with other countries. China's incremental adjustments since 1978 do not look like transitional measures toward a clear destination, but rather like a routine mode of Chinese economy today.

To explain the need for constant change and experimentation, William Easterly distinguishes between two approaches to development: that of planners and that of searchers. Institutions affiliated with the Washington Consensus are said to primarily use planner approaches, setting lofty goals such as the elimination of poverty,

[33] Yuen Yuen Ang, *How China Escaped the Poverty Trap*, p. 7.

[34] Ronald Coase and Wang Ning, *How China Became Capitalist* (Houndmills, Basingstoke: Palgrave Macmillan, 2012); Justin Yifu Lin, Fang Cai, and Zhou Li, *The China Miracle: Development Strategy and Economic Reform*, rev. ed. (Hong Kong: Chinese University Press, 2003); Jean Oi and AndrewWalder, *Property Rights and Economic Reform in China* (Stanford, CA: Stanford University Press,1999).

[35] Dani Rodrik, Second-Best Institutions, *American Economic Review* (2008) 98:2, 100–104; Justin Yifu Lin, *New Structural Economics: A Framework for Rethinking Development*, p. 78.

designing aid agencies, and administrating plans and financial resources. At the opposite end of the spectrum, searchers look for practical opportunities and do not become fixated on unreachable objectives.[36] Easterly considers structural adjustment and shock therapy to be social engineering projects similar to economic planning in communist countries. By these definitions, China's gradualist, piecemeal reform approach can be seen as a successful example of the searcher model. Nevertheless, China continues making socialist-style five-year plans. Government-led initiatives such as "Going Global" ("走出去") and Belt and Road Initiative ("一带一路") have a large influence on the overseas operations of Chinese firms. Although China does not make policy prescriptions to African countries in the form of conditionalities, the Chinese government and state-owned enterprises have their own means of economic planning in domestic and overseas operations. The gradualist, piecemeal reforms in China coexist alongside the government's strategic planning and guidance. Strategic divisions between planner and searcher are not clear cut in the Chinese approach, but subtly intertwined.

Recently, Justin Yifu Lin has proposed that to understand the success of China's development and its engagements in Africa one must look toward New Structural Economics theory. Lin argues that China has correctly promoted structural transformation in industry according to the principle of comparative advantage.[37] Per David Ricardo's original theory, comparative advantages of different countries should be decided by the free market. However, Lin points out that there are "binding constraints" in the development process, such as information scarcity, infrastructure backwardness, and the unwillingness of enterprises to invest in an undeveloped market. This collection of binding constraints cripples the ability of market mechanisms to allocate resources efficiently in developing countries.[38] Government intervention is therefore necessary in order to realize latent comparative advantages in these countries. East Asian countries such as Japan, South

[36] William Easterly, *The White Man's Burden: Why the West's Efforts to Aid the Rest Have Done So Much Ill and So Little Good* (New York: Penguin, 2006), pp. 11–12.

[37] *China's Miracle: Development Strategy and Economic Reform* (*Zhongguo de qiji: fazhan zhanlve yu jingji gaige*中国的奇迹：发展战略与经济改革) (Shanghai: Shanghai People's Publishing Press, 1999), pp. 195–199.

[38] Justin Yifu Lin, *New Structural Economics: A Framework for Rethinking Development*, pp. 20–30.

Korea, and China each similarly leveraged their respective comparative advantages in labor-intensive sectors at different times. This phenomenon has been dubbed the "flying geese pattern." Lin, along with Wang Yan, argues that Chinese investments and commercial loans to Africa can help developing African nations overcome binding constraints to structural transformation, nurturing a new flock of flying geese.[39] Sino-African engagements, in line with China's own development path, are accelerating African structural transformation.

New Structural Economics offers a new angle to see the relationship between market and state. State efforts to "pick winners" by facilitating certain industries are justified, but the industries should be identified with economic analysis of each country's endowment structure.[40] This approach creates a dilemma. In proposing to follow each country's comparative advantage, it seeks to emphasize the role of the market. However, by calling for industrial policy to overcome market constraints, it seems to support government intervention in the market, in defiance of market logics. In Dani Rodrik's words, "Lin wants to argue both for and against comparative advantage at the same time."[41] Indeed, to resolve this paradox, Lin borrows the idea of dynamic comparative advantage. As pointed out in his book with Wang Yan, China tends to view its development model as a dynamic process, not a static framework.[42] Nonetheless, the distinction between static and dynamic (or latent) comparative advantages remains unclear. Rodrik views the difference between static and dynamic comparative advantage as whether the advantage is calculated according to today's prices or intertemporal relative prices. Dynamic comparative advantage is nothing more than the overall advantage across an extended period. Whether industrial policy defies static or dynamic advantages is a secondary question. Rodrik considers industrial policy as universally contradictory to

[39] Justin Yifu Lin and Wang Yan, *Going Beyond Aid: Development Cooperation for Structural Transformation* (Cambridge: Cambridge University Press, 2017), pp. 107–115.

[40] Justin Yifu Lin and Célestin Monga, Growth Identification and Facilitation, The Role of the State in the Dynamics of Structural Change, Policy Research Working Paper 5313, World Bank, May 2010.

[41] Dani Rodrik, Comments on "New Structural Economics" by Justin Lin, *The World Bank Research Observer* (2011) 26.2, 227–229, Oxford University Press on behalf of The World Bank.

[42] Lin and Wang, Going Beyond Aid, p. 107.

market economies.[43] Although Justin Lin meaningfully attempts to theoretically explain the mixture of government intervention and market economy, his argument is neither consistent nor satisfactory.

Remarkably, the Chinese government has kept a consistent stance of nongeneralization of China's development model. This position makes it even more difficult to define the China Model. As early as 1985, Deng Xiaoping told the then Ghanaian head of state Jerry Rawlings, "Please don't copy our model .... If there is any experience on our part, it is to formulate policies in light of one's own national conditions."[44] When the debate about the Beijing Consensus heated up in the mid-2000s, Chinese leaders reiterated the viewpoint that China does not have a general development model and does not recommend other countries to follow any models. For instance, Premier Wen Jiabao put it at the Fourth FOCAC in 2009, "(Chinese) support the African people in exploring development paths that suit their national conditions. We firmly believe that Africa is fully capable of solving its own problems in an African way."[45] Similarly, Xi Jinping stressed at several occasions that China's unique history and conditions decide a development path fitting only for itself and each country should choose its own path accordingly.[46] Since no universal principles are drawn from the development practices, China cannot provide any defined model to other countries like the Washington Consensus, but only individual experiences.

Thus, there is a puzzling gap between the conceptual elusiveness of the "China Model" and the factual effectiveness of China's development practices. China's phenomenal economic growth and its rapidly expanding influences in the developing regions such as Africa

43 Dani Rodrik, Comments, 2011.

44 中国网[China.com], "2005专题"[2005 Special coverage], September 18, 1985, www.china.com.cn/zhuanti2005/txt/2004-08/04/content_5627003.htm (accessed January 18, 2019).

45 Speech at the Opening Ceremony of the 4th Ministerial Conference of FOCAC, November 10, 2009. www.focac.org/eng/zywx_1/zyjh/t627391.htm (accessed January 18, 2019).

46 习近平在莫斯科国际关系学院的演讲, 2013/03/24[Xi Jinping's Speech at the Moscow Institute of International Relations] 新华网 [Xinhua], http://politics.people.com.cn/n/2013/0324/c1024-20892661.html (accessed January 18, 2019); 习近平出席中国共产党与世界政党高层对话会开幕式并发表主旨讲话 [Xi Jinping Attends the Opening Ceremony of the High-level Dialogue between the Chinese Communist Party and World Political Parties and Delivers a Keynote Speech], December 1, 2017; 新华社[Xinhua] www.gov.cn/xinwen/2017-12/01/content_5243832.htm (accessed January 18, 2019).

demonstrate the impressive achievements in practice. Despite easily identifying differences between Western and Chinese development approaches, researchers still encounter huge difficulties when attempting to precisely define the so-called Beijing Consensus. While previous debates focus mainly on China's domestic experience, I propose to examine China-Africa engagements in depth to understand the manners and impacts of the Chinese-style development. As noted, the economic ties between China and Africa have witnessed remarkable growth and impacted significantly the development process across the continent. The study of this relationship can thus shed light on what is effective in China's development approach. Meanwhile, the study is not limited to China itself, but observes the Chinese-style engagements in a broader context. Going beyond the specific experience and conditions of a country, the study aims to explore the general implication of China's development approaches, for African countries as well as for other developing countries.

1.3 Evolution of China-Africa Pragmatism

A number of researchers have offered their comments on the nature of the growing China-Africa ties. Yet, the views are so divergent that careful scrutinization is required. A popular view is that China utilizes Africa for resource extraction. For instance, Denis Tull states that "there is little doubt that natural resources are at the core of China's economic interests in Africa." He even suggests that resource acquisition may be China's "overall interest in the [African] continent."[47] Likewise, Chris Alden, Ian Taylor, Sanusha Naidu, and others all claim that interests involving oil and other natural resources dominate Sino-African relationships.[48]

However, this view is not empirically supported. Until 2011, for instance, more African oil was exported to the United States than to China. Following 2012, both China and the United States reduced

[47] Tull, Denis M., China's Engagement in Africa: Scope, Significance and Consequences, *The Journal of Modern African Studies* (2006), 44.3, 459–479.

[48] Chris Alden, *China in Africa* (London: Zed Books, 2007), pp. 11–15; Sanusha Naidu and Daisy Mbazima, China–African Relations: A New Impulse in a Changing Continental Landscape, *Futures* (2008) 40:8, 748–761; Ian Taylor, China's Oil Diplomacy in Africa, International Affairs (2006) 82:5, 937–959.

their crude oil imports from Africa.[49] According to the Carnegie Endowment for International Peace, extractive industries accounted for only about 29 percent of China's FDI to Africa in 2009, whereas that same year, about 60 percent of American FDI to Africa went to the mining sector.[50] Not only are Chinese natural resource investments in Africa no more significant than those of other major powers, but Beijing also has sizable investments elsewhere in the African economy. The Chinese government's 2013 white paper on Sino-African cooperation confirmed the broad spread of Chinese economic engagement across many economic sectors in Africa. As of 2011, finance, construction, manufacturing, service, trade, agriculture, and real estate accounted for nearly 70 percent of Chinese FDI in Africa. In addition, China offered large amounts of commercial loans and official assistance for African infrastructure, education, and healthcare-related projects.[51] Although natural resources obviously constitute a substantial part of the China-Africa economic ties, it is insufficient to attribute the growing engagements primarily to resource acquisition.

Another interpretation, as expressed by Naazneen Barma and Ely Ratner, posits that China seduces corrupt and illiberal governments in Africa "into its orbit." "Through a wide array of bilateral and multilateral arrangements, the Chinese government has begun to build an alternative international structure anchored by these illiberal norms. Nowhere is this trend more evident than Africa."[52] Peter Brookes and Ji Hye Shin bluntly pose the same argument, declaring that "China (PRC) aids and abets oppressive and destitute African dictatorships by legitimizing their misguided policies and praising their development models as suited to individual national conditions." They continue their argument by declaring that "China rewards its African friends with diplomatic attention and financial and military assistance, exacerbating existing forced

[49] UN Comtrade, by 2018.

[50] Keith Proctor, China and Africa: What the U.S. Doesn't Understand, Fortune, July 2, 2013. fortune.com/2013/07/02/china-and-africa-what-the-u-s-doesnt-understand/ (accessed July 11, 2020).

[51] Economic and Trade Cooperation Between China and Africa (2013), The Information Office of the State Council, August 29, 2013.

[52] Naazneen Barma and Ely Ratner, China's Illiberal Challenge. *Democracy: A Journal of Ideas* (Fall 2006) 2. democracyjournal.org/magazine/2/chinas-illiberal-challenge/ (accessed July 11, 2020).

dislocations of populations and abetting massive human rights abuses in troubled countries such as Sudan and Zimbabwe."[53]

These critical observations are untenable when we examine data and statistics. China's largest trade partners and investment destinations in the continent have a variety of sociopolitical systems. There are functioning democracies such as South Africa and Ghana, developmental states such as Ethiopia and Algeria, as well as fragile states such as Democratic Republic of Congo (DRC) and Zimbabwe. These countries also have different ranks in the "Ease of Doing Business" index of the World Bank (see Table 1.1), which measures regulation burden, business environment, and performance of bureaucracy. The result shows that China's comprehensive economic ties with Africa have little correlation with the political systems and cannot be explained by China's connections with a few authoritarian governments.

Proponents of Sino-African cooperation cannot provide satisfactory explanations for the extraordinary growth of this relationship either. Chinese scholars often emphasize that China's well-intentioned policies forge long-lasting friendships with African countries. For example, Li Anshan asserts that "the most important element in Sino-African relations" is "that the development of the relationship over the past 50 years has been based on 'equal treatment, respect for sovereignty and common development.'"[54] He Wenping pushes a comparable narrative, holding that "China's policies toward Africa have been unfailingly based on ... China's respect for African countries' sovereignty, territorial integrity and national dignity."[55] Views such as these sound more like political statements than critical analyses. Although China has maintained quite consistent political policies toward Africa for more than fifty years, the strong growth of bilateral ties is a rather recent phenomenon. The foregoing statements cannot explain why an old but lukewarm friendship suddenly turned into a dynamic comprehensive partnership.

[53] Peter Brookes and Ji Hye Shin, Backgrounder 1916, China's Influence in Africa: Implications for the United States, Washington, DC: Heritage Foundation, February 22, 2006. www.heritage.org/asia/report/chinas-influence-africa-implications-the-united-states (accessed July 11, 2020).

[54] Li Anshan, China and Africa: Policy and Challenges, *China Security* 3.3 (2007), 69–93.

[55] He Wenping, The Balancing Act of China's Africa Policy, *China Security* (2007) 3.3, 23–40.

Table 1.1a *China's top ten trade partners in Africa*

Country	Trade Volume (US$ million) 2017	Doing Business Rank 2018
South Africa	39,197.36	82
Angola	22,956.16	175
Nigeria	13,777.21	145
Egypt	10,827.58	128
Algeria	7,233.07	166
Ghana	6,677.74	120
Kenya	5,201.47	80
Congo Brazzaville	4,459.90	179
DRC	4,259.97	182
Zambia	3,832.22	85

Table 1.1b *China's top ten investment destinations in Africa*

Country	FDI Stock (US$ million) 2017	Doing Business Rank 2018
South Africa	7,472.77	82
DRC	3,884.11	182
Zambia	2,963.44	85
Nigeria	2,861.53	145
Angola	2,260.16	175
Ethiopia	1,975.56	161
Algeria	1,833.66	166
Zimbabwe	1,748.34	159
Ghana	1,575.36	120
Kenya	1,543.45	80

Source: China Statistics Year Book 2017; Doing Business Report 2018, World Bank

Li Anshan divides the development of the Sino-African relationship into three stages: a period of steady development (1956–1978), a period of transition (1978–1994), and a period of rapid growth (1995–the present). He accredits the rapid growth of bilateral ties over the past two decades to a weakening of socialist ideology on the Chinese side and an expansion of cooperation from mere aid to activities with mutual benefits, such as trade and investment.[56] Similarly, Chris Alden also noted that the desire to capture new markets drives the growth of Chinese businesses in Africa after Deng Xiaoping's reform.[57] While the policy changes did occur, they are not sufficient to elucidate the rapid expansion of Chinese engagement in Africa relative to that of other countries, especially those that have been active in doing business with Africa for far longer. As the second largest economy in the world, China has overwhelmed all other national economies in terms of trade and construction contracting in Africa. Chinese investment and influence in Africa have not only caught up with but have also begun to overshadow and surpass those of traditional Western powers.

Thus, it is necessary to examine the characteristics of the changing China-Africa relationship to reveal its unique dynamism. Just after the founding of the People's Republic of China in 1949, Chinese foreign policy toward Africa focused on supporting socialist movements in the struggle against imperialist hegemony. Premier Zhou Enlai visited ten African countries between 1963 and 1964 and announced five principles to guide China's relations with African and Arab countries, the first being that "China supports the African and Arab peoples in their struggle to oppose imperialism and old and new colonialism and to win and safeguard national independence." Premier Zhou also made a diagnosis that resonated with African audiences, saying that "[r]evolutionary prospects are excellent throughout the African continent."[58] Because of ideological opposition to colonialism, before the 1970s, China particularly supported African partners that had communist or socialist inclinations, such as in Guinea, Ghana, Mali, Tanzania, and Zambia.

Ideological enthusiasm metamorphosed into economic pragmatism following China's market reform in 1978. Four years after China's economic reforms began, from late 1982 to early 1983, then Chinese premier Zhao Ziyang visited eleven African countries. A notable outcome from this tour was the announcement of new guidelines for

[56] Li Anshan (李安山), The Origin of China-Africa Cooperation Forum and Thoughts on China-Africa Strategy (*Lun Zhongfei hezuo luntan de qiyuan: jiantan dui Zhongguo Feizhou zhanlve de sikao*论中非合作论坛的起源 -- 兼谈对中国非洲战略的思考, 外交评论 [*Foreign Affairs Review*] (2012) 第3期, 16.

[57] Chris Alden, China in Africa, p. 37ff.

[58] Philip Snow, *The Star Raft: China's Encounter with Africa* (New York: Weidenfeld & Nicolson, 1988), pp. 75–76.

bilateral cooperation; documented as the Four Principles of Economic and Technological Cooperation. These new principles did not replace previous ones, but instead supplemented them. Previous stances such as the Eight Principles for Economic Aid and Technical Assistance to Other Countries and the Five Principles Guiding China's Relations with African and Arab countries continued to shape China's interactions with the world. Beijing insisted on the friendship and nonconditionality principle and continued to provide foreign aid to Africa after the 1980s. The new principles built upon this relationship, adding new dimensions and cooperative avenues. The changes are summarized in the following principle:

> China's economic and technological cooperation with African countries takes a variety of forms suited to the specific conditions, such as offering technical services, training technical and management personnel, engaging in scientific and technological exchanges, undertaking construction projects, entering into cooperative production and joint ventures ...[59]

The forms of cooperation listed above illustrate China's first attempts to work with Africa beyond political alliances and aid. Subsequently, China expanded economic cooperation with the continent in the following manners. First, Beijing shifts gradually from foreign aid in the strict sense to business cooperation.[60] A significant number of previous aid projects were salvaged or rejuvenated through commercial restructuring. For example, in 1984, Mali requested that China provide further assistance for a pharmaceutical factory and a leather factory, both of which were Chinese aid projects that had fallen into operational difficulties. Dozens of Chinese experts were sent to help manage and restructure the businesses. Mali paid their salaries and living costs, as they were not aid workers but employed professionals. This employment model secured the timely use of China's managerial and technical workforce. Both factories turned a profit within three years and attracted a considerable amount of foreign exchange for Mali. The case, called a "second kind of aid," was acknowledged by then Malian president Moussa Traoré, as a successful example of reform among state enterprises.[61]

[59] Four Principles of Economic and Technological Cooperation 1983, number 3.
[60] Foreign aid by the definition of OECD DAC.
[61] Kong Weishi (孔维实), The Practice of Economic and Trade Integration in Mali (*Jingmao jiehe zai Mali de shijian*经贸结合在马里的实践), *Journal of International Economic Cooperation* (1996) 5, 23–24.

After engaging in management cooperation on several projects, including textile mills, sugar factories, and tea farms, Chinese firms took a step further. In 1996, two former Chinese aid projects – a sugar plantation and a refinery – became a joint venture between Sinolight Co. (a 60 percent stake) and the Malian government (a 40 percent stake) called the Sukula Sugar Complex.[62] Both China and Mali benefited from this partnership. According to a statement by Sinolight Co., "The Chinese partner had obtained lucrative profit from the Malian sugar complex" by 2008. For the Malian government, the sugar complex purchased local supplies worth $6 million and hired about 10,000 seasonal workers every year. It was also the third largest taxpayer in the country, generating tax revenue and dividends of about $6 million annually.[63] Because both partners were satisfied with the results of cooperation, a new, larger joint venture sugar complex was built in 2009. Some other notable instances of Chinese aid projects being converted into joint ventures include Urafiki Textile (Tanzania), Mulungushi Texile (Zambia), Lokossa Textile (Benin), and Anie Sugar (Togo).

Second, China is constantly adjusting its cooperation manners through trial-and-error experiments. For instance, although some of the joint venture projects have been successful, other projects have failed or experienced significant setbacks. The Urafiki Textile Mill in Tanzania and the Mulungushi Textile Mill in Zambia both started as aid projects from the Chinese government. Facing operational difficulties in the late 1990s, these textile mills were converted into joint ventures with Chinese companies. However, after a short revival, Chinese managers soon found that the local sociopolitical structure did not allow them to fully implement their market-oriented plans. Political considerations and a cultural gap added too much complexity to the entrepreneurial operation. Mulungushi stopped operating nine years after the formation of joint venture and Urafiki continues to struggle for survival. Nonetheless, China found new paths to work in

[62] Mali Kara Sugar Union plans to build a third sugar factory (*Mali shangkala tanglian jiang jian disan tangchang*马里上卡拉糖联将建第三糖厂), Bureau du Conseiller Economique et Commercial de L'Ambassade de la Republique Populaire de Chine en Republique du Mali, March 19, 2006. ml.mofcom.gov.cn/aarticle/jmxw/200603/20060301709328.html (accessed July 11, 2020).

[63] Sugar Union Affairs Department, CLETC （糖联事务部, 中国轻工业对外经济技术合作公司), 2008. www.cletc.com/364-908-10270.aspx (accessed May 20, 2012).

both countries with the experiences of Mulungushi and Urafiki. A former Chinese employee of Mulungushi, for example, set up a ginnery called China-Africa Cotton, which with the investment of the China-Africa Development Fund, has become a major player in southern Africa's cotton sector. China-Africa Cotton also partnered with Tianjin Tianfang Investment to establish a new textile mill in Malawi in 2018. Similarly, Chinese investors were not deterred from implementing this new approach in Tanzania due to the failure of the Urafiki project. Instead, two large private enterprises invested in Tanzania's cotton and textile sectors by using market information and logistical support from Urafiki in their preparation phase.[64]

Third, Chinese business collaborations with Africa borrow many practices from China's own market reform and opening. One example of this is the resource-for-project deal. At the beginning of China's market reform, Beijing agreed to send $10 billion worth of oil and coal exports to Japan between 1978 and 1985. In exchange, China could purchase an equivalent amount of technology, equipment, and construction machinery. Since China did not have sufficient foreign exchange reserves to pay in advance of the oil sales, Japan allowed China to acquire the desperately needed equipment first and pay with oil and coal revenue later.[65] China quickly applied similar practices to its relations with African countries. When Chinese companies carried out technological cooperation with Mali and Tanzania, they sent spare parts and production equipment there first, but also asked for leather, cashew, and other products for repayment.[66]

Over time, this style of business arrangement would evolve into resource-financed infrastructure deals between China and Africa. In 2004, the China Exim Bank signed an agreement with Angola to provide a loan of $2 billion. It was a commercial loan with a preferential interest rate and a long repayment period. The repayment of the loan was secured with revenue from Angola's oil exports. It was

[64] Tang Xiaoyang, Investissements chinois dans l'industrie textile tanzanienne et zambienne. De l'aide au marché (From Aid to Market: Transformation of Chinese Textile Investments in Zambia and Tanzania) *Afrique contemporaine* (2014) 2.250, pp. 119–132. DOI: 10.3917/afco.250.0119.

[65] China and Japan Long-Term Trade Agreement (*Zhongguo he Riben changqi maoyi xieyi*中国和日本长期贸易协议), February 16, 1978. China's foreign exchange reserves in 1978 totaled a mere US$167 million.

[66] Deborah Brautigam, The Dragon's Gift: The Real Story of China in Africa (Oxford: Oxford University Press, 2009), pp. 55–56.

used to finance as many as 107 infrastructure projects, ranging from hospitals and schools to roads and power transmission infrastructure.[67] This deal was a huge success for both China and Angola. On one hand, the deal allowed China to increase oil imports from Angola to meet its own voracious energy demands. On the other hand, Angola received the infrastructure necessary for a rapid national reconstruction following its decades-long civil war. Because this kind of loan arrangement was commercially profitable and politically beneficial for both sides, China Exim Bank later named it *huhui daikuan* (互惠贷款mutual benefit loan). This represents a type of loan in which commercial lending is secured by endowments of natural resources and used to finance a set of infrastructure projects and equipment purchases from Chinese firms. The China Exim Bank signed *huhui* loan agreements with Angola, Sudan, Equatorial Guinea, Congo Brazzaville, and Ethiopia between 2004 and 2014. The total sum of these loans exceeded $10 billion.

Fourth, Chinese government and enterprises utilize experiential learning to make flexible adjustment to diverse contexts. Following no universal rules or fixed models, Chinese players strive to make projects feasible through case-by-case learning and discussion. *Huhui daikuan* terms and conditions, for example, are not uniform, but often change to accommodate the needs of China and her partner countries. Ethiopia does not produce oil and is usually not considered for resource-backed lending by international banks. Yet, China Eximbank signed a loan agreement in 2006 to allow Ethiopia to use all its exports, mainly sesame, as collateral to secure a loan of $500 million. The loan was mainly spent on improving the country's power transmission network. The then vice president of the Commercial Bank of Ethiopia, Mohammed Nuredin, noted the unprecedented nature of a resource-backed loan for Ethiopia. In his opinion, it established a good mechanism, claiming that resource-backed lending "facilitate[s] [Ethiopian] exports to China," which would be "both [mutually] profitable and good for development."[68]

The DRC also intended to use resource-backed loans to finance its postwar reconstruction, but unfortunately the production level of

[67] Linha de credito com o Eximbank da China, Relatorio II Trimestre de 2008, Ministry of Finance Angola, June 30, 2008.

[68] Mohammed Nuredin, vice president of Commercial Bank Ethiopia, Addis Ababa, November 14, 2011.

Gecamines, its state-owned mining enterprise, was too low to provide sufficient collateral. Instead, China Exim Bank brought in two enterprises, the China Railway Group and Sinohydro, to set up a joint venture with Gecamines to extract and sell copper and cobalt from the still undeveloped Kolwezi region. The income from this mining joint venture would then be used to repay the Chinese infrastructure loan. The deal was signed in 2008 and, by early 2012; approximately $1 billion of the loan had already been utilized to fund mining projects and infrastructure facilities, such as municipal roads and bridges.[69] In the DRC's case, a pragmatic revision of the original loan deal had been made to allow underground resources to take the place of production resources as loan collateral.

1.4 Pragmatism in Structural Transformation

The four characteristics described in Section 1.3 demonstrate a very pragmatic style of facilitating changes and flexible adaptation. Indeed, researchers such as Deborah Brautigam, David Shinn, and Joshua Eisenmann noted that the spirit of pragmatism can be found in numerous Chinese engagements in Africa during past three decades.[70] Faten Aggad-Clerx as well considered pragmatism to be the main characteristic of the China-Africa relationship today.[71] Official statements, along with politicians' comments, confirmed the significance of pragmatism in this bilateral relationship too. Chinese and African governments hailed FOCAC as a platform for "an effective mechanism for pragmatic cooperation."[72] The FOCAC Johannesburg Action Plan (2016–2018) aimed at promoting and strengthening "practical cooperation" between China and Africa in terms of politics, economy, social development, and culture.[73] South

69 Johanna Jansson, China-DRC Sicomines Deal Back on Track, *The Africa Report*, August 4, 2014. www.theafricareport.com/Central-Africa/chinadrc-sicomines-deal-back-on-track.html (accessed July 11, 2020).

70 Dragon's Gift, p. 62, China and Africa: A Century of Engagement, p. 6.

71 Faten Aggad-Clerx, Africa and China: It's All About Pragmatism Silly!, Marc h 27, 2013, ecdpm.org/talking-points/africa-and-china-its-all-about-pragmatism-silly/ (accessed July 11, 2020).

72 Declaration of the Beijing Summit of the Forum on China-Africa Cooperation 2006; Beijing Declaration of the Fifth Ministerial Conference of the Forum on China-Africa Cooperation 2012.

73 The Forum on China-Africa Cooperation Johannesburg Action Plan 2015.

Africa's State Enterprises Minister Malusi Gigaba explicitly stated that "Chinese pragmatism has certainly enabled broader infrastructure and investment in a range of African countries."[74]

However, an emphasis on practical effects is not a policy option employed exclusively by China, but a guideline frequently opted for in international politics. In questions of foreign intervention, global governance, transnational institutions and diplomacy, Western countries often focus on solutions to particular problems without appealing to grand theories or universal ideals.[75] In the field of international development, agencies, such as the World Bank or UK's Department for International Development (DFID), also frequently adopt a pragmatic strategy to boost economic growth and raise per capita income in African countries.[76] What is unique for Chinese pragmatism vis-à-vis the pragmatism of other countries?

As discussed in Sections 1.2 and 1.3, Chinese development practices do not appear to have well-defined models or to be guided by specific principles. This is the main reason that has led many to label China's engagement as being pragmatic, since the Chinese appear to focus solely on making individual commercial deals and projects feasible and successful. By comparison, Western development agencies may have pragmatic attitudes when they implement projects, but these projects are designed under certain frameworks such as the Washington Consensus or foreign aid policy. Pure case-by-case pragmatism is usually criticized for lacking coherent principles. Yet, the Chinese practices at home and in Africa show that the development generated by this "pure" pragmatism can sustain and expand for decades. The effects of these seemingly scattered and incremental

[74] See Kenneth Kidd, "China and South Africa: An alliance of 'pragmatism'", November 12, 2011. www.thestar.com/news/world/2011/11/12/china_and_south_africa_an_alliance_of_pragmatism.html (accessed July 11, 2020).

[75] See Pragmatism in International Relations Theory. *Millennium: Journal of International Studies* 200231.3. www.lse.ac.uk/internationalRelations/Journals/millenn/abstracts/31-3.aspx (accessed July 11, 2020).

[76] Francis Owusu, Pragmatism and the Gradual Shift from Dependency to Neoliberalism: The World Bank, African Leaders and Development Policy in Africa, *World Development* (October 2003) 31.10, 1655–1672; Duncan Green, Politics, Economists and the Dangers of Pragmatism: Reflections on DFID's Governance and Conflict Conference, 2014, blogs.worldbank.org/publicsphere/politics-economists-and-dangers-pragmatism-reflections-dfids-governance-and-conflict-conference (accessed April 5, 2018).

activities are more consistent and remarkable than those with a clearly defined ideology. What is the reason for this puzzling contrast? [77]

In this context, we need to trace the origin of Chinese pragmatism in contemporary times. Two famous quotes from the architect of the post-1978 reform, Deng Xiaoping, shed light on the essence of Chinese pragmatism. The first states, "It doesn't matter whether the cat is black or white, as long as it catches mice" ("不管白猫黑猫，捉到老鼠就是好猫"). It was originally used in Deng's speech at the Communist Youth League conference of July 1962 and emphasized that increased productivity was the ultimate goal and criterion of social development.

> What form of mode of production is exactly the best one? Perhaps we should take such an attitude, namely what form can relatively easily and quickly recover and develop agricultural production in a place, this form should be adopted; the people are willing to use what form, this form should be used, if it is not lawful, we can make it legitimate.... Comrade Liu [Deng's colleague and friend] often says a Sichuan idiom: 'Yellow cat, black cat, as long as it catches mice, it is a good cat.' He said that about fighting.... Now when we want to restore agricultural production, it also depends on the circumstances. We cannot completely take a fixed form of the mode of production. Let's see what form can mobilize the enthusiasm of the people, then we use that form.[78]

Deng's original quote made one thing clear: he did not have a definitive plan to improve production, but rather preferred adjusting the current plan based on feedback. This quote is often used interchangeably with another, "cross the river by feeling the stones" ("摸着石头过河"). "Feeling the stones" refers to trial-and-error experiments as well as case-by-case solutions. Failed experiments are to be studied and revised to further align with the concrete, situational reality. In the end, the goal can be achieved only through incremental steps. This attitude also implies openness to various kinds of tools so long as they help to achieve economic growth.[79]

[77] The following analysis on the role of pragmatism in structural transformation can also be extended to the relationship between China and other developing countries. Please see Tang Xiaoyang (2020): Co-evolutionary Pragmatism: Re-examine "China Model" and Its Impact on Developing Countries, Journal of Contemporary China, DOI: 10.1080/10670564.2020.1744381.

[78] How to Restore Agricultural Production (*Zenyang huifu nongye shengchan*怎样恢复农业生产), Selected Work from Deng Xiaoping, Volume 1, July 7, 1962.

[79] Joseph Stiglitz, Globalization and Its Discontents (New York: Norton, 2002), p. 184.

These two interrelated quotes suggest that Chinese pragmatism of the reform is not completely void of principles. "Catching mice" and "crossing the river" indicate the unambiguous goal of development and growth. Pragmatism simply leaves the path to this destination wide open and relies on individual experiments and diverse activities. By comparison, the Washington Consensus and other development policies lay emphasis on defining the path, in addition to the goal, of development. On understanding Chinese pragmatism as such, we can also explain why all previous efforts to define the Beijing Consensus or China Model have failed, because the essence of China's development experience is indeed to reject consensus or models for a development path.

However, this explanation certainly raises as many questions as it answers: Can people reap transformation and growth by simply setting a goal for development? How can development work without clear plans for action? Why are all development models, not just some of the failed ones, ineffective? Finally, how can this explanation account for those models that functioned successfully in certain countries and periods, such as institutional reform and developmental states?

Before providing a systematic explanation of the dynamics of Chinese pragmatism, I would like to first address these questions and clarify the argument. (1) The rejection of a defined path does not mean only setting a goal, but stresses the stimulation of numerous experiments and transformations toward the unchanging goal of productivity growth. (2) Good plans are of course needed for each experiment but in the case of China, the experiments are so diverse and dynamic that they go far beyond any predesigned master plan. Meanwhile, the Chinese are open to unconventional attempts as long as they contribute to the goal of productivity growth. (3) Chinese pragmatism does not deny the value of good development experiences. The Chinese have indeed studied many useful socioeconomic models from the advanced economies and their developing neighbors. The China-Africa cooperation also borrows experiences from China's own development. Yet, China refuses to stick to any specific models, as doing so would constrain the possibility of experiments and transformations based on situational needs. (4) Likewise, development models are not universally applicable. The World Bank admitted in a 2005 report that "there are no best practice policies that will always yield the same positive result – there is no unique way to succeed."[80] This view echoes what Deng Xiaoping said in 1985 in a meeting with the Ghanaian delegation, "Please don't copy our model …. If there is any experience on our part, it is to formulate policies in light of one's own national conditions."[81] For him, there is no one path that will guarantee successful development. The so-called successful models are just achievements of others, and so their validity cannot be guaranteed elsewhere.

That being said, we need to investigate *why the goal of productivity growth matters* and *why many diverse experiments and incremental changes are required to reach this goal.*

The first question may seem banal at first glance. In today's world, almost every country sets growth of productivity as its goal. However, such a common pursuit for productivity growth is just a recent phenomenon, and even now not all countries can effectively mobilize their people to strive for this goal in their daily practices. In the 1960s and early 1970s, Deng's view on "catching mice" was severely criticized by Mao Zedong, who believed that class struggle and pursuit of communist ideology should be the country's top priorities, whereas productivity growth was just a means to support the political agenda of the Chinese Communist Party. Similarly, a number of African countries placed political goals before economic growth in their agenda, particularly during the Cold War era. This order of priorities in China reversed after Deng launched the market reforms. Economic development has since become the central task of the Communist Party, which believes that its political power ought to be used to achieve this goal.[82]

There are also many social and cultural values hindering the prioritization of productivity growth. Confucianism has had a strong tendency to disregard the pursuit of economic and material gain. The Confucian classic text *Great Learning* (大学) taught that "a state does not take material gain as its interest, but takes righteousness as its interest" ("国不以利为利，以义为利也") and "Virtue is the root, and wealth is the end of the branch." ("德者，本也；财者，末也")

80 World Bank, *Economic Growth in the 1990s: Learning from a Decade of Reform* (Washington, DC: World Bank, 2005), p. 80.

81 September 18, 1985. www.china.com.cn/zhuanti2005/txt/2004-08/04/content_5627003.htm (accessed January 18, 2019).

82 1987: One central task and two basic points, www.china.org.cn/features/60years/2009-09/16/content_18535066.htm, China.org.cn. September 16, 2009 (accessed July 11, 2020).

Taoism expressed similar disdain toward economic and material pursuits, instead placing emphasis on spiritual life. It described an ideal state as follows: "Though they had boats and carriages, they should have no occasion to ride in them...They should think their (coarse) food sweet, their (plain) clothes beautiful, their (poor) dwellings places of rest, and their common (simple) ways sources of enjoyment." ("虽有舟舆，无所乘之 ... 甘其食，美其服，安其居，乐其俗。" *Tao Te Ching* Section 80.) The ideal Taoist state is a state of self-sufficiency and self-contentedness, which rejects any temptations and demands of unnecessary material enjoyment.

It is, in fact, a common phenomenon of traditional cultures of the world to stress spiritual and ethical values over material wealth. The Qur'an explicitly calls wealth and property (ghina) as the source of man's rebellion against God. [83] Swahili proverbs in East Africa as well say that wisdom and charity transcend wealth. (Akili yatpita mali or Hisani ni bora zaidi ya mali) Pre-modern European society attached little importance to the wealth accumulation either. For instance, when St. Thomas Aquinas discussed the fulfilment of a human being's perfection, he quickly rejected the attainment of wealth and concluded that "perfect happiness can consist in nothing else than the vision of the Divine Essence."[84] For him as well as for ancient Greek thinkers, a society should primarily be concerned with justice, and in the case of individuals, with their virtues. Unlimited accumulation of wealth was considered the cause of injustice that ought to be reined in.[85] Viewing material wealth as an insignificant target in the life, traditional societies put little effort to elevate productivity as well. According to the estimates by economists such as Agnus Maddison, Elio Lo Cascio, and Paolo Malanima, the level of per capita output in the world did not see any real long-term progress until the sixteenth century.[86]

[83] The Qur'an96:6,7. See Murtadha Mutahhari, "Islam and Historical Materialism," www.al-islam.org/society-and-history-ayatullah-murtadha-mutahhari/islam-and-historical-materialism (accessed July 11, 2020).

[84] St. Thomas Aquinas, Summa Theologica trans. Fathers of the English Dominican Province (New York: Christian Classics, 1948), p. 802.

[85] Tang Xiaoyang, Political Duty, 2011, pp. 20–21; Michael J. Hagan, St. Thomas Aquinas: Economics of the Just Society, Austrian Student Scholars Conference, 2012, pp. 8–9.

[86] Angus Maddison, *The World Economy: A Millennial Perspective* (Paris: OECD, 2001); Elio Lo Cascio and Paolo Malanima, GDP in Pre-Modern Agrarian

Only in the modern era has the constant pursuit of gaining higher value, both in terms of societies as well as individuals, been popularized and legitimized. This is closely related to the rise of capitalism. To be sure, there are numerous definitions of capitalism. What I mean by capitalism refers to the intrinsic nature of capital, which is the money (M) invested into commodities (C) for the purpose of generating more money (M'), namely M-C-M', as Karl Marx illustrated.[87] In a precapitalistic society, trade usually took place when there were concrete needs for exchange, namely C-M-C. Exchanges occurred as different commodities were exchanged for their concrete utility. By comparison, capitalistic exchange is driven by the desire to increase abstract exchange value, which does not see a natural end like concrete utility. Accordingly, the essence of capitalism is the endless pursuit of surplus value M-C-M' -C-M"-C-M'"- …

The endless pursuit of value increase consequently stimulates constant productivity growth. With the ever-growing productivity, capitalism has gradually expanded across the world, forcing countries, capitalist or noncapitalist, to attach importance to productivity growth. Those that neglect productivity growth, because of political ideology or cultural values, face being overwhelmed by other advanced economic and technological powers. China used to rigidly resist the ideas and influences of capitalism in the modern time. In the late Qing dynasty, the government and society put more emphasis on preserving the indigenous old traditions rather than pursuing economic growth. In the Republic period (1911–1949), frequent wars distracted people from focusing on production and development. In the pre-1978 socialist period, the dominating ideology of class struggle put productivity growth only on a secondary role. When the Chinese society finally prioritizes productivity growth and economic development, it signifies a fundamental shift to accept the goal of capitalism.[88] As Figure 1.1 illustrates, the productivity growth rates before 1978 were not merely low, but also violently fluctuating. After 1978, especially after 1992,

Economies (1–1820 AD): A Revision of the Estimates, *Rivista di storia economica* (2009) 25.3, 391–420.

87 Karl Marx, The Capital, chapter 4.

88 Although other forms of societies, for example the former USSR, may also stress productivity growth sometimes, they only consider the growth as one of their targets, along with other political and cultural goals. By contrast, capitalism takes constant value increase and productivity growth as the primary goal, because the pursuit is the nature of capital by definition.

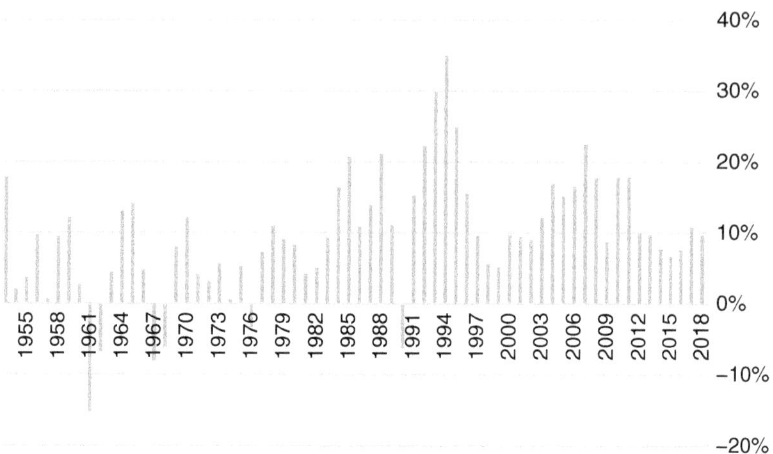

Figure 1.1 Annual growth rate of labor productivity in China, 1953–2018. (Labor productivity is measured by GDP per labor annually.)
Source: China Statistics Year Book

the consensus on promoting economy and the corresponding reform led to continuous productivity growth.

It is an enormous challenge to achieve sustainable productivity growth, because it requires comprehensive changes to the socioeconomic relationship. In the eighteenth century, the division of labor was broadly identified as the cause of "the greatest [improvement for] the productive powers."[89] Adam Smith's famous example of a pin factory demonstrates that productivity can increase exponentially through the division of labor.[90] Today, the application of machinery and advanced technology also largely depends on the division of labor into single steps and objects. Meanwhile, elevated production capacity creates sales and distribution problems. Adam Smith rightly observed that large-scale division of labor could make sense only when large-scale markets are in place.[91] Sustainable productivity growth must be supported by an expanding and well-functioning market. The production mode, namely M-C (investment to produce commodities), must be coupled with the distribution mode, namely C-M' (sales to realize value increase), so that the production growth can continue. When socialist

[89] Adam Smith, *Wealth of Nations* (Edinburgh: Thomas Nelson Press, 1843), p. 3.
[90] Wealth of Nations, pp. 14–15. [91] Ibid., chapter 3.

command economies intended to increase production through planning instead of through market forces, they caused overproduction in certain sectors and shortages in others. Solely stressing the production mode (labor, technology) and neglecting the distributive mode (ownership, market), traditional socialist economies, including pre-reform China, could not sustain growth and failed without exception.[92]

Therefore, comprehensive change must extend to societal structures in order for sustainable productivity growth to occur. The advance of production methods, such as division of labor, professional specialization, usage of machinery, and technological progress, should take place along with the transformation of societal structure and living style, such as increasing trade activities, rising consumption demands, and enhanced distribution channels. Furthermore, improvement of market regulation, protection of private property, construction of infrastructure, the breakdown of household production, standardization of education, and efficient administration is all also vital. As Max Weber pointed out, the "forever renewed profit" of capitalist enterprises is not individual matter, but deals with an order of society.[93] Similarly, Emile Durkheim argued that the complex division of labor led to a new type of social solidarity in the modern world, transitioning from a society with rigid social controls and uniform beliefs (mechanical solidarity) into one with more autonomous individuals, increased differentiation, and frequent interactions between citizens (organic solidarity).[94] Using eighteenth-century England as an example, Karl Polanyi illustrated that comprehensive societal and cultural transformation, not a simple "market" system, is required to make the industrial revolution possible.

> In an agricultural society such conditions (for selling large amounts of goods) would not naturally be given; they would have to be created. … … The transformation implies a change in the motive of action on the part of the members of society: for the motive of subsistence that of gain must be substituted. All transactions are turned into money transactions, and these in turn require that a medium of exchange be introduced into every articulation of

92 Moishe Postone, *Time, Labor, and Social Domination* (Cambridge: Cambridge University Press, 2003), pp. 10–11.

93 Max Weber, *The Protestant Ethic and the Spirit of Capitalism* (London: Routledge, 2001), pp. xxxii ff.

94 Emile Durkheim, *The Division of Labour in Society* (London: Macmillan, 1984), pp. 83–86.

industrial life. All incomes must derive from the sale of something or other, and whatever the actual source of a person's income, it must be regarded as resulting from sale. No less is implied in the simple term "market system," by which we designate the institutional pattern described.[95]

Today, the transition from a traditional socioeconomic relationship to a modern society that centers on productivity growth is named by development economists as structural transformation. On the one side, this term refers to the expansion of highly productive industries and other modern sectors in the place of subsistence agriculture. On the other hand, it describes the related alterations in economic, political, and social frameworks, including urbanization, secularization, and so on.[96] China has experienced effective structural transformation during the rapid growth of the past four decades, significantly reducing its agricultural sector and rapidly increasing urbanization. In contrast, Africa (with several exceptions, such as South Africa) has seriously lagged in industrialization[97] (see Table 1.2).

In this connection, diverse experiments and incremental changes are crucial to achieving comprehensive structural transformation and sustainable productivity growth. First, because comprehensive transformation touches all aspects of society, policy change must be incremental – no single policy can bring about comprehensive structural transformation. Second, every developing nation must approach structural transformation differently given their unique traditions and societal forms. Indeed, every society needs to explore its own development path without copying previous models. Finally, comprehensive transformation also generates the "chicken-and-egg" dilemma. When one part, for instance industrial capacity, is growing, it is affected and constrained by many other parts in the society, such as a nation's infrastructure and labor force. However, the construction of infrastructure and the development of labor skill are conversely limited by the lack of industrial activities. The sophisticated division of labor and corresponding distributional network require all the related

95 Karl Polanyi, Great Transformation, p. 41.

96 Simon Kuznets, Modern Economic Growth: Findings and Reflections, 1971. www.nobelprize.org/nobel_prizes/economic-sciences/laureates/1971/kuznets-lecture.html (accessed July 11, 2020).

97 Margaret McMillan, Dani Rodrik, and Inigo Verduzco-Gallo, Globalization, Structural Change, and Productivity Growth, with an Update on Africa, *World Development* (2014) 63, 11.

Table 1.2 *Percentage of urban population and agriculture in China and Major African Countries*

	Agriculture Value Added (% GDP)			Urban Population (% of Total Population)		
	1979	2000	2015	1979	2000	2015
China[a]	30.70	14.68	8.88	18.6	35.8	55.6
Egypt	20.91	16.74	11.18	43.8	42.8	43.1
DRC	28.32	32.33	20.63	26.8	35.1	42.5
Ethiopia		47.76	40.97	10.2	14.7	19.5
Ghana	63.39	39.41	20.99	30.9	43.9	54.0
Nigeria		26.03	20.86	21.5	34.8	47.8
Tanzania		33.48	31.08	14.1	22.3	31.6
South Africa	5.97	3.29	2.37	48.3	56.9	64.8
Sub-Saharan Africa		19.85	17.50	21.9	30.8	37.8

[a] As China uses the stubborn Hukou registration system to prevent farmers from moving to the cities, the official statistics of urban population is probably underreported.

Source: World Development Indicators Database, May 2018

components to perform their functions appropriately, but it is impossible to enable all actors simultaneously with new skills and knowledge, especially when the collaborating synergism is still new to them. Societal members must be gradually acclimated to their new roles in order to work effectively and in coordination with their peers. A country must solve the "chicken-and-egg" dilemma in order to have successful structural transformation. As we will see in this book, Chinese pragmatic approaches to development not only played a key role in solving China's "chicken-and-egg" dilemma, but also in assisting Africa on its own path toward structural transformation.

1.5 Solve the Chicken-and-Egg Dilemma

Indeed, some researchers have already noticed the chicken-and-egg dilemma in the structural transformation. For instance, Gunnar Myrdal pointed out that the socioeconomic system has the nature of self-reinforcement. Social inertia makes it more difficult for the non-industrialized countries to shift to industrial society than the industrialized countries to continue industrialization. This is the notion of circular cumulative causation. Accordingly, Myrdal was pessimistic about the growth prospect of the Third World and believed that weak institutions in almost all the political, economic, social, and cultural frontiers tend to keep these countries in low-level equilibrium.[98] Yuen Yuen Ang sees as well that all wealthy capitalist economies are necessarily supported by good institutions, such as protection of private property rights, professional bureaucracy, formal accountability, and so forth, but "attaining these preconditions also appears to depend on the level of economic growth."[99] However, China's rise from backward socioeconomic conditions to a global industrial powerhouse during past four decades offers an invaluable example of how a country can effectively escape the vicious circle of poverty and bad governance. Ang reveals that, in the case of China, markets and the state agencies interacted and adapted to each other. This coevolutionary process manifested itself in diverse forms, over the course of different periods of development. In her view, the practices showed that "weak" institutions and state capacities actually help *build* markets when none exist, whereas "strong" governance preserves existing markets. In particular, improvisation among ground-level agents spurred the coevolution of markets and states.[100] The coevolution on the ground level must be diverse and incremental, as the specific agents need time to undergo mutual adaptation in their own manner. Such a coevolution resonates with Deng Xiaoping's philosophy of "white cat and black cat" and "crossing river by touching stones."

However, Yuen Yuen Ang investigated only the interactive relationship between government agencies and market. Structural transformation involves changes in many more aspects of society. As noted in Section 1.4, a modern industrial system with sustainable productivity growth requires not only a functioning market and efficient administration, but also skilled workers and infrastructure facilities. Additionally, entrepreneurship, professionalism, consumerism, and urbanization are also important components. All these factors are interdependent and mutually impact one another. In Adam

[98] Gunnar Myrdal, *The Challenge of World Poverty* (London: Allen Lane, 1970), p. 268.

[99] Yuen Yuen Ang, *How China Escaped the Poverty Trap* (Ithaca, NY: Cornell University Press, 2016), p. 1.

[100] Ibid.

Przeworski's words, "In the end, the motor of history is endogeneity. From some initial circumstances and under some invariant conditions, wealth, its distribution, and the institutions that allocate factors and distribute incomes are mutually interdependent and evolve together."[101] In the development process of China and Africa, numerous challenges precisely lie in the difficulty of forming coevolutionary dynamism between modern economic activities and the relevant social-political environment. As we will analyze with concrete cases in the following chapters, wherever mutual adaptation is made possible, the growth drive becomes self-reinforcing and sustainable. Wherever the changes fail to interact with the surrounding environment, the effect of the changes cannot last long.

The revelation of the coevolutionary complexity indeed explains why many previous development programs failed. Since the transformation of a society is not determined by any independent primary cause, attempts to launch a designed program or set definite conditions, either by foreign agents or local authority, cannot shift the entire society rooted in traditional life directly into a new system of modern production. To understand the mutual causation, Yuen Yuen Ang made an artificial but meaningful distinction between "complicated" and "complex." The former refers to a system composed of many parts, but it can be determined by a linear causation. For example, pressing a button can launch a rocket. By contrast, in a complex system the components "interact with one another and change together."[102] I think that a soccer team is a good example to illustrate what a complex system looks like. A good pass cannot be decided by a single factor but depends on the position and action of the player who passes the ball as well as those of the player who receives the ball. Any change of these elements may turn a good pass to a bad one or conversely. A good pass refers to a harmonious coordination of all the changing factors at the same time, not a definite pattern of actions. The relationship in a complex unity, like a soccer team, is not one-dimensional but interdependent.

The build-up of a soccer team is thus a chicken-and-egg dilemma too. Everyone learns how to play soccer by first working within a team. Initially, there must be numerous misunderstanding and

[101] Adam Przeworski, The Last Instance: Are Institutions the Primary Cause of Economic Development? *European Journal of Sociology* (2004) 45.2, 185.
[102] Yuen Yuen Ang, *How China Escaped the Poverty Trap*, p. 10.

miscommunications. Yet, as the experiments continue, the players get familiar with each other and begin to form a cohesive team. They enhance their skills through team practice. A similar approach can be found in China's structural transformation. The market-oriented reform started with incremental experiments in diverse fields such as market liberalization, loosening of price control, establishment of private enterprises, introduction of performance-based bonuses, opening for FDI, and so on. A large variety of players, from farmers, workers, and entrepreneurs to scientists, officials, and foreign investors, were involved in this process. All of them made changes simultaneously and they gradually learned to adapt to each other under the new circumstances. Most of these adaptations, not prescribed by existing rules or theories, were improvised in practices. Through trial-and-error, different stakeholders have learned to work with each other to achieve better productivity. Then they continue to evolve and adapt for further productivity growth.

In the coevolution process, it is critical to ensure all the stakeholders stick to a common target so that synergism can be forged. For a soccer team, only when all the members strive to score and not be scored do their training exercises for cooperation and mutual adaptation make sense. Likewise, the stakeholders of structural transformation need to explore the appropriate manner of division of labor and market functioning with the goal of promoting sustainable productivity growth. However, the nature of interdependent coevolution makes it challenging to achieve the goal. Using the soccer team again as an example, more than 90 percent of the actions in a match do not directly lead to goals, but the passing and running are necessary preparation for scoring goals. Therefore, instruction and coaching are needed to unite the team and advance toward a single objective. When it comes to structural transformation, most individual actors cannot observe the overall long-term productivity growth, but only local actions and ad hoc gains, which, albeit necessary for the overall transformation, are likely to deviate from the general goal as well. Strategic direction is thus needed to keep the coevolving synergism on the track toward structural transformation.

Yet, a strategic direction for the coevolving synergism is not a linear mechanism either. The direction should indeed be an organic component of the coevolution so that it can effectively guide the constantly changing components. It is not enough to coach the soccer players on just the basic rules of the game. Similarly, the direction for the structural transformation cannot be limited to mere theories or prescribed instructions, but instead must be absorbed and integrated into the active socioeconomic synergism. The Chinese government used the combination of national-level reform design, corporate style evaluation of local cadres, and interregional balance to stimulate and coordinate continuous growth.[103] The national-level design sets the target and criteria for all the other activities, but it is also relatively broad and flexible, leaving plenty of space for the local officials and enterprises to improvise, with the exception of a few areas marked with "red lines," for example, land use. Consequently, although China's market reform was initiated by the central government, the exact outcome of the reform often surprised the central government. This in turn forced the central leadership to learn from the practice and give new policy guidance to keep the development on track.[104] In this manner, the strategic direction and the grassroots changes form a synergism of mutual adaptation, in which the general growth goal gradually merges with the various aims of diverse actors in the country.

To be sure, the relationship between general direction of state strategy and grass-root socioeconomic transformation is not a fixed one either. In similar manner that a soccer team can in some cases develop better through playing actual matches rather than coaching, the structural transformation of a society may also move forward through long-time interactions between diverse capitalist-minded actors with little state intervention. An active state may play a bigger role to accelerate the learning process in the late-industrialized countries and promote the overall productivity growth. However, no matter which role the state may play, the critical point is that the general direction and grassroots changes should build an interactive coevolving relationship, not a mechanical linear one.

In this connection, we can understand the mistakes of some previous development theories. The advocates of the Washington Consensus rightly see that market mechanism can promote growth, but they wrongly assume that the institutions in the developed countries, such as independent judiciary, clear property rights, and liberalization of

[103] Eric X. Li, "The Life of the Party"; Yuen Yuen Ang, *How China Escaped the Poverty Trap*, pp. 48–68.

[104] Yuen Yuen Ang, *How China Escaped the Poverty Trap*, pp. 73–75, 88–102.

financial markets, can directly cause development in other societies.[105] Consequently, the advocates of the Washington Consensus tend to impose conditionality on the developing countries, expecting to stimulate development, but often end up stagnating. This miscalculation is due largely to the methodology used by the mainstream economists in the Washington-based institutions, which basically prescribes a linear mechanism. In Kindleberger's words, "The missions bring to the underdeveloped country a notion of what a developed country is like. They observe the underdeveloped country. They subtract the former from the latter. The difference is a program."[106] The Washington Consensus has a clear theoretical model of how a market economy should function, but does not realize the organic complexity of market functioning in diverse practices.

Similarly, the Modernization Theories described specific development patterns of the so-called modern society, largely according to the existing Western socioeconomic structure, and used these patterns to design development paths for other traditional societies.[107] The patterns identified for modern society, including universalism, achievement orientation, and self-orientation, were criticized for being imprecise and flawed. This was especially the case in the way that traditional societies were simplistically compared with the developed industrial West. The diversity and originality of these traditional societies were neglected and all these countries were assumed to follow along the Free West model.[108] The logic underlying the Modernization Theories is also that of social engineering. Not only does this approach ignore the complex cultures and histories of developing countries, but it also asserts that the modernization of Western society, as well as that of other societies, is a predestined mechanical process. Although these theorists discern that modernization as a global phenomenon has

105 Adam Przeworski, The Last Instance, p. 182.

106 Charles Kindleberger, Review of The Economy of Turkey; The Economic Development of Guatemala; Report on Cuba, *Review of Economics and Statistics* (1952) 34, 391–392. Quoted by Adam Przeworski, pp. 182–183. Przeworski points out that this kind of practice is still widely used in the Bretton Woods institutions in the twenty-first century.

107 G. Hawthorn, *Enlightenment and Despair* (Cambridge: Cambridge University Press, 1976), p. 242; W. W. Rostow, *The Stages of Economic Growth: A Non-Communist Manifesto* (Cambridge: Cambridge University Press, 1960), pp. 1–14.

108 Preston, pp. 170–175.

special characteristics, their depictions suggest a merely passive stereotypical mechanism rather than an active, diverse, and organic societal transformation.

By witnessing China's development, Justin Yifu Lin understands that the transformation toward a market economy is not uniform. He argues that the state should play a role in the development process of emerging countries. However, his perspective is still largely rooted in the concept of direct causation, as outlined in orthodox economic theory. Assuming that the market mechanism works automatically, Lin believes that comparative advantages of endowment, such as cheap labor cost, can lead to the growth of related industrial sectors as long as state support can help overcome the initial infrastructure and informational hurdles.[109] He fails to note that the functioning of the market is not simply a given, but requires time and multilateral effort. Consequently, Lin's theory designs narrow and definite paths for all the developing countries and regions. Lin and Monga suggest that a developing country should identify which countries and industrial sectors to emulate based on resource endowment, tradable goods, and per capita income.[110] In this manner, the unique sociopolitical structure, history, and culture of developing countries are not addressed. The paths of structural transformation in a society are solely evaluated by economic calculation.

Therefore, the inconsistency between Lin's effort to break the uniform pattern of Washington Consensus economics and his assumption of universal economic mechanism generates the paradox of "both for and against comparative advantage" in New Structural Economics, as Rodrik pointed out.[111] In addition to the contradictory logic, Lin's theory fails to explain the diversity and comprehensiveness of

[109] Lin, *New Structural Economics*, p. 29.

[110] Lin and Monga, Growth Identification and Facilitation, Policy Research Working Paper 5313, World Bank 2010, pp. 12–20. Justin Lin also talks about endogeneity, stating that exports and imports, financial structure, industrial structure, and corporate behaviors are endogenous to factor endowment such as labor, capital, and natural resources. However, his analysis of the endogenous relationship suggests rather a linear mechanism between these factors. The factor endowment determines the industrial sectors and financial structure. When these industrial sectors grow, they will certainly increase capital and labor costs. In turn, the new factor endowment will determine new suitable sectors. The endogeneity here is just a temporal linear mechanism, not an interactive coevolution.

[111] Dani Rodrik, Comments on "New Structural Economics," pp. 227–229.

structural transformation. Structural transform does not just depend on winner-picking industrial policy. China's economic reform during the preceding four decades covered a vast range of issues, including change of government functions, adjustment of income and welfare system, restructuring of enterprises, legislation for property rights, and nurturing of business and professional culture. Without these changes, industrial growth would not have taken off. Furthermore, the process of socioeconomic changes in different countries and in different regions of China have various forms. By reducing the success factor of transformation to mere comparative advantages, New Structural Economics does not give sufficient consideration to the complexity and diversity of the structural transformation.

The aforementioned development theories strive to find a straightforward approach to make policies and promote development. However, the methodology of attempting to identify direct causations is simplistic and mechanical. Theory and general mechanism are not even sufficient to build a good soccer team, let alone the transformation of societies. When mechanical rules are imposed on actual people and societies, they may not only fail to get the expected outcome, but also generate conflicts. To be sure, the analysis of statistics and mechanical causation is a valuable tool. In a system of coevolution, the analytical tools can assist people to identify weak linkages so that mechanical measures can be taken to strengthen and balance the linkages. Yet, the mechanical assistance should be limited to parts of the system and should not be regarded as the guiding principle for the entire synergism. Coevolution requires interactive coordination rather than fixed one-dimensional rules.

Relatedly, the role of foreign aid in a developing country ought to be strictly limited to the activities that are temporary and necessary for building a synergism with sustainable productivity growth. Foreign aid allocates resources according to the sociopolitical agendas that are not seeking profit or value increase. Such external assistance may provide capital, knowledge, and infrastructure for the underdeveloped countries to initiate production and market activities (threshold effects).[112] However, long term, extensive aid can also create a state of aid dependency. When foreign aid is systematized and regularized, the aid

[112] Jeffrey Sachs, *The End of Poverty: Economic Possibilities for Our Time* (New York: Penguin Press, 2005), pp. 249–250.

recipients may turn their attention to applying for grants rather than promoting productivity growth. Unnecessary aid such as donation of clothes may even kill local manufacturing industries.[113] Therefore, foreign aid is not always good for a recipient country's development when its amount increases. The effects of foreign aid depend on whether it contributes to the recipient country's own efforts of socio-economic transformation. If foreign aid, serving external ethical or political standards, distracts the recipient country from building its own synergism of modern economy, then these well-meaning donations may actually harm the development.

This being said, we can examine how Chinese engagements interact with Africa's structural transformation. As noted in Section 1.3, corresponding to the reform at home, the Chinese engagements in Africa have shifted their attention to economic benefits since the 1980s. Bilateral commercial collaborations thus grow rapidly instead of politically motivated aid. While Western institutes impose rules on African countries, Chinese government and firms experiment actively to make business deals possible in diverse places, from urban centers to remote rural area, and in various sectors, from trade and infrastructure to agriculture and manufacturing. These commercial activities, albeit trivial as individuals, substantially impact African economies and societies as a whole. They expand the scope of market exchange and enhance the industrial base of the continent. Through concrete practices on the ground, not through defined policies or models, Chinese pragmatism promotes structural transformation in Africa in a more comprehensive and effective manner.

To be sure, there are also companies from Western countries doing business in Africa. They contribute to Africa's economic transformation too. Nonetheless, Chinese firms are more willing to take risks in challenging business environments than the Western counterparts. The difficult political-economic conditions in Africa, such as ineffective administration, regulation loopholes, financial volatility, and so forth indicate high risk. A large number of Western firms therefore choose to avoid sub-Saharan countries, because the small market size cannot justify the risks.

113 Dambisa Moyo, *Dead Aid: Why Aid Makes Things Worse and How There Is Another Way for Africa* (London: Penguin Books, 2010).

By comparison, Chinese firms, from banks and traders to construction contractors and industrial investors, are all willing to accept the high risks in Africa, because of the substantially lower competition in comparison to the Chinese market. For them, the challenging business environment is not necessarily an obstacle but presents some opportunities. They themselves experienced the growth of the Chinese market not long before and remember similar regulation challenges and macroeconomic risks during the transition process. China's own structural transformation provided Chinese enterprises with the experience and confidence necessary to do business in Africa's structural transformation. As China itself has been still undergoing structural transformation, it even forms an interactive coevolving synergism with Africa. Not only do Africans get support from Chinese regarding market development and industrial production, but Chinese also greatly strengthen their international business capacity through engagements with Africans. China's structural transformation helps Chinese firms better understand the demand and prospect of Africa's structural transformation and develop an approach of mutual adaptation. In this manner, China and Africa's transformations eventually converge into one synergism.

This book aims to demonstrate how, in the context of the structural transformations for both China and Africa, concrete practices on the ground effectively advance socioeconomic coevolution on both sides. The interactive synergism can be seen in a wide array of aspects, from trade and infrastructure to agriculture, manufacturing, and urbanization. In each aspect, I will present a chicken-and-egg dilemma to exemplify the prevailing challenge of mutual causation in the development process. Then, by analyzing the real cases of China-Africa engagements, we can see how incremental practices produce reciprocal changes in the thoughts and behaviors of related stakeholders, and consequently facilitate mutual adaptation for the purpose of sustainable growth. It is through these tangible cases that the essential characteristics of pragmatism in China's own reform, as well as in China-Africa engagements, can fully unfold. The flexibility and diversity of the efforts to explore market opportunities and seek sustainable economic growth can be grasped through nothing but the examination of various live practices.

Since 2007, I have traveled to nearly twenty African countries to investigate hundreds of Chinese projects in Africa, and I have closely observed the interactions between Chinese and Africans at these sites by interviewing more than 2,000 officials, entrepreneurs, professionals, workers, farmers, and scholars – both Chinese and African. For this book, I have collected large amounts of first-hand information and cases that have never been used elsewhere. The raw data gained from the field research have been analyzed and organized to present the main features of Sino-African economic interactions, as well as project the trajectory of the sociopolitical evolutions driven by them.

In the following chapters, I will detail the unique aspects of China-Africa economic partnership. Chapter 2 will focus on trade, which is usually the first form of business interaction between Chinese and Africans. We will observe how pragmatism is employed to facilitate the formation of transcontinental markets and tackle accompanying problems. Chapter 3 examines infrastructure construction, shedding light on how the relationship between infrastructure and development is perceived and constantly revised by Chinese and Africans during their collaborations. Chapter 4 focuses on agriculture, analyzing how the Chinese government and the private sector engage with Africa's rural regions through methods that promote market practices. Deep-rooted traditions and unpredictable environments in the rural areas make such interactions even more challenging. Chapter 5 looks at increasing Chinese investment in Africa's manufacturing industries. For decades, Chinese firms have explored the potential of Africa's manufacturing sector with pilot investment projects. These ventures stimulate active responses from African actors and contribute to African industrialization. Chapter 6 studies a particular model of Chinese engagement: special economic zones (SEZs). The Chinese government and enterprises choose to construct SEZs in Africa in order to support manufacturing investment. The SEZs often tend to diverge from the original model and emerge as new patterns of industrial development through experiments known as "feeling-the-stones." The last two chapters will investigate two hotly debated social issues. Chapter 7 addresses the issue of work ethics. Industrialization requires special work practices and ethics. I present various experiments that have taken place at Chinese factories to show how qualified African workers are trained and how cultural values influence each other in the process. Chapter 8 examines Chinese firms' environmental and social responsibility practices in Africa. The relationship between environmental protection and economic development is not decided by linear causation either. Pragmatism is likewise applied by Chinese firms in environment-related issues.

The chapters are arranged in a way to illustrate the evolving stages of China-Africa interactions, from trade deals with quick returns to long-term investments or from foundational infrastructure projects to industrial complexes and urban construction. Additionally, this book outlines the shift of ethical values and social consciousness in the transformation. In this manner, the book suggests that the China-Africa interactions gradually move structural transformation forward and spread the impact of this transformation to various aspects of African society. Although mining is an important sector for many African economies, as well as for Chinese investment in Africa, its impact on social transformation is relatively limited and isolated. Therefore, I will not cover mining sector investments in detail in this book. Likewise, China's official development aid will be discussed only insofar as it is related to structural transformation in China and Africa.

2 Trade

2.1 The Chinese Story of African Markets

In June 2007, shortly after I arrived in the Angolan capital of Luanda, I was made aware of an informal market in the city that was known to be the largest in Africa: Roque Santeiro. Owing to a lack of standardized commerce during the twenty-seven-year-long Angolan civil war, which lasted from 1975 until 2002, multitudes of people began to trade in various goods and eventually established a large-scale open-air market. I had seen images of it in aerial photographs, the uneven layers of colorful tin roofs stretching toward the distant horizon, like an undisturbed, jungle wilderness. Curious to know more about the market, I asked my hosts, Ghassan, a burly Lebanese restaurant owner, and Paula, his statuesque Angolan wife, if they had ever been there. Paula laughed and told me that Roque Santeiro had a nickname, the "stock exchange," because it was fully stocked with every kind of product, from weaponry to narcotics. She had never been there, though, and said that most white-collar residents of Luanda would not go, because it was known to be an extremely disorderly and dangerous place with almost no police supervision. Ghassan said that he had only driven past one time but had never entered the market. Then Paula smiled mysteriously, and added, "I've heard that there are Chinese people there doing business."

I was surprised to hear this, "Really? Are they not worried about security?"

Paula laughed, "They are not afraid. Angolans say they all know kung-fu!"

Unfortunately, I am far from skilled in martial arts, and therefore I never mustered the courage to pay my respects to those daredevil fighting masters. Instead, I visited the residence of President Xu Ning of the Chinese Chamber of Commerce, and from his explanation came to a general understanding of local Chinese business operations. Xu

Ning started out as a playwright for the Children's Art Theater in Beijing, but later gave up writing to become the manager of an affiliated trading company. At the end of the 1990s, while selling aluminum alloy doors and windows, he heard by chance that these products were selling for an extremely high profit on the Angolan market. He bought a ticket and went to Angola to investigate. At the time, there was still conflict in certain areas of the country, but the capital was calm, and reconstruction work had already begun. Many years of wartime chaos had nearly destroyed local industry, and consumer goods were in desperately short supply. However, as Angola is blessed with a wealth of natural resources, holding rich supplies of both oil and diamonds, it was far from lacking in US dollar reserves. These two factors combined to result in highly elevated commodity prices. At the time, a window frame with a production cost of 100 RMB could be sold in Angola for close to 100 US dollars, six or seven times the price for which it would be sold in China. Xu Ning realized he had stumbled upon a goldmine. Immediately after returning to China, he quit his job, made some basic preparations, and rushed back to Angola, where he began to put down roots. His company imported various small commodities, from decorating materials to clothing and shoes to office supplies. These proved so popular on the local market that demand for his merchandise surpassed supply, and nine years later, the company's annual sales had exceeded 100 million USD. After the year 2000, Angola's rapidly growing market attracted more and more Chinese businesspeople, including both large-scale importers and small-scale retail vendors who set up stalls in markets such as Roque Santeiro.

That said, behind these high profits lay high risks, especially in terms of security. Many weapons leftovers from the long civil war had made their way into the hands of local civilians. Moreover, many demobilized soldiers who had failed to receive appropriate accommodations were left drifting through the city, sometimes causing security problems. Robberies specifically targeted foreigners, the majority of whom were engaged in commerce and therefore relatively wealthy. During the five short weeks I spent in Luanda, I was robbed, twice, in the city center, in broad daylight. Luckily, I was never injured. Xu Ning's residence, like those of many other foreign businessmen, was equipped with a thick iron gate and watched over by armed private security guards. Despite these precautions, up to twenty or thirty Chinese expatriates were murdered in Angola every year, in addition to countless thefts and robberies. Extortion from local police and diseases like malaria could also result in damages to property and health. The costs and hardships necessary for opening up this fertile new market were extraordinary.

A few months later, in Kinshasa, capital of the Democratic Republic of Congo (DRC), I saw with my own eyes the legendary Chinese market vendors of Africa. Since the 1996 revolt against Mobutu Sésé Seko, the country went through more than a decade of war and upheaval, and intermittent conflict continues in the eastern region today. In March of 2007, brief clashes took place in Kinshasa when antigovernment forces took control of the city and plundered a large number of shops, but by the time I arrived, the situation had stabilized somewhat. With blue-helmeted United Nations soldiers patrolling the city, foreigners could at least walk the streets with ease. After several attempts, I was finally able to speak with Wu Ruisan, Secretary-General of the local Chinese Chamber of Commerce. Following his direction, I made my way to a large market at the center of town, which even on a Thursday was full of people jostling for space in the crowd. The narrow street was lined with four rows of shops and the two exterior rows made up of the original street-facing buildings. The doors and windows of some of these were left open to welcome business, while others remained closed, though customers still pushed their way in from time to time. Along the innermost edges, simple stalls occupied the center of the road, selling items such as coarse cloth, denim jeans, or artificial leather shoes. Because of the heat, many people wore sleeveless shirts, and their shiny, sweaty arms rubbed against one another as they squeezed through the crowd. Under the scorching sun, a thick odor of perspiring bodies, combined with the smell of cheap leather, emanated through the air. Trying to dodge puddles in the muddy ground, I alternated between lowering my head to watch the road, looking for a dry place to jump to, and observing my surroundings to avoid collisions with sweaty bodies. After ten or so minutes like this, I progressed about 400–500 meters to reach a large covered area, the center of the market, then I turned right and walked another 20-something meters to where I noticed a two-story house on the other side of the street. A faded red banner of Chinese characters had been hung on its door frame, reading "Wealth and honor, peace and safety." This was the place I had been looking for.

The door was open, but since there were no windows it was very dark inside. A wall separated the room into two sections, with customers restricted to the outer area and two African salesclerks working inside. A large hole had been cut into the wall and installed with iron bars. Customers selected their purchases by looking between the iron bars at shoe samples hung from the wall, then calling for an employee to bring them the merchandise. When I entered the store, there were quite a few customers keeping the salesclerks busy. I waited for five or six minutes until I was able to take advantage of an argument between two customers to ask one of the employees where Manager Wu was. Seeing a Chinese person, he turned his head toward the ceiling and gave a shout. This was followed by the creaking sounds of someone walking down the stairs: a forty-something man of medium stature, Manager Wu. After hearing me introduce myself, he opened a side door to let me into the inner chamber of the room, and then had me follow him upstairs. There, I met a young man of tall and sturdy build named Xu Zhiyong. He had come over from Shenyang only two years before, and was also a member of the Chamber of Commerce. Wu Ruisan was from Wenzhou, and when I met him he had already been in the country for six years.

The two men explained that Chinese businesses in the DRC had come in three waves: the first group consisted of people who had come in the 1980s, sent by the Chinese government to work on aid projects, who had stayed behind to start their own businesses.[1] These included medical personnel, employees of construction companies, and diplomatic staff. President Liang of the Chamber of Commerce, who had been in DRC for more than nineteen years, had previously been a cadre of a foreign aid program for the Agriculture and Forestry Bureau of Gansu Province. There were around 300–400 of these "old Congos" in the DRC. The second wave of Chinese migration had come at the end of the 1990s, when some people who had encountered difficulties "jumping into the sea" (*xiahai*) of domestic private business came to DRC to try their luck. The third and most recent wave of business from China had peaked around 2005, when enterprises, already successful in China, sought to expand their operations abroad.

Chinese aid and economic cooperation had left a positive impression among high-level members of the DRC government, and the president

[1] In the 1960s and '70s, staff for aid projects were required to return to China once their work was finished; government rules stipulated that they were not allowed to remain in Africa. However, beginning in the 1980s there was relatively more freedom.

and ministers all held friendly attitudes toward China. Lower-level officials, however, were not interested in diplomatic relations; to them, all that mattered was the practical reality of money. Although ministers had agreed to speed up customs procedures and improve infrastructure, the staff members who actually oversaw regulation refused to implement such measures. Instead, they made excuses to create difficulties, hoping to garner profit through extortive activities. For example, they refused to recognize receipts issued in China, or arbitrarily arrested and imprisoned Chinese businesspeople. On recommendation by the Chinese embassy, Chinese business representatives organized a Chamber of Commerce in order to form a united response to such abuses of power by local officials. However, neither Secretary Wu nor young Xu had a positive outlook on the future of the DRC market. Previously, there had been no Chinese importers in any of Congo's neighboring countries, including Angola, Burundi, and Rwanda. DRC-based importers of Chinese clothing and footwear therefore not only supplied the local market but also distributed to other countries. Now, however, large numbers of Chinese had also entered those countries, and the number of Chinese importers in the DRC market had decreased. Facing rampant corruption and bureaucratic red tape, many Chinese companies were finding it hard to make a return on their investments.

When we finished talking, Xu Zhiyong invited me to visit his shop. Again, we made our way through the crowded, muddy streets until we reached a small building facing the road. The door was closed and there was not even a sign in front. As Xu gently pushed open the door and led me in, I found an entirely different world, ablaze with color from the brightly shining satins and silks arranged on the shelves. Xu's young wife and a young local woman busied themselves attending to several elegantly dressed female customers. I could not help but exclaim in admiration, "Really, I never would have imagined that in these harsh conditions it would be possible to decorate a store so beautifully!"

Xu Zhiyong laughed softly. He didn't respond, but the look in his eyes betrayed a feeling of bitterness and confusion.

In many African countries, the government does not allow foreign businesses to engage in retail trade, but even in those places I spotted Chinese shadows in the markets. Wandering the streets, the footprints of Chinese distributors and salesmen could be found everywhere, and now, increasing numbers of African merchants are driving sales of

Chinese products. In a market in the Nigerian capital of Abuja, I found a street peddler selling books. Beside stacks of colorful entertainment magazines and popular fictions, I was astonished to see a photocopied book entitled "How to Become a Millionaire by Importing from China." In Addis Ababa, the capital of Ethiopia, I wandered through Merkato, a sprawling open-air market. There, shop owners not only rushed over to greet me warmly with a "*nihao*" in Chinese, but also used basic Chinese words like *shoutao* (gloves) or *maozi* (hat) to show me their products.

> I took an interest in a wallet, and the shopkeeper quickly explained in Chinese, "*Yangpi de, hao*" (It's sheepskin, good).
> "*Duoshao qian?*" (How much?) I asked.
> "*Jiushi*" (Ninety).
> I shook my head, "*Liushi*" (Sixty).
> "*Buxing, buxing, qishiwu, zui pianyi*" (No way, no way, seventy-five, cheapest price).

Just like that, he and I were able to conduct a business transaction completely in Chinese. Later on, he told me that he had been to China and imported many of his goods from Yiwu.

Indeed, few of the Africans I met abroad had heard of any large Chinese cities besides Beijing, Shanghai, and Guangzhou, but many people knew about Yiwu, a county seat of only several hundred thousand residents. There, at the largest distribution hub for small commodities in the world, African importers could find anything they might be looking for. It was said that one was limited only by one's imagination, not the actual range of products. More than 50,000 African traders are reported to visit Yiwu every year.[2] In China, they also tend to concentrate in Guangzhou. As southern China's strategic gateway, Guangzhou is well positioned in terms of geography and transportation to receive visitors from Africa. Moreover, the types of products manufactured in the Pearl River Delta region, such as household appliances, mobile phones, and clothing, are precisely the commodities most sought after by African consumers. According to official statistics, beginning in

[2] Yiwu sets up African goods exhibition center (*Yiwu she feizhou shangpin zhanlan zhongxin* 义乌设非洲商品展览中心), October 21, 2011. www.yiwuen.com/zh-hans/yiwu-set-up-the-african-goods-exhibition-enter-cn_17222.html (accessed May 18, 2012).

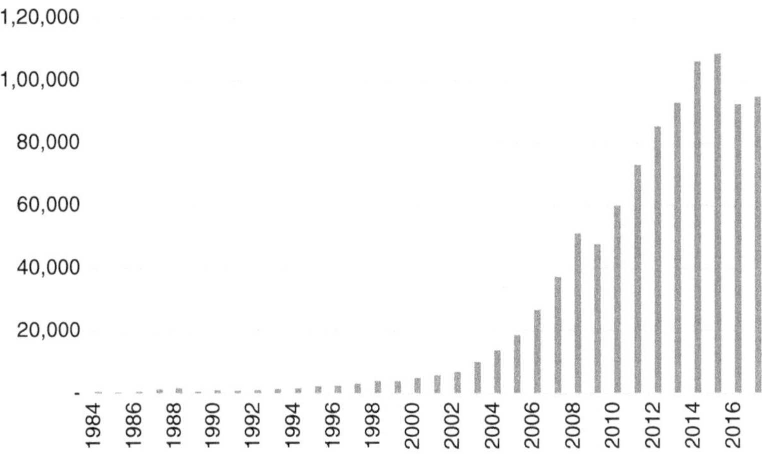

Figure 2.1 Chinese exports to Africa, 1984–2017. Unit: million US$.
Source: *China Statistical Yearbook, China Customs Statistics*

2003, the number of African visitors to Guangzhou increased by 30 to 40 percent every year.[3] The majority of these traders move frequently back and forth between China and Africa, carrying sacks filled with merchandise that they ship back to Africa to sell. Many of them have truly gotten rich from this trade, transforming themselves into local "millionaires." Meanwhile, through the transport and distribution work performed by these traders, Chinese-made products have penetrated every corner of life on the African continent.

Figure 2.1, compiled from yearly customs statistics, clearly indicates the explosive growth of Chinese exports to Africa over the past three decades, especially since 2000. In 1984, the entire African continent imported goods worth 820 million USD from China. By 2000, this number had just surpassed 5 billion USD. In the 1980s and '90s, exports from China to Africa tended to include textiles, clothing, and

[3] Chocolate City: Africans Follow Their Dreams in China (*Qiaokelicheng – feizhouren xunmeng zhongguo*巧克力城 – – 非洲人寻梦中国), *Southern Weekly* (*Nanfang zhoumo*南方周末), January 23, 2008. www.infzm.com/content/6446 (accessed July 12, 2020); Sights and Sounds from the African Neighborhood of Guangzhou (*Guangzhou feizhouyi jujiqu jianwen* 广州非洲裔聚集区见闻), *Economic Information Daily* (*Jingji cankao bao* 经济参考报), October 14, 2009. news.sina.com.cn/c/2009-10-14/034018823281_2.shtml (accessed July 12, 2020).

manufactured goods. After 2000, there was a striking increase in the proportion of exports of home appliances, communications equipment, and machinery and automobiles. And by 2012, machinery and electronics made up 45.9 percent of Chinese exports to Africa.[4] Although African streets are still overrun with Japanese-made cars, now one frequently sees Chinese motorcycles from brands like Lifan, Jialing, and Jincheng, as well as pickup trucks from Great Wall and Jiangling. With the relentless dynamism of entrepreneurs, attractive low prices, and a vast product range, Chinese commodities can overcome linguistic, cultural, and geographical barriers to yield exceptional results on the African market. Their expansion into more localities seems unstoppable, as they advance into newly emerging areas of these economies.

2.2 "Bad Quality": A Double-Sided Coin

As Chinese imports have rapidly expanded into African markets, a major problem is that of "inferior goods." Complaints about the quality of Chinese products are common in African popular discourse, including stories of mobile phones breaking after a week of use, or construction materials disintegrating as soon as it rains. These have amounted to a kind of truism within public opinion: Chinese goods may be cheap, but you get what you pay for in terms of quality. I believe there are two main explanations for the bad reputation that Chinese products have garnered among African public opinion. First, as African purchasing power is generally low, consumers are usually able to purchase only low-grade products. Although they may complain loudly about the "bad quality" of Chinese products, when people have only a few dollars in their pockets, they will ultimately still choose to buy cheap Chinese goods. As Mr. Adma Issara, an official in charge of the Asia-Pacific Region for the Tanzanian Ministry of Foreign Affairs, astutely pointed out in an interview, China also manufactures and exports products of first-rate quality, such as the iPhone.[5] Manager Yang Xiao, who once ran a shoe factory in Uganda, told me that the leather sandals she produced were of excellent quality and would last more than three years, but they came with a price too high for local customers to afford. Instead, they preferred cheap rubber sandals

[4] China-Africa Trade Cooperation 2013, Ministry of Commerce, August 2013.
[5] Dar es Salaam, Tanzania, September 29, 2011.

imported from China, whose soles could be patched or repaired when they inevitably cracked after about a month of use – better than having no shoes at all.[6] Similarly, most Africans preferred a crudely constructed, unattractive mobile phone with only basic functionality that could at least provide a basic means of communication. This, for many ordinary Africans, was already quite sufficient.

Although the majority of commodities exported from China to Africa are low-level products, these kinds of products are not necessarily a bad thing. The option to buy cheap Chinese products offers multitudes of ordinary Africans their first opportunity to use a mobile phone, wear leather shoes, watch television in their homes, or to wear new cloths during holidays. Western brand-name products, on the other hand, though superior to Chinese products in terms of design, style, materials, and durability, have a far higher price tag and far surpass the purchasing power of the average African consumer. Even the *New York Times* has admitted that imports from China "give Africans access to goods and amenities that developed countries take for granted but that most people [in Africa] could not have dreamed of affording just a few years ago."[7]

There is, however, another reason for the poor reputation of Chinese products. This stems from the actions of deceitful merchants who price inferior products at the level of first-rate goods. Some deliberately purchase substandard products, but market them as quality goods sold at a slightly lower price. They thereby capture a large share of the market and swindle their customers in order to reap higher profits. Some defective goods that have not met factory standards might harm customers or their property. For example, Chinese national standards require liquefied gas tanks to be of a certain thickness, but there are African importers who insist that their suppliers in China manufacture gas tanks of substandard thickness in order to reduce costs. Subquality gas tanks are ticking time bombs, waiting to explode at any moment. When customers attracted by low prices are unable to differentiate between various products or lack key information, they may suffer great losses by purchasing inferior goods.

[6] Kampala, Uganda, July 19, 2009.

[7] Lydia Polgreen and Howard French, China's Trade in Africa Carries a Price Tag, *New York Times*, August 21, 2007. www.nytimes.com/2007/08/21/world/africa/21zambia.html?pagewanted=all&_r=0 (accessed July 12, 2020).

Therefore, quality issues cannot be resolved with a "one size fits all" solution. Superior quality cannot be upheld at all costs, since high prices would deny many low-income consumers access to commodities they need. At the same time, businesses cannot be left free to reduce costs by any means possible, thereby cheating customers and harming consumers' interests. The precise measures of action must be evaluated and controlled by supervisory branches of government.

The popularity of low-quality Chinese goods in African markets has also been a mixed blessing for China. Exporting these products certainly generates income for businesses for the country. However, if immediate profits, however petty, are valued at the expense of reputation or consumer safety, the image of "Made in China" could be devastated. Customers who distrust Chinese goods will choose to buy products from other countries as soon as they can afford to. Perhaps even worse than this, some factories falsely promote their products as merchandise from other brands. This kind of unfair competition disrupts the market and causes harm to other businesses. In addition to international brands, a considerable number of Chinese companies also suffer from the production of counterfeits. For example, Manager Zhou Yong, General Representative for Holley Pharmaceuticals in Tanzania, told me that in recent years he has frequently found "pirated" versions of the company's brand-name antimalaria drug Cotexcin being sold in East African markets. As a result, the company has suffered significant losses due to rampant counterfeiting.

At present, market regulation is the weakest link in Sino-African trade. Domestically, China has worked to establish strict product standards and a system of market supervision, but in the face of rapidly increasing exports to Africa, customs inspections seem to be sorely insufficient. However, many African countries have only recently begun to develop their markets and still have not established comprehensive standardization systems. Some might exist in name only, without any means to effectively carry out corresponding inspection procedures. Bilateral coordination on these issues is unprecedented and remains in an exploratory stage. Some traders have thus taken advantage of loopholes to export large amounts of counterfeit and low-grade products to African markets. With the continuous growth of bilateral economic exchange, negative side effects have appeared with increasing frequency.

To ensure that Sino-African trade is mutually beneficial, government agencies in China and African countries have continually sought out practical means of effectively managing the market. Customs departments in some African countries have strengthened their inspections, in terms of both manpower and procedures. New monitoring and testing equipment have been installed. China has also enhanced examination of cargo before it is loaded onto ships. Companies that violate quality regulations are sometimes blacklisted, and their products are forbidden from entering the country. In 2010, for example, the Egyptian government penalized 257 Chinese enterprises for forging inspection certificates.[8] On the Chinese side, 204 cases were discovered related to quality and counterfeit of products exported to Africa that dealt with 660,000 products in 2016 alone.[9] In late 2010, nine Chinese government agencies, including the Ministry of Commerce and Ministry of Foreign Affairs, collectively issued a "Notice Regarding Special Measures to Combat Violations of Intellectual Property Rights and Export of Counterfeits or Low-Grade Products to Africa" (关于开展打击对非洲出口假冒伪劣和侵犯知识产权商品专项治理的通知). A series of reforms were established to address the particularities of African markets, and inspections of products bound for Africa were enhanced at major shipping ports. In Guangdong, Fujian, Zhejiang, and Henan – the main provinces conducting trade with Africa – private enterprises and independent merchants with business in Africa were thoroughly reviewed. Any such businesses or merchants found to have unsatisfactory records were restricted from exporting. Trade associations for such sectors as light manufacturing, textile, or healthcare were all called upon to self-regulate in order to safeguard the interests of the industry overall. As a result, the disqualification rate of exports

8 Notice Regarding Appeals Hearing for Enterprises Penalized by Egypt (*Guanyu kaizhan youguan bei aiji chufa qiye shensu shouli gongzuo de tongzhi*关于开展有关被埃及处罚企业申诉受理工作的通知), *Quality Inspection Letter* (*Zhijian jianhan*质检检函) (2010), p. 981, General Administration of Quality Supervision, Inspection and Quarantine of the People's Republic of China (*Guojia Zhijian Zongju* 国家质检总局).

9 Director of AQSIQ, Zhi Shuping, talks about quality improvement (*Guojia zhijian zongju juzhang Zhi Shuping deng tan zhiliang tisheng*国家质检总局局长支树平等谈质量提升), March 14, 2017. live01.people.com.cn/zhibo/Myapp/Html/Member/html/201703/7_3089_58c39d600c3d2_quan.html (accessed July 12, 2020).

Figure 2.2 A trade fair to promote good-quality Chinese products in Dar es Salaam, Tanzania, 2014.

to Africa decreased from 7.52 percent in 2014 to 4.6 percent in 2015 and 3.2 percent in 2016.[10]

Chinese and African governments have also actively collaborated to develop cooperative action on quality control issues. China General Administration of Quality Supervision, Inspection and Quarantine (AQSIQ) has signed cooperation agreements in regard to quality control with fourteen African countries, including Sierra Leone, Ethiopia, Algeria, Kenya, Burundi, Guinea, Egypt, and others. In addition, since 2006, AQSIQ and the Ministry of Commerce have conducted trainings programs for inspection and quarantine officials from African and Middle Eastern countries. This has allowed African personnel to acquire a deeper understanding of Chinese quality control policies, inspections operations, and production conditions.[11] By March 2017,

[10] Ibid.

[11] Wang Xin: Perfecting the Inspection and Supervision System, Performing a Professional Service to Guarantee Quality (*Wang Xin: Wanshan Jianyan Jianguan Tixi, Lüxing Baguan Fuwu Zhineng* 王新：完善检验监管体系，履行把关服务职能), *China Quality News* (*Zhongguo Zhijian Wang* 中国质检网), January 12, 2011. m.cqn.com.cn/zj/content/2011-01/17/content_1145560.htm (accessed July 12, 2020).

more than 1,000 officials from more than 50 African countries have taken part in such training.[12]

2.3 Dilemma of "Market Activeness" and "Regulation"

The popularity of Chinese products in Africa, and the accompanying regulatory problems makes up a dilemma of mutual causation between market activeness and regulation. While Chinese supply a wide range of products to African markets, the loosely regulated commercial environment suffers from substandard products and irregular activities. Consequently, market prosperity may not be sustainable without effective regulation. However, the effectiveness of market regulation is dependent on the increase of market exchange activities. Successful markets in advanced countries usually correspond with skillful market regulation, whereas the underdeveloped markets often lack proper order and public management. Therefore, some of the challenges facing China-Africa commercial ties include developing the market in spite of ineffective regulating circumstances as well as strengthening the regulatory capacity in an underdeveloped market.

Similar challenges existed in the early period of Chinese market reform in the 1980s. At the time, when the country faced severe shortages of material supplies, a group of audacious entrepreneurs launched an attack on the planned supply system. Carrying their heavy sacks north and south, they left footprints in cities and towns across the country. Through their persistent attempts, they uncovered consumer demands and facilitated market distribution, in the same way that Chinese businessmen now make their way to countless markets scattered across Africa. In the early stages of the transition into a market economy, supply and demand were both constrained and dispersed. It was the vast number of nimble private individual entrepreneurs who facilitated market circulation by effectively connecting supply to demand. Their contributions to the development of early networks for the circulation of products and sales must not go unrecognized.

12 Director of AQSIQ, Zhi Shuping, talks about quality improvement (*Guojia zhijian zongju juzhang Zhi Shuping deng tan zhiliang tisheng*国家质检总局局长支树平等谈质量提升), March 14, 2017.

However, the flexibility of small and medium-sized businesses is also their fatal weakness. Because of their focus on individual short-term profits, they are used to making a steal in one place and then quickly moving elsewhere without considering overall interests in the long term. Thus, individual and small-scale enterprises tend to disregard matters of reputation, sometimes engaging in deceitful or illegal activities. This is one of the causes behind congestion of the market with large numbers of fake or low-quality goods during an initial period of economic development. Thirty years ago, Chinese consumers were on constant alert for "daily shoes," "weekly shoes" (shoes that would last only one day or one week before falling apart), or other poor-quality products rampant at the time. To guarantee that all sides benefit from the exchange of commodities as well as sustainably develop market circulation over the long term, governments need to effectively regulate market activities. An appropriate equilibrium between market activity and product regulation is critical for market development.

Long-term continuity and sustainable growth are critical to the development of a market. The problem is that individual traders tend to prioritize their own immediate aims, by driving down cost in order to gain greater profit. Even if some businesses consider more long-term interests, they do so only for a specific firm. Of course, short term, individual profits do not necessarily conflict with long-term, general interests. In a market economy, the general interest is achieved precisely through the satisfaction of the majority of individual interests most of the time. However, short-term individual interests also clearly do not always coincide with the long-term general good. Peddling fake merchandise, cutting corners in the production process, or engaging in unfair competition may result in small immediate, profits, but ultimately harms the long-term health of the market. However, "regulation" is not exactly the opposite of "market activeness." "Regulation" appears to restrict business activities by adding administrative obstacles. It also creates a fair market environment for long-term sustainable development, such that all businesses can benefit from a growing market and overall productivity can increase in the long run. "Regulation" is not antimarket; rather it works through market activities to enable a functioning market. "Activeness" on its own does not represent the market either, since exchange and circulation must follow regulations; together they constitute an orderly market whole.

In the concrete practices of Sino-African trade, people often find it difficult to achieve a harmonious balance between "market activeness" and "regulation." Often there is either too much "activeness," leading to a chaotic and disorderly market, or too much "regulation," for example, banning of certain types of low-end products, leading to suppression of economic vitality. One of the reasons for this is that many complex modern products require deep professional knowledge in order to verify whether they conform to standards and satisfy customers' needs. For example, although standards exist for chemical or medical products in many African countries, there may be a lack of clarity as to how to assess products not produced or rarely used domestically. Similarly, testing the functions of machinery or electronics requires specific skills and equipment. Countries with a low level of technological development therefore tend to find themselves at a loss when attempting to combat illegal activities involving technology. In some cases, they might even abandon regulatory efforts and instead institute sweeping bans, thereby shutting their doors to perfectly good products. Another major challenge is the complexity of the modern trading system. The transnational business practices involve different languages, various agents, numerous products, and diverse social aspects. The regulating agencies need to develop highly professional skills in order to handle all these issues. When the authorities in China and Africa are unable to control all of these procedures precisely and efficiently, loopholes may emerge and disrupt the market.

This constitutes a kind of chicken-and-egg dilemma. On the one hand, a healthy functioning market requires effective regulation and management. On the other hand, this kind of expertise and ability need to be generated through concrete and gradual practices within the market. It is only when industrial or technological products already exist in a market that regulatory organs of government can begin to understand these kinds of products by accumulating relevant experience. The regulating authorities will likely not comprehend the complexity of the modern trading system until transnational businesses practices grow to a certain scale. Neither appropriate market behaviors nor the fitting market regulation can be acquired without concrete market practices.

Facing such a dilemma, the Chinese government adopted the principle of "crossing the river by feeling the stones," gradually deepening its understanding of market mechanisms in China's own development over the past thirty years. In the initial stages of market reform in the 1980s, the government did not ban the activities of small vendors on the basis of difficulties of regulatory administration, but instead paid attention to learning lessons from the ongoing market practices themselves. New measures and regulations were implemented from time to time to tackle emerging problems, including the establishment of the China Association for Quality Promotion in 1992, as well as the implementation of the Consumer Rights Protection Law since 1994. Meanwhile, some of the once unscrupulous traders also gradually recognized the long-term advantages of a sustainable market, such that, to a certain extent, they began to voluntarily uphold the order of the market. After a protracted struggle between the production and sale of fakes and administrative attempts to curtail such activity, the anarchic market environment slowly began to assume some semblance of order.

Gradualism is as well employed in the regulation of China-Africa trading activities. As noted in Section 2.2, bilateral authorities have incrementally improved technical capacity and regulatory coordination between each other. Additionally, diverse approaches are experimented in the China-Africa commercial world, since it involves players from diverse backgrounds and transnational administration. No standard institution or pattern has been established for all fifty-four African countries. For instance, although nearly all Chinese embassies in African countries encourage Chinese firms to form associations in order to organize and discipline themselves, the forms vary. In Tanzania, there used to be only one association for all small and medium-sized Chinese businesses, consisting of about 100 members. However, the secretariat of the association was not able to keep up with the large number of newcomers from China. After Ambassador Lü Youqing arrived in 2013, he vigorously pushed for all the Chinese businessmen to join organized associations. A few new associations were set up to cover those businessmen who had been affiliated with the original organization. They are organized either according to sectors – for example, there was an association of traders at the Kariako market, and an association of shoemakers – or according to their place of origin in China, such as Wenzhou or Fujian. "As long as people are organized, messages from the (Chinese) government can be sent to them ... Disputes between (Chinese) competitors can also be coordinated or mediated (by the association)," an official in the Chinese embassy explained.[13]

For the business associations in some other countries, their main function is to facilitate communication between Chinese traders and local authorities. Ma Futao, the general secretary of the Chinese Chamber of Commerce in Ethiopia said, "The (Chinese) embassy represents the government. The way it works with local authority is too formal. The chamber of commerce is semi-official. It can thus have more flexibility to make suggestions or requests to local authority."[14] Besides, the Chamber of Commerce also regularly invited Ethiopian customs, tax, and other government officials to clarify relevant market regulation policies. However, since the business associations are essentially voluntarily self-organized entities, they do not always work in the same manner in every country. In Zambia, no chamber of commerce had been set up. In Uganda, multiple associations compete with each other and have even caused chaos among themselves.

African authorities have also actively communicated with Chinese businesspeople. As an example, in Botswana, when new standards for import inspection were issued, the Bureau of Standards held a training to specifically ensure a smooth transition for Chinese firms.[15] Chinese businesspeople are also keen to share their opinions and insights with local officials, and several experienced entrepreneurs even serve as advisers to host country governments on matters of economic policy and regulation. One of the more famous examples is Nigerian "Chief" Hu Jieguo, who became a Special Adviser to President Olusegun Obasanjo. He was thus able to interface directly with the president, provincial governors, and other high-ranking officials on issues such as whether taxes were burdensome to the point of negatively affecting

[13] Chen Chao, third secretary in Chinese embassy, Dar es Salaam, July 2014.

[14] Ma Futao, general secretary of Chinese Chamber of Commerce in Ethiopia, Addis Ababa, June 2009.

[15] Botswana Bureau of Standards holds training on import inspection standards regulations for Chinese businesses (*Bociwana biaozhunju wei huashang juban jinkou heyan biaozhun guize peixunban* 博茨瓦纳标准局为华商举办进口检验标准规则培训), Economic and Commercial Counsellor's Office of the Embassy of the People's Republic of China in the Republic of Botswana (*Bociwana Jingshangchu* 驻博茨瓦纳经商处), July 28, 2010. bw.mofcom.gov.cn/aarticle/jmxw/201007/20100707048349.html (accessed July 12, 2020).

enterprises.[16] In Uganda, I also met a female business owner named Jing Hong who served as adviser to the Ugandan National Assembly Committee on Trade, Tourism and Industry. At a meeting in her office, which was decorated with multiple photos of her with President Museveni, she told me that she has regular discussions with government ministers and members of the National Assembly on how to change Ugandan economic reasoning. She uses the experience of China to illustrate the process of market development to these government officials. She also encourages them to be more open minded in regard to foreign businesses, instead of sticking firmly to outdated conventions out of fear of dynamic market fluctuation.

Diverse forms of communication have facilitated mutual understanding and agreements between the two sides. In November 2008, the Tanzanian government raided foreign businesses in the Kariakoo market in central Dar es Salaam, confiscating merchandise and detaining and fining several Chinese business owners and employees who lacked proper documentation. This incident was described in some media outlets as an anti-Chinese action.[17] But only a few months later, when I spoke with the president of the Chinese Chamber of Commerce in Tanzania, Zhu Jinfeng, he stated plainly that the Tanzanian government had done the right thing, and that the Chamber of Commerce supported such regulatory action. Some Chinese merchants, along with Indian and Lebanese merchants, had ignored government regulations that prohibited foreigners from conducting retail sales in Kariakoo market. They invited widespread resentment across local society by exploiting relaxed supervision on open stores, thereby encroaching on local market share. This investigation upheld the regular order of the market and could benefit foreign businesses and their harmonious relations with local society in the long run. Sure enough, when I returned to Kariakoo in 2011, the market was noticeably more orderly than it had been before. Local retail traders kept delightfully busy, while Chinese wholesalers enjoyed steady sales,

[16] Peng Zike (彭子珂), Hu Jieguo: I Am an African Chief (*Hu Jieguo: Wo zai feizhou dang qiuzhang* 胡介国：我在非洲当酋长), Bizmode (*Shangjie Shishang* 商界时尚), April 13, 2007. http://m.fx361.com/news/2007/0416/5764778.html (accessed July 12, 2020).

[17] Tao Duanfang (陶短房), Chinese workers held captive in Africa in 2008 (*2008 nian zhongguogongren zai feizhou mengnan ji* 2008年中国工人在非洲蒙难记), *Southern Reviews* (*Nan Feng Chuang* 南风窗), January 4, 2009. news.sina.com.cn/c/2009-01-04/114716974059.shtml (accessed July 12, 2020).

this time on a solid basis. Mutual understanding had resulted in an orderly development of the market and benefits for traders who observed the regulations.

2.4 The Challenge of Trade Structure

In comparison with that of the Western industrialized countries, China's trade in the African continent is more scattered to various partners, particularly to the sub-Saharan underdeveloped countries. For example, 72 percent of US trade with Africa in 2016 was concentrated in six countries (South Africa, Nigeria, Algeria, Egypt, Angola, and Morocco), whereas 72 percent of China's trade with Africa is distributed to eleven countries (South Africa, Angola, Egypt, Nigeria, and Algeria, Ghana, Kenya, Congo Brazzaville, DRC, Zambia, and Tanzania). In addition, the volume of China-Africa trade was much larger than that of US-Africa trade. The European Union (28 members) has a similar trade structure to that of the United States. Its trade with six African countries (South Africa, Algeria, Morocco, Egypt, Nigeria, and Tunisia) made up 70 percent of the EU-Africa trade 2016.[18] The comparison shows that China tends to do business with a broad range of countries, whereas the United States and EU concentrate on several better-off and large countries in Africa.[19] Apart from the factor of economic complementarity, the intrepid Chinese businessmen greatly facilitate the trade deals. Their devotion to seeking business opportunities and their flexible manners of doing business spread the made-in-China products all over the continent.

Positive outcomes notwithstanding, when Chinese businesses enter the underdeveloped African markets they unavoidably enter into competition with local firms, greatly impacting the original economic structure. While consumers may be happy to be able to purchase cheap goods, some African manufacturers complain that competition from China has devastated local industry. In 2005, the Africa chapter of the International Textile, Garment and Leather Workers' Federation, representing countries such as South Africa, Zimbabwe, Mozambique,

[18] UN comtrade: /comtrade.un.org/dbi.

[19] Nigeria, South Africa, Egypt, Algeria, Angola, and Morocco are among the top seven countries in terms of GDP in Africa 2016 (IMF data). The only country in the top seven that did not trade with the United States and the UK was Sudan because of sanctions.

Lesotho, Swaziland, and Zambia, issued a joint statement declaring that "Chinese imports flooding into global and local markets . . . [are] a fundamental challenge for the industry, its workers and their jobs."[20] Ethiopia's *The Reporter* magazine asserted that "Products produced from fake and cheap materials in China . . . are saturating the market . . . and as a direct result of this, homemade products have been thrown out of the competition."[21] At the same time, Nigerian media lamented, "Nigeria is fast becoming a dumping ground while indigenous companies are dying."[22] This kind of thinking has become common among African publics. In Maseru, capital of Lesotho, fifty-nine-year-old Mathabo Mabekhla once owned one of the finest women's clothing stores in the city, but her sales dropped and she ended up having to close her business. She blamed her misfortune on an increase in Chinese retailers in the area, "Chinese are selling very cheap and not good quality things, and they are killing local businesses." At the end of 2007, this kind of hostility triggered a small-scale riot in Maseru, when local hawkers marched the streets shouting slogans and throwing rocks at Chinese shops.[23]

Business competition understandably generates some friction. That said, it is important to clarify, first, that Chinese products have impacted African industry only in a few specified sectors, namely, textiles, garment, and shoes. Many African countries, especially south of the Sahara, never developed very strong industrial foundations. For many years, apart from the textile industry and simple agriculture, there were almost no decent factories, and basic commodities were all imported. Thus, cheap Chinese goods have either filled a gap in the market or replaced expensive products that were previously imported from developed countries. British scholar Ian Taylor has observed that some African countries have consciously encouraged trade with China in order to reduce dependence on trade with other partners. Namibia, for example, was extremely reliant on South African and European

[20] *Business Day*, September 27, 2005. Cited in Ian Taylor, *China's New Role in Africa* (Boulder, CO: Lynne Rienner, 2010), p. 63.

[21] *The Reporter*, June 30, 2007. Cited in Ian Taylor, *China's New Role in Africa*, p. 64.

[22] *Daily Trust*, February 23, 2007. Cited in Ian Taylor, *China's New Role in Africa*, p. 64.

[23] Lesotho: Anti-Chinese resentment flares, *IRIN News*, January 24, 2008. www.irinnews.org/report/76405/lesotho-anti-chinese-resentment-flares (accessed July 12, 2020).

imports. Now, trade with China has not only helped the government save foreign currency through the purchase of cheaper goods, but also diversified import channels, contributing to the country's autonomy.[24]

Second, the severely impacted African textile industry was able to survive in the past only due to extraordinary historical circumstances. From 1974 to 2004, the World Trade Organization's Multi-Fiber Arrangement (MFA)[25] governed international trade in textiles and clothing. It determined quotas for the export of textile products from developed countries and required major textile-exporting countries such as China and India to limit their exports. The majority of African countries, however, were not constrained by quotas. Moreover, in 2000, the United States passed the African Growth and Opportunity Act (AGOA), granting duty-free and unrestricted entry of certain African exports into the United States, among them textiles and garments. These policies attracted many Asian textile and garment factories to relocate part of their production base to African countries so that they could benefit from preferential trade with Europe and America, resulting in a minor surge in textile production for sub-Saharan Africa.[26]

However, on January 1, 2005, the MFA expired, and all quotas for import and export of textile products were cancelled. African textiles lost their superior position and their share of Euro-American markets plummeted (see Figure 2.3). In contrast, there was a huge increase in the volume of textiles exported from China to Europe and North America. Figure 2.3 clearly indicates the decline of textile exports from sub-Saharan Africa. From 2000 to 2010, exports to the United States experienced a particularly violent shock.

To add insult to injury, textile products from Asian countries flooded into Africa's domestic market, further threatening the existence of the remaining textile industries in that region. China poses the largest threat to Africa's textile and apparel industries. For example, textile imports to southeast Africa exceeded US$3.23 billion in 2017.[27] That

24 Ian Taylor, *China's New Role in Africa*, p. 65.

25 Actually, after 1995 the Agreement on Textiles and Clothing replaced the Multi-Fiber Arrangement, but the name MFA continued to be widely used to refer to this framework.

26 Louis Curran, Clothing's Big Bang: The Impact of the End of the ATC on Developing Country Clothing Suppliers, *Journal of Fashion Marketing and Management* (2007) 11.1, 122–134.

27 The countries include Botswana, Lesotho, Malawi, Mozambique, South Africa, Swaziland, Tanzania, Zambia, and Zimbabwe. Commodity HS 50–63.

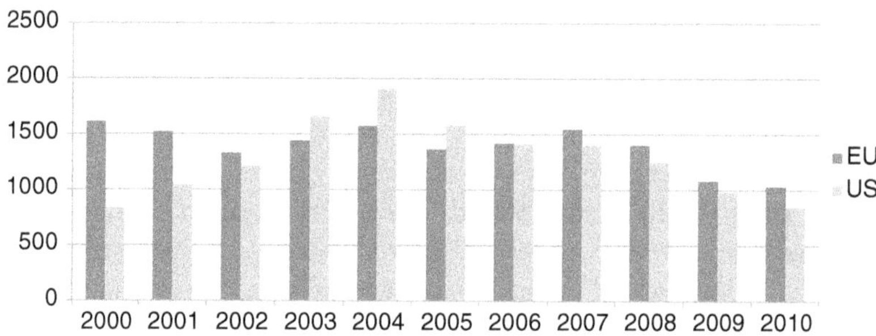

Figure 2.3 Sub-Saharan African textile and clothing exports to the United States and EU, 2000–2010. Unit: 1 million US$.
Source: United States Department of Commerce, UN Comtrade

is an increase of 71 percent over its US$1.89 billion in imports in 2007. China is not the only Asian exporter of textiles and apparel to southeast Africa, though the next largest exporters, India and Pakistan, rank far behind, at US$548 million and US$139 million, respectively, as of 2017 (see Table 2.1). In 2006, China actually limited the amount of textiles it exported to South Africa to protect local manufacturers from being completely overwhelmed by Chinese imports, but this policy was stopped in 2009 because it was found to be ineffective. During the period that Chinese imports were limited, other Asian investors continued to enter the South African market and seize market share from local manufacturers.[28]

The export data in Figure 2.3 show how the African textile industry developed with the aid of quota systems and preferential trade terms, not from its own competitive power. The elimination of restrictions on international trade immediately exposed the weakness of African countries' textile industries. The California-based Institute of Development and Education for Africa (IDEA) attributed the tragedy of African textile industries to a lack of skilled labor, insufficient technical knowledge, and small scale.[29] Other researchers have indicated that

[28] China expressed no interest in extending the quota of textile exports to South Africa, China Garment Net, September 16, 2009. www.51fashion.com.cn/HtmlNews/New/2009-9-16/265253.html (accessed September 4, 2013).

[29] Institute of Development & Education for Africa, Inc. The Tragedy of African Textile Industries, February 14, 2005, press release. www.africanidea.org/tragedy.html (accessed July 12, 2020).

Table 2.1 *Textile and apparel imports to southeast African countries from Various Asian Countries, 2006–2017 (in million US$)*

	2006	2009	2011	2013	2015	2017
China	1,888.7	1,892.8	3,246.9	3,454,6	3,741.9	3,239.1
South Korea	51.2	51.2	76.4	77.0	72.7	59.1
Malaysia	8.7	11.2	16.6	26.8	45.1	33.7
Pakistan	138.8	138.0	190.9	179.2	160.5	138.8
India	230.7	360.1	511.8	501.4	547.9	548.0
Vietnam	7.0	15.8	28.6	48.1	53.4	44.4

Source: UN Comtrade database.

exorbitant prices and unstable supplies of electricity, deteriorated road and port infrastructure, and low government service capacity have all contributed to extremely costly industrial production in many African countries, along with their inability to contend with Asian counterparts.[30] As for those foreign investors who had set up factories in African countries benefiting from the MFA, as soon as the policy expired, they returned to Asia.[31]

Thus, the decline of the African textiles industry actually stems from the removal of trade barriers in the international market as well as the strengthening of global commodity circulation, rather than an influx of Chinese goods. In a globalized market, commodity production tends toward specialization; regions that can produce at lower cost and higher efficiency will naturally outcompete manufacturers in other regions to capture world markets. Africa was not the only place to be negatively affected by the end of the MFA; many American and European textile and garment firms were also forced to shut down. However, these countries can export their own competitive products and therefore the ultimate impact has not been nearly as severe. Developed countries may have lost a labor-intensive, low-end textile industry, but this process allowed capital to concentrate on new high-technology, value-added industries. With the income from high-end products, these countries can buy even more traditional low-end commodities. Former minister of commerce Bo Xilai once calculated that

30 Ian Taylor, *China's New Role in Africa*, p. 73.

31 Institute of Development & Education for Africa, Inc. The tragedy of African textile industries, February 14, 2005.

one European Airbus could be exchanged for 800 million Chinese shirts.[32] This is supposed to be a win–win transaction, because the price of an airplane would yield less than one-tenth of that amount in European-made shirts, while, on its own, China would probably not be able to produce a similarly comfortable, reliable aircraft at the same costs. The transnational division of labor should maximize profit for participating countries.

Similarly, limitations on skill, management, transportation, and energy supplies make textile and garment production in Africa less efficient than in Asian countries. With further opening and integration of global trade, these industries will transform in the face of comparative advantages from Asian countries, at least for the upcoming years. The operative mechanism of market economy and the overall interests of the global market may hurt African industries in the short run, but in the long term they will contribute to a more sustainable industrialization in the continent. Chapters 5 and 6will have more in-depth investigations on how market-oriented Chinese investments impact Africa's manufacturing and industrial sectors. Before that, it is meaningful to first examine what role African countries currently play in the global division of labor. The remaining part of this chapter will discuss Africa's export to China and its implications.

2.5 African Exports to China

Just as Chinese exports to Africa reflect the comparative advantage of China in global manufacturing, the current situation of African exports to China reflects the position of Africa in the global market. First, from a quantitative perspective, Figure 2.4 shows that trade between China and Africa is basically balanced overall. Before the year 2000, China enjoyed a trade surplus, with fewer imports from Africa. But over the past few years, African imports to China skyrocketed, even surpassing exports from China to Africa. Yet this situation changed dramatically after 2015 as the commodity price in the global market plunged and China's industrial upgrading reduced its need for raw materials.

32 How to Change the Reality of "Eight Million Shirts for One Airplane (*Ruhe gaibian "ba yi chenshan huan yi jia feiji" de xianshi*如何改变'八亿衬衫换一架飞机'的现实), *Beijing Youth Daily*, May 19, 2005. http://finance.sina.com.cn/review/20050519/08471601737.shtml (accessed July 12, 2020).

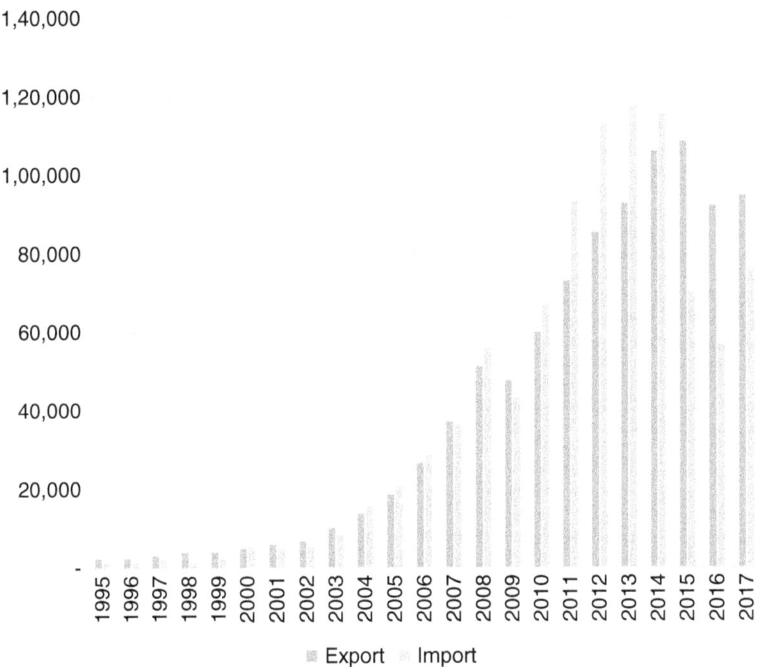

Figure 2.4 Imports and exports from China to Africa, 1995–2017. Unit: million US$.
Source: China Statistical Yearbook, China Customs Statistics

Inspecting the composition of African exports to China is instructive. Figure 2.5 clearly shows that mineral products and petroleum take up the lion's share of African exports to China. Moreover, oil imported from Africa to China is sourced from only a few countries: in 2017, Chinese imports of crude oil from Angola amounted to 50,416,004 tons, making up more than 61 percent of total imports of African oil to China. Crude oil imported from South Sudan, Gabon, and Ghana constituted another 13 percent.[33] Such a composition of Chinese imports from Africa has also led researchers like Denis Tull and others (see Chapter 1, Section 1.1) to claim that natural resources are China's key interests in Africa. Yet, it is just one aspect of the current China-Africa economic ties. There are many other areas of collaboration such as infrastructure construction and

[33] UN Comtrade.

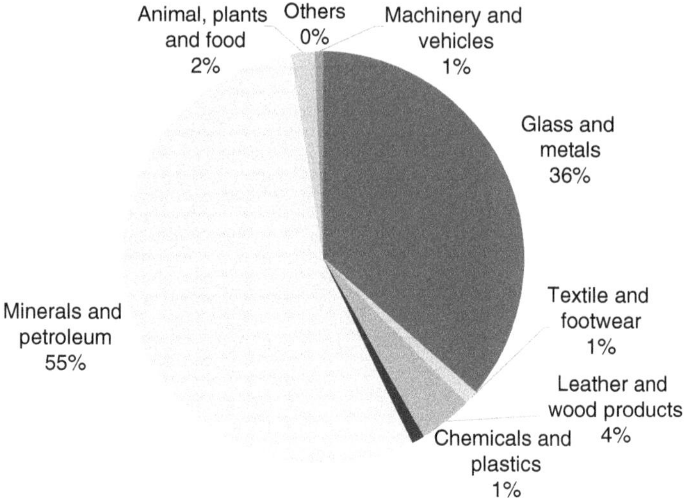

Figure 2.5 Composition of exports from Africa to China, 2016 (US$ values).
Source: UN Comtrade

investment. A closer analysis of the trade figures also reveals diverse interests among China and African countries.

First of all, the appearance of an overall trade balance between China and the African continent actually conceals a great imbalance. Apart from disparities in the type of commodities, with oil and minerals composing the bulk of exports, there is also great variety among different African countries' trade relations with China (see Table 2.2). Countries rich in oil, gas, and mineral resources such as Angola, Gabon, South Africa, South Sudan, and Zambia have very favorable trade balances with China. On the other hand, resource-poor countries, such as Benin, Ethiopia, Liberia, and Tanzania, have huge trade deficits. They demand great numbers of Chinese-made low-cost industrial products, while they cannot provide anything in exchange except a small number of agricultural goods. To assist those countries that cannot achieve trade balances, since 2004, China, under the framework of FOCAC (the Forum on China-Africa Cooperation), exempted imports from the least developed countries in Africa from customs tariffs. At the 2006 FOCAC summit in Beijing, the number of duty-free products was expanded from 190 to 400, and in 2009, the Sharm

Table 2.2 ***Trade Surpluses Between China and Select African Countries, 2017 (in US$)***

Country	Import from China	Export to Chinas	Trade Balance
Algeria	6,784,746,250	448,323,792	-6,336,422,458
Angola	2,257,453,225	20,698,709,467	18,441,256,242
Benin	1,926,508,591	91,590,374	-1,834,918,217
Ethiopia	2,664,554,880	357,582,736	-2,306,972,144
Gabon	446,190,755	2,293,610,995	1,847,420,240
Kenya	5,034,650,207	166,820,240	-4,867,829,967
Liberia	2,103,670,654	28,857,194	-2,074,813,460
South Africa	14,808,766,628	24,388,596,208	9,579,829,580
South Sudan	51,942,094	1,270,049,729	1,218,107,635
United Rep. of Tanzania	3,119,554,166	335,859,050	-2,783,695,116
Zambia	709,467,936	3,122,754,433	2,413,286,497

Source: UN Comtrade

el-Sheikh Action Plan promised to further remove tariffs on 95 percent of imports from undeveloped African countries with which China has established diplomatic relations. The 2018 FOCAC Beijing summit announced tax exemption policies on 97 percent of exported products from the 33 most underdeveloped African countries.

However, as discussed in Section 2.4, African manufacturing is weak to begin with, often struggling to survive even within the domestic market, let alone export to other countries. Agriculture is also relatively backward. Basic levels of cultivation and subsistence are often unachievable due to natural disasters. The development of large-scale production and export of cash crops has been slow. With agricultural production requiring great costs in time and labor, while acquiring little added value, significant profits from trade in agricultural products seem nearly impossible. On the other hand, countries with plentiful natural resources are concerned that mineral reserves will not last, and that heavy reliance on a single or several commodities makes their economies vulnerable to volatile prices. Ultimately, they are afraid that the pattern of exporting natural resources to China and importing finished products will further exacerbate the "resource curse" that has plagued several African countries for decades.[34]

These problems are not limited to Sino-African trade. Oil and mineral resources made up 47 percent of exports from African countries to the United States in 2016 and 50 percent of exports to the EU in 2015.[35] Economists have long understood that trade imbalances are a widespread problem for African countries, but this issue is often simplistically blamed on industrialized countries' plundering of African natural resources or suppression of local industry. Calestous Juma, a professor of Kenyan descent at the Harvard University Kennedy School of Government, wrote, "The worst that China can do is to continue Africa's mineral and plantation economies. China needs to complement its raw material imports with serious efforts that help African countries become exporters of finished goods to the Chinese market. Failure to do so will reinforce the perception that China's involvement in Africa will undercut the continent's efforts to increase its participation in the global economy."[36]

On the one hand, Professor Juma is correct to point out that exporting only natural resources or unprocessed raw materials will prevent African countries from building broad, sustainable commercial relations with other countries, and restrict Africa's reentry into the global division of labor. If this situation continues, African industry will inevitably be inhibited from reaping the gains of market globalization, which will lead to the further marginalization of Africa in the world economy, as well as significant income disparity. On the other hand, his belief in the power of a single country's unilateral intentions and actions to change this situation is far too simplistic. The global market follows neither the will nor the capabilities of individual countries or

34 Aderoju Oyefusi, Oil-Dependence and Civil Conflict in Nigeria, CSAE WPS/2007-09, p. 2; Jeffrey Sachs and Andrew Warner, The Curse of Natural Resources, *European Economic Review* (2001) 45, 827–838, pp. 833–834.

35 UN Comtrade. This is already a large decrease from several years ago due to the revolutionary use of shale gas. In 2012, the import of oil and minerals counts 78 percent of US total imports from Africa and 66 percent of EU imports. See also Lauren A. Johnston, Stephen L. Morgan, and Yuesheng Wang, The Gravity of China's African Export Promise, *The World Economy* (2015), 913–934.

36 Calestous Juma, China Should Import Africa's Finished Goods, Op-Ed, *Business Daily* (Nairobi), September 27, 2007. belfercenter.hks.harvard.edu/publication/17530/china_should_import_africas_finished_goods.html?breadcrumb=%2Fproject%2F46%2Finternational_security (accessed July 12, 2020).

groups, but rather economic rules. Investors must pursue greater efficiency in order to increase profits; otherwise, they will be eliminated from the market. Even though the Chinese government is conscious of trade imbalances and has even given preferential treatment to African imports, in the face of such a huge gap in manufacturing productivity between China and Africa today, capital flow cannot change its course.

I am absolutely not claiming that African countries are doomed to be merely providers of raw materials. China itself has, over the past forty years, forcefully proven how relations of comparative advantage or division of labor between countries can change dramatically. In the early 1980s, crude oil was also China's largest export commodity, but after 2000, machinery, electronics, and other industrial products took the lead. Notably, this shift was not driven by a single foreign country or set of policies; rather, it was mainly based on the effort and transformation of the society as a whole. The improvement of infrastructure in such areas as energy, transportation, and water supply; the increased technical capacity of the labor force; and the strengthening of legal regulations, along with the assembling of complete production lines, have all greatly strengthened China's manufacturing sector and blustered global competitiveness. These major developments helped China transition from being an importer of industrial products into becoming "the world's factory," exporting various products across the globe. The challenge of increasing industrial competitiveness for African countries and thereby transforming present trade imbalances between Africa and China, in addition to other countries, is immense and complex. It is only through an understanding of the concrete interactions between China and Africa in various domains that we can make accurate, in-depth assessments of China's impact on African economic development. Can the practices and knowledge that transformed China also turn Africa into a modern industrial powerhouse? The following chapters will examine several related areas one by one, noting China's impact on African progression toward industrialization. A pragmatic solution to the problem of structural asymmetry is not a simple task, but rather involves a series of consistent, meticulous efforts.

3 *Infrastructure*

3.1 Reflections on the Tan-Zam Railway

In August 2013, I boarded a train on the world-famous Tan-Zam Railway (Tanzania-Zambia Railway Authority; also called TAZARA) and began a 1,860-kilometer journey from Zambia to Tanzania. The railway's starting point in Zambia had been built at New Kapiri Mposhi, near the Copperbelt Province. The station was a square-shaped concrete building with pale yellow walls and light green window frames; reminiscent of the train or bus stations of small Chinese towns in the 1970s and '80s. Up to 200 people sat in the waiting hall – I guessed around 70 percent were locals, while the remaining 30 percent appeared to be European or East Asian. When a bell signaled that it was time to board the train, the travelers held in their hands or balanced on their heads packages of every size, fastened children too small to walk onto their backs, and surged toward the gate, filing through one by one.

The train was divided into several classes: there were first-, second-, and third-class seated cars, as well as first- and second-class sleeper cars. First-class sleeper cars were the most comfortable, but not that expensive either – with a round-trip ticket costing around 50 US dollars, they tended to be fully booked a month in advance. I originally only managed to get a second-class sleeper ticket, but luckily someone's reservation was cancelled, and at the last minute I made my way onto a first-class car. The service was excellent, with blankets and bottled water provided. Each compartment held four passengers; my fellow travelers included a local pastor vacationing in Tanzania, a Korean backpacker touring the continent, and a Zambian businessman. The businessman had made frequent trips between Tanzania and Zambia over the past several years, riding the train once every month or two. He said the railway remained the most convenient means of transportation between the capitals of the two countries. Flights were not only expensive but also required a transfer. (Direct flights between the two cities did not begin until October 2013.) Long-distance buses took six or seven hours less than the train, but the bumpy roads were intolerable. So the man preferred to take the train, even if a one-way trip took more than two full days and nights.

Not many passengers on the train were long-distance business travelers like this man. Most people in the sleeper car were tourists, groups of friends, or families on vacation. The train would pass by stunning mountain peaks, deep valleys, and gushing rivers. It would also traverse national parks, where wild animals fleetingly appeared. These were some of the colorful scenes and unique experiences that had been recorded by countless famous travelers. Those passengers going short distances were mostly locals visiting family or friends. Conditions in the seated cars were significantly inferior to those of the sleeper cars. Some looked like the old "green cars" in China, with seat covers worn to tatters and windows full of cracks, or in some cases simply the empty window frames. Others resembled the Chinese "blue cars" of the 1990s, with newer interior and more comfortable seats. These were the first-class cars, while the older, dilapidated cars were third-class. The entire train was composed of roughly twenty cars of different colors, a motley crew that together formed a mobile museum of railroad car history.

The train moved neither quickly nor slowly, chugging along rhythmically at around 50 or 60 kilometers per hour. There were many brief stops on the way; we arrived at a small village or town every hour and a half to two hours. When the train stopped, local vendors squeezed against the train windows, peddling bananas, corn, peanuts, or other simple food items. Naturally, the liveliest faces were those of the village children. As soon as they saw a train approaching in the distance, they would start to shout and jump for joy, arms held high in the air. Then when the engine started again and the train began to depart, they would wave goodbye to the passengers, looking as if they could not bear to see them go. The Tan-Zam Railway runs only twice a week, but for these children of the remote mountainous wilderness, without access to any outside information, each train that stopped for a few minutes was their only chance to connect with the world beyond their village. Therefore, they were always very excited.

After crossing the border between Zambia and Tanzania, the train stopped at a large station called Mbeya. Here, trains from Tanzania and from Zambia changed tracks, so there was a relatively long wait. As I waited, I saw two Chinese-looking mechanics inspecting the train. Their uniforms had the letters CSR (for China South Railway) printed on them. I struck up a conversation with the two engineers. Their surnames were Huang and Ding, and they had come to Tanzania with six other coworkers, for a period of one year, to do maintenance work on TAZARA trains. They told me that TAZARA also had cargo trains that should have been able to run once a day, but because of frequent delays, often took a whole week to get from Zambia to the border with Tanzania. The railway authority suffered from poor management – unable to make ends meet, it had already stopped issuing salaries. Cargo transport workers were on strike, and only the passenger trains continued to run. Another major problem in the operation of the railway was the frequent occurrence of accidents. On dangerous mountain passes, excessive speed could cause a train to derail. Aging engines and tracks only contributed further to possible malfunctions. I remember during my trip, now and again, seeing abandoned train cars and engines on either side of the tracks. These wreckages were often left corroding into scrap metal on the side of the tracks.

Even more concerning was the fact that the entire length of the Tan-Zam Railway ran on a single track. This meant that a single accident could paralyze the entire railway. Ordinarily, it should take about forty-nine hours to get from New Kapiri Mposhi to Dar es Salaam, but trains rarely arrived on time. My own journey ultimately lasted fifty-five hours, a relatively fortunate occurrence. Someone in my sleeper cabin had heard of other travelers experiencing 100-hour-long train rides. The two Chinese engineers said there were even trains that, because of accidents on the tracks, had to stop and turn back midway through a journey, leaving passengers on their own to find an alternative route to their destination.

The final station in south Dar es Salaam was rather impressive, far more magnificent than the initial starting point in Zambia. Two broad avenues intersected at a large public square surrounded by tall trees with lush green foliage. At the far end of the square, an imposing building stood in the shape of the Chinese character for "mountain" (山), a faint shadow of the Beijing Railway Station. An old train chassis and a section of track had been placed in the corner of the square as a historical display. Carved into the heavy, black iron frame were the Chinese characters for "People's Republic of China Sifang Locomotive and Rolling Stock Factory." A stone plaque erected at the base bore a description in English, roughly stating: "This memorial was inaugurated by the Economic and Trade Delegation of the People's Republic of China to commemorate the 25th-year anniversary of the Tan-Zam Railway, and to pay respects to the brave Tanzanian, Zambian, and Chinese leaders and workers who lost their lives in the construction and operation of the railway." The date inscribed was July 19, 2001.

After the trip, I checked the appropriate sources and found that a total of sixty-five Chinese aid workers had lost their lives during the construction of the Tan-Zam Railway. Their remains were buried around the outskirts of Dar es Salaam or in Zambia, never to be reunited with their families in China. From October 1970, when construction began, to June 1975, when the railway was opened to traffic, China sent up to 56,000 managers and technicians to assist in construction, while Tanzania and Zambia mobilized a total of 100,000 workers.[1] At the same time, across the Indian Ocean came numerous vessels transporting large quantities of materials, equipment, and provisions from China to East Africa. Whatever equipment or machinery wasn't able to be produced locally, China purchased on the international market and had delivered directly to construction sites. China funded the entire project, a cost that ultimately reached 1.094 billion RMB. Of this, 988 million was provided through interest-free loans; while the remaining 106 million that was added due to rising commodity prices was given for free.[2] At the time, China's domestic economy faced a crisis of stagnation resulting from effects of the Cultural Revolution. From 1972 to 1975, government revenue amounted to a deficit of 1.24 billion RMB,[3] roughly the cost of building the Tan-Zam Railway. In other words, the Chinese government continued its efforts to expand East African transportation infrastructure, despite putting itself in debt.

1 Little-Known Facts about TAZARA (*Xianweirenzhi de tanzantielu shi* 鲜为人知的坦赞铁路事), *Xinhua*, October 17, 2006. http://news.sohu.com/20061017/n245844624.shtml (accessed July 13 2020).

2 Zhou Boping, *Diplomatic Life in a Time of Emergency* (*Feichang shiqi de waijiao shengya*非常时期的外交生涯) (Beijing: World Affairs Press, 2004), pp. 129, 137.

3 China Statistical Yearbook, 1986.

Why did China decide to make such sacrifices, and even risk lives, to build a railway for another country? The reason, naturally, was that the project held crucial strategic significance. Newly independent Tanzania and Zambia desperately needed to develop their national economies. Tanzania's founding president, Julius Nyerere, firmly believed that national self-sufficiency could not be achieved without a robust economy, and he hoped to use the railway to develop the southern part of the country, which had been neglected during the colonial era.[4] Landlocked Zambia, for its part, had been relying on Mozambican and South African seaports, both to export copper, its economic lifeline, as well as to import petroleum and other necessities. However, after independence in 1964, transporting goods through neighboring European colonies became extremely risky. This was especially the case after a group of white settlers in neighboring Rhodesia (modern-day Zimbabwe) declared independence from Great Britain in 1965, and international sanctions were put in place against them. As a result, and through no fault of its own, Zambia's southern routes were almost completely cut off.[5]

Under the complicated and difficult conditions of southern African international relations, construction of the Tan-Zam Railway was never a simple question of economics. Although the World Bank and United Nations had declared the project untenable, Nyerere and his Zambian counterpart Kenneth Kaunda continued to actively pursue international support. Kaunda later said, "Every time there is a communication network between African countries, that is a step nearer the end of our continent's balkanization on which imperialism has fattened itself."[6] Colonial policies of "divide and conquer" had not only isolated and divided various regions of Africa, but also made them excessively economically dependent on the metropole. The United States provided aid to reconstruct a Great North Road between Zambia and Tanzania, but the transport needs of the two countries vastly exceeded the road's capacity. Particularly during the muddy rainy reason, passage along the road could not be guaranteed. The Tan-Zam Railway thus came to hold great significance in the liberation

[4] Zhou, *Diplomatic Life*, p. 130.

[5] Jamie Monson, *Africa's Freedom Railway* (Bloomington: Indiana University Press, 2009), p. 23.

[6] Monson, *Africa's Freedom Railway*, p. 21.

movement among African nations. Local people called it the "Uhuru railway," using a Swahili word, *Uhuru*, meaning "freedom."

Just as the "Great Proletarian Cultural Revolution" was spreading like wildfire across China, the Chinese government made a firm decision to support the liberation movements of its African brothers. At a moment when former colonies across Africa were achieving independence and establishing self-government, colonial rule and racial apartheid in Southern Africa emerged as a focal point of international struggle. Consequently, China sent large quantities of materials and military assistance to resistance movements in the region. In 1965, a request came from Tanzania for aid in building the Tan-Zam Railway, and after careful consideration, Premier Zhou Enlai decided that, regardless of the enormous cost and the many difficulties involved, the potential influence of this project surpassed that of many small projects combined.[7] Indeed, throughout the 1970s and '80s, most people's knowledge of Chinese aid to Africa was limited to the Tan-Zam Railway. Some would have been surprised to discover that China also provided other forms of aid.[8]

Construction of the Tan-Zam Railway had a massive impact on African political and economic development. In his 1986 address to celebrate the ten-year anniversary of the railway, Kenneth Kaunda praised the railway both for helping frontline states of Africa liberate themselves from colonial rule and for stimulating the integration of trade in eastern and southern Africa.[9] American historian Jamie Monson has also documented how construction of a new mode of transport allowed trade to flourish and improved the lives of tens of thousands of local peasants living along the railway.[10] Indeed, by its fortieth anniversary in 2016, the railway had transported a total of 28.40 million tons of cargo and more than 47.50 million passengers.[11] Construction of the Tan-Zam Railway also greatly enhanced the prestige of China, both in Africa as well as on the international stage. In 1971, Tanzania actively supported the restoration of China's seat at the

[7] Zhou Boping, *Diplomatic Life*, p. 132.
[8] Brautigam, *The Dragon's Gift*, p. 40.
[9] Zhou Boping, *Diplomatic Life*, pp. 129–130.
[10] Monson, *Africa's Freedom Railway*, pp. 100–122.
[11] Tan-Zam Railway Past and Present (*Tanzan tielu jinxi*坦赞铁路今昔), *Southern Weekly* [*Nanfang Zhoumo*], September 17, 2009. http://news.sina.com.cn/o/2009-09-17/111916313516s.shtml (accessed July 13, 2020).

United Nations. On the day of the vote, the Tanzanian representative to the United Nations, Salim A. Salim, dressed in a Maoist styled suit for the occasion, performed an impromptu dance of celebration in the assembly hall.

However, from its inception, the railway faced numerous difficulties. Transportation efficiency was hindered by a lack of experience in managerial and technical matters, as well as problems of coordination between Tanzanian and Zambian sides. For example, a large load of fertilizer and food supplies, urgently needed in Zambia, was delayed at a station in Tanzania for several months.[12] By the time both sides agreed to bolster their efforts, new challenges arose. Owing to falling copper prices on the international market, Zambian copper exports drastically decreased, and the railway found itself with no viable commodities to transport. At the same time, formerly colonized Angola, Mozambique, and Zimbabwe, along with other neighboring countries, began to achieve independence. Meanwhile, South Africa abolished the system of apartheid. With an economic blockade no longer in place, fierce competition emerged among multiple transportation routes, diverting a portion of Tan-Zam's passenger flow. The railway had originally been designed to transport 2 million tons annually, but even in 1977, its busiest year; it carried only 1.27 million tons. By the end of the 1980s, freight volume was falling with each passing year. By fiscal year 2014–2015, it had dropped below 90,000 tons.[13] Moreover, because of aging equipment and loss of staff, operational efficiency has gone from bad to worse. During fiscal year 2017–2018, the railway bore a deficit of 12.68 million dollars.[14] Even with 1.2 billion Tanzanian shillings of government subsidy funds, wages for October and November 2018 were not paid until mid-December, which led to a strike resulting in the cancelation and alteration of several routes. On the brink of bankruptcy, the Railway Authority is counseling the Chinese government on ways to inject more funds as of 2020.

12 Monson, *Africa's Freedom Railway*, pp. 101–102.

13 Tazara records drop in freight, *Zambia Daily Mail*, December 16, 2015. www.daily-mail.co.zm/?p=52844 (accessed July 13, 2020).

14 The director of the Tanzania branch of the Tan-Zam Railway Bureau expressed difficulties (*Tanzan tieluju tansang fenju juzhang biaoshi tanzan tielu mianlin kunjing*坦赞铁路局坦桑分局局长表示坦赞铁路面临困境), December 29, 2018. tz.mofcom.gov.cn/article/jmxw/201812/20181202821384.shtml (accessed July 13, 2020).

The ups and downs of the Tan-Zam Railway over the past several decades provide important lessons for development cooperation between China and Africa. First, large-scale infrastructure construction is a highly important affair; lines of communication such as railroads or highways are the major arteries of a nation, and they play a crucial role in a country's political, economic, and social development. Similarly, water supplies, electrical power, and communications networks all constitute basic conditions for the survival and development of modern societies. Therefore, a proper evaluation of the function of infrastructure must go beyond purely economic considerations. Although the Tan-Zam Railway has been suffering losses for a long time now, its contributions to national liberation movements in southern Africa, as well as to the development of neglected parts of Tanzania and Zambia, make it a substantial milestone in the history of China-Africa cooperation.

That said, the construction of large-scale infrastructure demands enormous investments, not only financially but also in terms of labor and time. Projects often take years or decades to be completed, and maintenance costs can be exorbitant. Therefore, in the policy planning stages, costs must be carefully calculated, and revenues and expenditures should be managed with discretion. A moment of negligence could lead to heavy financial burdens down the road. Owing to the emphasis on politics, combined with lack of experience, when China agreed to aid in the construction of the Tan-Zam Railway, it did not make sufficiently comprehensive economic calculations. As a result, not only did the actual cost of completion amount to 100 million RMB more than what had been projected, but also maintenance aid has added up to more than 1 billion RMB.[15] Meanwhile, owing to changes in international and domestic circumstances, as well as poor management, the railway's revenue has continuously fallen, leaving the governments of the three countries with a heavy financial burden.

Thus, it becomes apparent that, while infrastructure construction brings far-reaching benefits, it is often accompanied by enormous costs and risks. Through long periods of construction and use, changes in external circumstances unavoidably lead to the emergence of additional variables. It follows that the costs and benefits of large-scale

[15] Introduction to the Tan-Zan Railway Project, Embassy of the People's Republic of China in the United Republic of Tanzania, March 13, 2008. tz.china-embassy.org/chn/ztgx/wsyzyfx/t414461.htm (accessed July 13, 2020).

infrastructure construction cannot be conclusively determined through a set of standard measurements; rather, many contributing factors must be observed and analyzed over the long term. Today, forty years after construction of the Tan-Zam Railway, the need for a comprehensive understanding of infrastructure and its uses is all the more pressing. As Chinese enterprises have already become the principal force in African engineering and construction, such knowledge couldn't be more pertinent. There are currently hundreds of thousands of Chinese construction workers on the continent, working day and night to open up roads; dam rivers; and make extensive changes to local transportation, water, energy, and communication systems. But how will these Chinese-built projects ultimately impact African societies? Will they truly be able to promote economic development and industrialization? Can the errors and losses of the Tan-Zam Railway be avoided?

3.2 The Predicament of African Infrastructure

With few exceptions, the infrastructure of most African countries leaves much to be desired. As soon as one sets foot on the continent, the outdated and inconvenient nature of African infrastructure is quite apparent. Airports consist of only one or two small buildings, often dimly lit, with cracks and stains on the walls and floors. Roads in and around cities, unable to keep up with the pace of urbanization, are congested with vehicles, rendered immobilized due to constant traffic jams. In rural areas, roads consist of only muddy dirt paths, often littered with potholes. Whether in a five-star hotel or a government office, the electricity could go out at any time, leaving everyone in pitch-black darkness. Thus, self-provided generators have become a necessity for every enterprise and institution, even if the cost is exorbitantly high. Water supplies are not stable either. The vast majority of villages, and even some towns, still do not have water plants or running water facilities. Residents either walk several kilometers with a heavy container balanced on their heads to fetch water from a well or river, or they line up early every morning to wait for a truck to arrive and distribute water. The piles of trash accumulating around cities are not disposed of, and the toxins that emanate from them spread through air and water, threatening residents' health. A fixed telephone line is a rare sight in many countries. To get online, one must go to one of the few internet bars scattered around and then endure the double torture of excruciatingly slow internet connections and ancient computers. Over the past ten years, mobile telephone use has spread quickly throughout Africa. Even among nomadic tribes one can find youth who have begun to fiddle with cell phones. Even so, internet connections are unstable, the quality of signals is hard to guarantee, and service coverage areas remain limited.

In 2010, the World Bank published a report titled, "Africa's Infrastructure." It stated that, in nearly every aspect, the infrastructure of African countries lags far behind that of other developing countries, not to mention the huge discrepancy with developed countries (see Table 3.1). Especially when it comes to roads and electricity, there is a wide gap between Africa and other regions. There are many reasons why African infrastructure development has fallen behind that of other developing countries. First, comparatively speaking, Africa is sparsely inhabited. In 2010, the population density of Asia was 134.4 people per square kilometer, while that of Africa was only 35.2 people per square kilometer.[16] At the same time, more than 60 percent of Africa's population resides in rural areas, and for sub-Saharan Africa specifically, the urbanization rate is even lower. By contrast, up to 80 percent of the population of Latin America is concentrated in cities, while even in Asia, the rural population has dropped below 60 percent.[17] With the majority of the population scattered across a large area, the cost of implementing networks for water, electricity, and telecommunications increases dramatically, as does the difficulty of providing accessible public transportation and health services. Moreover, African regional politics are extremely complicated. Looking at a map of the continent, one sees fifty-four countries coming together to form a combination of various colors and shapes – most are small countries with populations of less than 20 million. This is due, on the one hand, to the diversity of African indigenous societies, and, on the other, to the legacy of European colonial partitioning of Africa. Socioeconomic differences and administrative barriers between countries create serious impediments to the construction of transcontinental roads, telecommunications systems, electrical grids, or internet connections.[18] Lastly, much infrastructure in Africa today is left over from the period of colonial

[16] World Population Prospects, The 2015 Revision, *United Nations*. [17] Ibid.

[18] Vivian Foster and Cecilia Briceño-Garmendia, eds., *Africa's Infrastructure: A Time for Transformation* (Washington, DC: World Bank, 2010), p. 4.

Table 3.1 ***International perspective on infrastructure deficit in sub-Saharan Africa***

Measurement	African Low-Income Countries	Other Low-Income Countries	African Upper-Middle-Income Countries	Other Upper-Middle-Income Countries
Density of paved road network (km/1,000 km^2, 2001)	31	134	238	781
Density of total road network (km/1,000 km^2, 2001)	137	211	293	1171
Density of fixed-line telephones (subscribers per 1,000 people, 2004)	10	78	120	274
Density of mobile telephones (subscribers per 1,000 people, 2004)	55	86	422	554
Electrical generating capacity (MW per 1 million people, 2003)	37	326	246	861
Access to electricity (percent of households, 2004)	16	41	28	95
Water (percent of households, 2002)	60	72	90	93
Sanitation (percent of households, 2002)	34	51	39	90

Source: Tito Yepes, Justin Pierce, and Vivien Foster. "Making Sense of Sub-Saharan Africa's Infrastructure Endowment: A Benchmarking Approach." Working Paper 1, Africa Infrastructure Country Diagnostic (Washington, DC: World Bank, 2008), p. 7.

rule. However, European colonizers were primarily concerned with, on the one hand, transporting local raw materials to ports for export, and, on the other, serving the few large cities where colonial settlers lived. Therefore, transportation systems, energy sources, and urbanization infrastructure designed during that period were never sufficient to support the development needs of contemporary African societies.[19]

Deficiencies in infrastructure have severely obstructed African socioeconomic development. Inconvenient transportation forces both cargo and passengers to move at a slow pace, while the costs of transport remain highly elevated. This situation leads to many strange phenomena. For example, a shipment that takes less than a month to travel from Guangzhou to Africa might stay anchored outside the port for two months waiting to unload and clear customs. Similarly, the cost of transporting cargo from the port to a destination several hundred kilometers inland might exceed the cost of shipping more than 10,000 kilometers from China to Africa. Transportation bottlenecks lead to shortages of goods on the market, causing prices to skyrocket while exports lose their competitiveness. Furthermore, insufficient supplies of water and energy hinder the progress of large-scale industrial production. In a World Bank survey of companies with operations in Africa, more than half cited energy supplies as their largest constraining factor. Inefficiencies at ports and customs clearance, as well as delays in transportation and telecommunications, were also said to have marked negative effects on business development. The report stated that infrastructural problems caused these companies to suffer a roughly 40 percent loss in productivity.[20] Underdeveloped infrastructure also implies a low standard of living. Local people, lacking access to basic water, electricity, and sanitation facilities, as well as a means of transportation and communication, are cut off from the material wealth of modern society. They cannot enjoy any of the benefits brought by economic and technological advancement.

Actually, African states and international aid organizations long ago recognized the importance and urgency of infrastructure construction in Africa. As early as the 1950s and '60s, newly independent African countries actively requested aid from international organizations and other countries to repair and build infrastructure. In 1950, the World

[19] Michael Fleshman, Laying Africa's Roads to Prosperity, Africa Renewal, January 2009, Vol.22–4 p. 13. Laying Africa's Roads to Prosperity, *Africa Renewal*, January 2009, p. 13.

[20] Vivian Foster and Cecilia Briceño-Garmendia, *Africa's Infrastructure*, p. 2.

Bank gave its first loan to Africa in the form of 5 million dollars to rebuild a road in Ethiopia. Indeed, the Bank's early aid projects in Africa were practically all electrical power stations, roads, and railways. For example, in 1958, Sudan was granted a 39-million-dollar loan to enhance the capacity of railroads and water supply facilities, and in 1964, Nigeria was given 80 million dollars for construction of the Kainji Hydropower Station. In 1961, the Ghanaian government independently raised 98 million dollars and received loans of the equivalent amount from the United States, Great Britain, the World Bank, and the International Bank for Reconstruction and Development, ultimately spending a total of nearly 200 million US dollars to build the majestic Akosombo Dam.

However, these infrastructural projects have not resulted in the substantial increases in socioeconomic development that were anticipated. Searching for the root of this problem, some researchers found "widespread misallocation of resources" and "failure [of investment] to respond to demand" to be the primary causes.[21] Furthermore, they placed the blame on overinvolvement of the state in infrastructure construction management, criticizing government monopolies for making the aim of projects unclear and reducing motivation for high efficiency. They argued that political influence was especially strong in investment decisions, leading to a large waste of funds and a heavy burden on the public budget.[22] These criticisms are not entirely without merit, as the plight of the Tan-Zam Railway shows how, during the early wave of infrastructure construction, African countries were incomprehensive and shortsighted in their considerations. These early mistakes demonstrated a need for reflection and improvement. Unfortunately, however, the International Monetary Fund (IMF) and the World Bank used these early missteps as a basis for implementing "structural adjustment" policies. They required developing countries to drastically cut their financial expenses and promote privatization. African countries, suffering from deteriorating domestic economies, and with governments drowning in debt, had no choice but to accept externally imposed reforms, in exchange for which they received

21 World Development Report 1994: Infrastructure for Development (World Bank/Oxford University Press, 1994), p. 25.

22 Michel Kerf and Warrick Smith, Privatizing Africa's Infrastructure: Promises and Challenges, World Bank Technical Paper Vol. 23–337, World Bank: 1996, ix.

emergency funding. In accordance with "Structural Adjustment," major Western donor countries shifted the focal point of aid from infrastructure and economic growth to government administration and the provision of basic welfare services for the poor. As a result, in the 1980s and '90s, local governments and international aid organizations stopped making large investments in African infrastructure.[23]

However, more than two decades of "structural adjustment" have still not brought substantial development to Africa. A 2005 report by the British government admitted that the single-minded emphasis on privatization and reduction of public investment in infrastructure had been a "policy error." Indeed, the facts indicate that private enterprises cannot completely take over the government's role in properly managing infrastructure. Private capital may be relatively active in an emerging industry such as mobile communications, but it would have little interest in areas such as water supply or sanitation, which require high investments but yield little profit.[24] For a full twenty years, insufficient investment in infrastructure has left Africa with crippling limitations on transportation, energy, water provision, and sanitation; making it difficult to meet the demands of daily life let alone achieve economic development. Over half a century, government-led initiatives and free market strategies have been experimented, including large-scale investment and financial austerity, but all have been unsuccessful, leaving infrastructure to persist as a longstanding challenge to local development. But if balanced, sustainable economic development is to be attained in Africa and if people's standard of living is to be comprehensively improved then this stumbling block must be removed. Can China provide a more effective solution to the problem of African infrastructure in the new millennium?

3.3 Dilemma of Public and Commercial Interests

China's market reform provides a contrast to the experience of Africa. During that period, infrastructure emerged as the driving force behind economic growth and development in China. Infrastructure, consumption, and exports came to be known as the "troika" of Chinese economic development. In fact, prior to 1980, China's road density,

23 Brautigam, *The Dragon's Gift*, pp. 28–29.
24 Laying Africa's Road to Prosperity, *Africa Renewal*, January 2009, p. 13.

telephone usage rate, and electricity and water supplies were similar to those of sub-Saharan Africa; some indicators were even lower.[25] But from 1990 to 2005, China's power generating capacity jumped nearly 400 percent, and the total length of its roadways increased by more than three times.[26] By 2005, every 1,000-square-kilometer area in China had an average of 180 kilometers of paved roads, six times what low-income African countries had; its energy supply had reached 99 percent, while that of Africa was only 20–30 percent; the rate of fixed telephone line use was up to 42 percent, several times that of Africa.[27] Even more significant, infrastructure construction has been relatively effective in supporting China's rapid economic growth, while booming industry and commerce, along with rising incomes, serve as sources of financing further infrastructure development and stimulate additional investment. Although infrastructure investment has overheated in certain areas, resulting in wasted equipment and funds, an overall loss of control has been avoided, and national finances have not had to shoulder any heavy burdens.[28] Over roughly the same time period, building upon similarly weak foundations, China's development achievements paint a stark contrast to Africa's harsh predicaments, which leads one to ponder: how has the Chinese model of infrastructure construction been so successful? And would it be possible to replicate such a model to Africa?

To find the key to infrastructure success or failure, we must first understand the position and function of infrastructure in a modern market economy. Infrastructure is not simply a commodity on the market; rather, it is a precondition for the circulation of commodities and the immense logistics of industrial production. Its significance

[25] Vivian Foster and Cecilia Briceño-Garmendia, *Africa's Infrastructure*, p. 2; Tito Yepes, Justin Pierce, and Vivien Foster, Making Sense of Sub-Saharan Africa's Infrastructure Endowment: A Benchmarking Approach, Working Paper 1, Africa Infrastructure Country Diagnostic (Washington, DC: World Bank, 2008), p. 19.

[26] Rajiv Lall, Ritu Anand, and Anupam Rastogi, *Developing Physical Infrastructure: A Comparative Perspective on the Experience of the People's Republic of China and India* in Klaus Gerhaeusser, et al., eds., *Resurging Asian Giants: Lessons from the People's Republic of China and India* (Mandaluyong City, Philippines: Asian Development Bank, 2010), p. 58.

[27] Connecting East Asia: A New Framework for Infrastructure, Asian Development Bank, Japan Bank for International Cooperation, The World Bank, 2005, p. 9 (Chart 3.1).

[28] Lall, et al., *Developing Physical Infrastructure*, p. 58.

cannot be limited to that of an ordinary commodity. Whether referring to roadways, water and energy supplies, or waste management, infrastructure builds networks or frameworks that facilitate the efficient flow of all these aspects. Large initial investment, uncertainty of consumer demand, long-term market risks, or better business opportunities in other areas may all lead a company to delay plans for investment in a commodity, but infrastructure, especially in developing countries, should never be treated with such hesitation. For many underdeveloped regions, lack of investment in infrastructure would make it impossible to engage in industrial production or market exchange with the outside world, forcing production to remain at the level of agricultural or pastoral subsistence. Over the long term, underdevelopment and isolation would lead to stagnation in the local economy, making these places even less attractive for infrastructure investment. Thus, pure marketization might be appropriate in cases where small investments yield quick results and recognizable market returns, for example, mobile networks, but they cannot be applied wholesale to infrastructure construction.

That said, history has taught us how infrastructure construction that neglects economic returns can be equally treacherous. Although a popular saying, "要想富、先修路" (Want to get rich, build a road first), has circulated in China since the late 1980s, in reality, transportation infrastructure does not necessarily bring economic benefits. Immense infrastructure projects like TAZARA may not have the expected socioeconomic impacts on a community. Without accompanying economic growth, the facilities built may not generate sufficient revenue to sustain themselves, and the maintenance and operation costs of the facilities then become a chronic financial burden for the countries in which they are built.

This forms another chicken-and-egg dilemma in the development process. Market economy requires infrastructure as an enabling condition, but investment in infrastructure cannot generate good commercial return or be well maintained if the market economy is not yet fully developed. Premodern societies, which relied on relatively self-sufficient production, indeed did not have much demand for infrastructure for millennia. Therefore, in developing countries, which are shifting from traditional subsistence farming to industrial market economies, an unavoidable question emerges as to how infrastructure can be built when commercial prospects for the future market are in doubt but there is a potential impact on national economic transformation. In a transiting market economy, the uncertainty of the commercial prospects of infrastructure is much larger than that in an established market, because an unsuccessful transformation may leave most of the designed functions of the infrastructure unused. Meanwhile, the business revenue of infrastructure projects in developing countries is not necessarily high given the low income level, although the public benefits of socioeconomic transformation may be huge. It is not easy to achieve a balance between investment return and overall development. Failure to stimulate sustainable investments will lead to stagnation of both infrastructure construction and market development.

China encountered this problem during the initial stages of reform. From 1981 to 1990, when the national economy was growing at an annual rate of nearly 10 percent, investment in transportation infrastructure increased by only around 1.3 percent every year, placing a great strain on economic development.[29] The Chinese government at that time was incapable of measuring the exact needs for infrastructure. They either invested too much in a short period of time or radically cut the investment rate after witnessing the economy overheat.[30] The turning point was during the mid-1990s. Since then infrastructure has become one of the primary motors of economic growth in China. From 1998 to 2005, the annual increase in investment for infrastructure soared to 23.3 percent, almost twice the rate of overall economic growth. In 2006, China's spending on infrastructure accounted for more than 14 percent of the gross domestic product, the highest of any country in the world.[31] Moreover, increased investment in infrastructure did not derive from state expenditures. Whereas in the 1980s, the proportion of estimated state spending on fixed asset investment averaged 15–20 percent, after 1992, it fell to an average of under 4 percent.[32]

29 World Development Report 1994, p. 18.

30 Fang Weizhong (房维中), The Development of China's Economy in the 1980s and Chen Yun's Economic Guidance Thought (*20 shiji 80 niandai zhongguo jingji de fazhan lichen he Chen Yun de jingji zhidao sixiang*20世纪80年代中国经济的发展历程和陈云的经济指导思想), *Contemporary China History Studies* (2005), 12.3, 27–37.

31 Lall, et al., *Developing Physical Infrastructure*, p. 59. In these statistics, infrastructure included energy, natural gas, transportation, water supply, irrigation, and telecommunications.

32 Ibid., pp. 64–65.

The key difference between the 1980s and the years after 1990s is not simply the increase of investment in infrastructure, but the sustainability of such immense investments. Although not every project has been effective, China's infrastructure construction in general has formed a benign synergism with the country's industrialization process and broad economic growth. New infrastructure improves investment environment and facilitates business development, whereas revenue from booming businesses enables further investments in infrastructure. The coevolution is achieved through appropriate consideration of both commercial and public interests. A concrete approach is to encourage local governments and state-owned enterprises to become the main driving forces for the new wave of China's infrastructure investment.[33]

In the early 1990s, financial decentralization accelerated and local governments gained more decision-making power on infrastructure construction. On the one hand, in a period dominated by economics, local governments were, like enterprises, evaluated primarily according to economic performance. Just as enterprises must achieve a balance of payments and see their assets appreciate in value, local governments had to concern themselves with GDP and fiscal revenue growth. In addition, after the 1990s, most funding for infrastructure came from financial market. Borrowers, namely local governments and state-owned enterprises (SOEs), have had to think about the capability of repayment. On the other hand, China has kept political power highly concentrated in the central government. Beijing has the absolute authority to award or punish local officials. This system prevented local officials from exploiting the huge infrastructure investment for private interests as happened in Russia.[34] Both SOEs and local governments must strictly comply with instructions from the central government and coordinate with national development strategy. Officials therefore combine economic benefits with overall development goals in their objective for infrastructure investment.

[33] Zhang Jun, Gao Yuan, Fu Yong, and Zhang Hong, Why China Has Good Infrastructure (*Zhongguo weishenme yongyou le lianghao de jichu sheshi* 中国为什么拥有了良好的基础设施), *Economic Research Journal* (2007) 3, pp. 9–11; Lall, et al., *Developing Physical Infrastructure*, p. 67.

[34] Blanchard, O. and A. Shleifer, Federalism with and without Political Centralization: China versus Russia, 2000, Working Paper 7616, National Bureau of Economic Research.

Of course, such dual identity is a complex issue. Its implementation and evolution process had numerous varieties and constantly encountered challenges. Nevertheless, over the past twenty years, this mixed motivation has effectively driven sustainable development of infrastructure in China.[35]

In order to stimulate local economies, local governments actively invest in infrastructure. With economic development at the center of their concerns, public officials act like corporate managers and allocate funds at the most crucial points. However, as government agencies, their focus is not limited to short-term financial returns; rather, they have to align their goals with national strategies, which aim at long-term gains for a region or the entire nation, in addition to taking public welfare into consideration. Once an infrastructure project has been completed, local governments and SOEs must rely on taxes and tolls to generate the funds necessary for maintenance. Therefore, operations take on a relatively strong market quality. At the same time, however, the government must consider limitations on the adaptability of the domestic economy – fees completely determined by the market would scare off consumers and lower efficiency. Therefore, the state provides latent subsidies to lower costs, mainly in the form of financial support for selective investments in energy and roads.[36] This arrangement deploys the supply–demand relationship as a means of project evaluation while sustaining long-term, comprehensive guidance and support. Accordingly, the share of private enterprises and foreign investors in infrastructure is very small. As the state decentralizes and promotes market strategies, it remains conscious of the significance of infrastructure for the economy and society as a whole and therefore does not loosen its grip on construction. Through the controlled shift towards commercialization, China was able to create an effective synergy between infrastructure construction and economic growth.

Although the political and social systems of various African nations differ vastly from those of China, the two regions have conducted a series of experiments in infrastructure cooperation over the past twenty years; drawing upon practices and experiences from China's domestic reforms, while also implementing new practices specially conceived for an African environment.

[35] Zhang Jun, et al., Why China Has Good Infrastructure, p. 10.
[36] Lall, et al., *Developing Physical Infrastructure*, p. 67.

3.4 From the "Angola Model" to the Addis Ababa-Djibouti Railway

Departing from the aid model of the Tan-Zam Railway, which predominated through the 1960s and '70s, in recent years China has begun to provide commercial financing to Africa on a large scale. One well-known example of this was mentioned in Chapter 1: a framework agreement of "oil for infrastructure" signed with Angola.

In 2002, when the Angolan civil war ended, the country desperately needed a large amount of funding for reconstruction. However, the IMF and other Western donor countries would supply a loan on favorable terms only if several preconditions were met. They demanded that Angola accept monitoring by aid organizations, guarantee budgetary transparency, and undertake administrative reforms. Despite their best efforts, the Angolan government could not meet the criteria set by the IMF.[37] At the beginning of 2005, Angolan finance minister José Pedro de Morais said in despair, "We will never be able to provide all the economic and financial information the Fund needs, according to their codes of fiscal transparency or of monetary operations. . . . We are a developing country, our institutional infrastructure is not well developed and, on top of that, we recently had severe disruptions in our institutions. So the process of providing economic information is a gradual process."[38]

In severe need of assistance to sustain its finances, the Angolan government had no choice but to seek out expensive oil-backed loans on the international market. These loans generally came from commercial banks, carried high interest rates and short repayment terms, and were meant to be reserved for urgent needs. In March 2004, the Angolan Ministry of Finance signed a 2-billion-dollar credit line framework agreement with China Exim Bank. This loan also used oil as collateral. Angolans promised to deposit the sales revenue of 10,000 barrels of oil every day in an escrow account of to guarantee repayment. China Exim bank gave a quite favorable interest rate: Libor +1.5 percent, more than 1 percent lower than the average interest

[37] Transparency on oil money delaying donor conference, *IRIN News*, February 2, 2005. www.thenewhumanitarian.org/feature/2005/02/02/transparency-oil-money-delaying-donor-conference (accessed July 13, 2020).

[38] Angola Unable to Meet IMF Criteria, Finance Minister, *IRIN News*, February 15, 2005. https://allafrica.com/stories/200502150654.html (accessed July 13, 2020).

rates for Angola at that time. The repayment period was seventeen years plus five-year grace period, much longer than the common commercial loans. The most unique characteristic of the agreement was that the Chinese bank did not remit any amount of money to the Angolan government. The 2 billion US dollars served as buyer's credit, meaning Angola could use it when contracting Chinese companies to build infrastructure, and once Chinese construction firms finished their work, they would receive payments directly from China Exim Bank.

The components of this model are not actually new. Oil-backed loans are commonly seen in financial markets, and, as mentioned in Chapter 1, exchanges of oil for infrastructure between China and Japan, or between other countries, can be traced to economic aid practices of the 1980s or even earlier. That said, in the case of Angola, China Exim Bank made some adjustments to these two preexisting models. Oil-backed loans were originally used by commercial banks to generate hefty profits. China not only lowered interest rates and extended repayment terms, but also coupled the loans with infrastructure construction, turning them into a special fund to support local reconstruction. Still, these loans do not constitute development aid, strictly defined. According to the official definition of "aid" from the Organisation for Economic Co-operation and Development (OECD) Development Assistance Committee, loans can be considered aid only if the interest on them is lower than market rate and if they are not being used for commercial aims.[39] Compared to previous cases involving China and other countries, where aid projects were guaranteed or repaid by natural resources, the agreement with Angola is markedly commercial in nature. Although the interest rate is relatively low in comparison with loans from other commercial banks, it is not lower than the market rate; moreover, the agreement guarantees contracts for Chinese companies under Angola's National Reconstruction Program, thereby providing a means for Chinese enterprises to gain a foothold in the local market.

Why was China able to effect this transformation, to come up with a new means of combining commerce with aid? In 2007, China Exim Bank chairman Li Ruogu published an essay entitled "Correctly

[39] Official Development Assistance: Definition and Coverage, OECD. www.oecd.org/dac/stats/officialdevelopmentassistancedefinitionandcoverage.htm (accessed July 13, 2020).

Understanding the Debt Sustainability Problems of Developing Countries," in which he expounded on a comprehensive reflection on the new forms of credit that China has extended to African countries in recent years. The main points are as follows: (1) The aim of lending is development, because development is inseparable from funding. We cannot give up at the slightest obstacle, restricting or cutting off loans to developing countries because of their heavy debt burdens; this would have a negative impact on recipient countries' development, making it even harder for them to make timely repayments and causing them to fall into a vicious cycle. It is crucial to build sustainable development through loan investment. (2) Western financing organizations and donor countries are overly fixated on the assessment of static debt; they neglect to take into account dynamic development and the potential positive impact of new loans. They currently use quantitative and calculative methods, as well as evaluation criteria for government policies and programs, that mostly come from hypothetical linear models or their own past experiences. The particular situations of developing countries are often very different, making it difficult to establish objective and appropriate judgments. (3) When China Exim Bank assesses loans, it pays more attention to receiving countries' actual situations, and it grants loans for specific projects. Through lending, it connects resources to development, transforming "resource advantages" into "development advantages." Thus, it effectively promotes the economic and social development of receiving countries, strengthening their ability to pay off debts and establishing a virtuous cycle. (4) Commercial benefit and development aid are not in contradiction to each other. Credit-invested projects with positive economic benefits can aid in local economic growth. This is the basic aim of development aid. At the same time, such projects can also create profit for the lending bank; therefore, they are mutually beneficial. Even though some may be financially unfeasible, projects with substantial social welfare benefits should rely on concessional loans. Choices should be determined according to individual case analyses, rather than generalizations.[40]

[40] Li Ruogu, Correctly Understanding the Debt Sustainability Problems of Developing Countries (*Zhengque renshi fazhanzhong guojia de zhaiwu kechixu wenti*正确认识发展中国家的债务可持续问题), *World Economy and Politics*, April 2007.

The foregoing points reflect how the principles underlying China's method of financial support to Africa are derived from the same origins as its own experience of self-development. Having been through a process of transformational development, Chinese banking officials fully realize the coevolutionary dynamics during the socioeconomic transformation. One cannot use the criteria of a mature market to evaluate developing countries; instead, one must look at how improvements in infrastructure can contribute to fundamental changes in production and social structure. China Exim Bank did not rely on complicated linear models to calculate potential profits. Instead, it created a new type of lending practice by integrating the actual situations of China and Angola: by means of resource guarantees and lines of credit, it effectively reduced the risks of graft or loan defaults. At the same time, Chinese enterprises made gains in terms of energy resources and construction contracts, while Angolan infrastructure saw drastic improvements. Large-scale infrastructure construction truly transformed oil profits into a platform for mass social welfare, as well as industrial and agricultural production. From 2005 to 2007, Angola maintained an annual GDP growth rate of more than 20 percent.[41] A local economist remarked: "This is the first time the Angolan people have truly seen their own country's oil revenue spent to improve their own lives!"[42] Notably, that same finance minister, José Pedro de Morais, who was crestfallen when his government failed to meet the demands of the IMF, was recognized for his outstanding management of national reconstruction. In 2007, *The Banker* magazine named him Finance Minister of the Year.[43]

The mode of using natural resources as collateral for infrastructure funding has been replicated in Ethiopia, Sudan, Equatorial Guinea, Congo Brazzaville, DRC, Ghana, and other African countries.[44] This

41 International Monetary Fund.

42 Vicente de Andrade, Professor of Economics, Catholic University (Luanda, Angola), November 2007.

43 Finance Minister of the Year/Africa: Jose Pedro de Morais, Finance Minister, Angola, *The Banker*, January 2, 2008. www.thebanker.com/Awards/Finance-Minister-of-the-Year/Finance-Minister-of-the-Year-Africa-Jose-Pedro-de-Morais-Finance-Minister-Angola?ct=true (accessed July 13, 2020).

44 China Exim Bank signed resource-backed framework lending agreements ("Angola Model") with Ethiopia, Sudan, Equatorial Guinea, and Congo Brazzaville. It also signed a framework agreement for lending plus investment

approach has received positive evaluations from international policymakers and researchers, because it has helped developing countries make use of their future revenue to improve current infrastructure and accelerate development.[45] However, this type of lending has encountered several challenges recently. First, falling prices of oil and other commodities affect the ability for these countries to repay their loans. Second, the debts of African countries have reached a high level; they therefore face restrictions on further borrowing. African governments thus require Chinese constructors to share more responsibility in financing. Many African countries also prefer to use guarantees of sovereignty without adding resources as collateral. Third, Chinese firms used to serve as EPC (Engineering, Procurement, and Construction) contractors on resource-backed infrastructure projects. Not only was profitability low, but they also had no influence on the maintenance and operation of the finished projects. Mismanagement in operations may prevent the infrastructure from functioning properly. Additionally, African countries also face increasing demand for high-quality management and skill transfer in infrastructure operations.[46]

In this context, Chinese enterprises have explored new patterns of collaboration with African countries on infrastructure construction. In 2007, Shenzhen Energy Company decided to build a gas power plant in Tema, Ghana. The company invested US$60 million out of its own pocket and China-Africa Development Fund (CADF) contributed another US$40 million . The investors borrowed US$100 million from China Development Bank as well. After beginning operations in 2010, the plant has been managed by Sunon-Asogli Power (Ghana) Ltd., which is a joint venture of Shenzhen Energy and CADF. The plant has managed to run nonstop as long as gas is supplied and generates

with DRC. China Development Bank signed a framework lending agreement with Ghana. Exim Bank signed resource-backed lending agreements for individual projects in Ghana, Nigeria, and other African countries.

45 Håvard Halland, John Beardsworth, Bryan Land, and James Schmidt, *Resource Financed Infrastructure: A Discussion on a New Form of Infrastructure Financing* (Washington, DC: World Bank), 2014.

46 "Hematopoietic" Finance: BRI Upgrades Africa's Development (*"Zaoxue" jinrong: "yidaiyilu" shengji feizhou fazhan fangshi* "造血"金融："一带一路"升级非洲发展方式), Chongyang Institute for Financial Studies, Renmin University of China, Research Report, Vol. 23, May 3, 2017, pp. 24–29.

15 percent of the total electricity generated in Ghana. The second phase of the plant began operations in 2016.[47]

In one of the largest Chinese infrastructure projects ever in Africa, the Addis Ababa-Djibouti Railway, which is more than 750 kilometers long and cost US$4 billion in total, Chinese firms and African partners used multiple forms of financing and collaboration to make the project feasible. Funding for the Ethiopian section of the railway came from the Ethiopian government (30 percent) and a commercial loan from China Exim Bank (70 percent). Funding for the section in Djibouti was initially divided in a similar manner, 85 percent from a China Exim Bank commercial loan and 15 percent from the Djibouti government. However, the Djibouti government had difficulty providing its share of funding. The contractor, China Civil Engineering Construction Corporation (CCECC Group), decided to shoulder the financial burden by investing a 10 percent share into the Djibouti Railway. With such an arrangement, Djibouti authorities merely needed to finance 5 percent of the construction costs.[48] Moreover, in order to ensure the project's successful execution, CCECC and China Railway Group partnered to manage the Addis Ababa-Djibouti Railway for six years after its construction. It thus became the first railway project in Africa to involve Chinese engagement through the entire value chain, from financing and equipment to construction and operation.[49] The railway began its experimental operations in October 2016.

However, critics are pessimistic about the economic prospects of the railway. Dissenting Ethiopian academics, calling the project a "White Elephant," pointed out that freight and passenger transportation would not provide enough revenue to sustain the rail line, let alone

47 Yuan Jirong (苑基荣), Chinese Company Fulfills Ghana's Dream of Power Independence (Zhongguo gongsi yuan Jiana dianli zizhu meng中国公司圆加纳电力自主梦), *People's Daily*, December 29, 2012. www.sec.com.cn/queryNewsShowInit.do?id=33022 (accessed July 13, 2020).

48 Addisababa Djibouti Railway: Comprehensive Chinese Standard for Export to Africa (*Yaji tielu: Chukou feizou de quantao Zhongguo biaozhun*亚吉铁路：出口非洲的全套中国标准), *Xiaokang*小康, November 16, 2016. finance.sina.com.cn/manage/mroll/2016-11-16/doc-ifxxwrwh4488904.shtml (accessed July 13, 2020).

49 Shen Shiwei (沈诗伟), Addisababa Djibouti Railway: From Chinese manufacture to Chinese operation (*Yaji tielu: cong Zhongguo zhizao dao Zhongguo yunying*亚吉铁路: 从中国制造到中国运营), *International Herald Leader*, Vol. 25, August 12, 2016.

make it profitable.[50] A *New York Times* journalist also expressed concerns regarding the impact of the gigantic project on Djibouti and Ethiopia's foreign debts.[51] The Mombasa-Nairobi Railway, for which China Exim Bank provided 85 percent of the US$3.8 billion funding and the Kenyan government cofinanced the remaining 15 percent, sparked debt-trap fears too after starting operation in 2017.[52] Several other countries such as Angola, Zambia, and Cameroon also flagged risks of debt default related to China's infrastructure loans. Addressing these concerns, Chinese agents have quickly reacted. Several loans were renegotiated and restructured. China extended the repayment of the Addis Ababa-Djibouti Railway debt and cancelled interest-free loans for Ethiopia and Cameroon. Meanwhile, China significantly reduced loans for new projects in Africa.[53]

Yet, the change of the lending practice is a part of the solution to the chicken-and-egg dilemma rather than a shift of policy model. Based on its own development experience, China does not identify the cause of debt stress simplistically as overlending, because Africa still badly requires investments in infrastructure. The real problem is the lower-than-expected growth generated by the infrastructure projects, which derails fiscal consolidations. Some supporting services, such as power supply or rail-to-port logistics, were not ready as promised, interrupting the appropriate operation and affecting revenue. There were also sociocultural obstacles seriously hindering the operation of these projects. For instance, Ethiopian farmers often drive livestock to cross the railway and cause collisions with the train. Kenyan truck drivers took to the streets to protest against the government's directive to increase rail transportation. These unexpected incidents tempered the optimism of both Chinese and

[50] Alemayehu Mariam, Ethiopia: Another T-TPLF White Elephant for Sale? nazret, January 30, 2017. www.nazret.com/2017/01/30/ethiopia-another-t-tplf-white-elephant-for-sale/ (accessed July 13, 2020).

[51] Andrew Jacobs, Joyous Africans Take to the Rails, with China's Help, *The New York Times*, February 7, 2017. www.nytimes.com/2017/02/07/world/africa/africa-china-train.html?_r=0 (accessed July 13, 2020).

[52] A New Chinese-Funded Railway in Kenya Sparks Debt-Trap Fears, NPR, October 8, 2018. www.npr.org/2018/10/08/641625157/a-new-chinese-funded-railway-in-kenya-sparks-debt-trap-fears (accessed July 13, 2020).

[53] China Is Thinking Twice About Lending to Africa, *The Economist*, www.economist.com/middle-east-and-africa/2019/06/29/china-is-thinking-twice-about-lending-to-africa (accessed July 13, 2020).

Africans, cautioning them to slow down the pace of constructing more infrastructure.

In spite of the tactic revisions, Chinese have not deviated from their strategic vision of fostering infrastructure construction in Africa. Now more importance is attached to coordinating various factors to ensure the functioning and growth effects of the infrastructure. As a Belt and Road Initiative document states, "Productive investment, while increasing debt ratios in the short run, can generate higher economic growth ...... leading to lower debt ratios over time."[54] Learning from the lessons of TAZARA, Chinese and Africans have made plans to develop industrial projects along the railway to build "interactive mechanism between large-scale infrastructure and industrial development."[55] CCECC and Ethiopian Ministry of Industry signed agreements to build a series of industrial parks, including Hawassa, Dire Dawa, Kombolcha, and Adama. China Merchants Group was also brought in to build a new port in Djibouti in order to more efficiently handle the expected increased amount of freight from the new railway.[56] Relatedly, a Chinese-built free trade zone began construction in Djibouti in 2017. For the Mombasa-Nairobi Railway, China and Kenya as well signed contracts to upgrade the Mombasa port and establish a special economic zone nearby.[57] Adhering to the "experiment first" principle, such efforts have been concentrated on just a few selected projects and countries.

[54] Ministry of Finance of People's Republic of China, Debt Sustainability Framework for Participating Countries of the Belt and Road Initiative, §16, April 25, 2019.

[55] Lin Songtian, "在中非智库论坛第五届会议全体会上的发言" [Statement at the plenary session of the fifth session of the China-Africa Think Tank Forum], April 18, 2016. www.fmprc.gov.cn/web/wjbxw_673019/t1356262.shtml (accessed May 18, 2019).

[56] The Chess Piece that Invigorated the East Coast of Africa: Chinese Built Addisababa Djibouti Railway Now in Operation (*Yizi zuohuo Feizhou donghaian: Zhongguo xuetong de yaji tielu jin touyun*一子做"活"非洲东海岸中国血统的亚吉铁路今投运), CBN, October 6, 2016. www.yicai.com/news/5129772.html (accessed July 13, 2020).

[57] China Communications Group and Ken Industrialization Department Sign an Agreement in the Development of the Mombasa Special Economic Zone (*Zhongjiao jituna yu Ken gongyehua bu xiaoqian mengbasa jingji tequ kaifa xieyi*中交集团与肯工业化部小签蒙巴萨经济特区开发协议), Economic and Commercial Counsellor's Office of theEmbassy of the PRC in the Republic of Kenya, September 24, 2015. www.mofcom.gov.cn/article/i/jyjl/k/201509/20150901121630.shtml (accessed July 13, 2020).

Chinese government announced a new debt sustainability framework for overseas lending April 2019, which states, "[I]t should be noted that an assessment for a country as 'high risk' of debt distress, or even 'in debt distress', does not automatically mean that debt is unsustainable in a forward-looking sense" (§35).[58] This indicates that Chinese banks have not ignored the debt risks or the criticisms on rising debts, but they insist on judging loans and investments through the angle of coevolutionary development, as opposed to IMF's debt limit policy. While IMF's policy is based on assumed universal standards and linear mechanism, Chinese practitioners focus on the possibility of projects to catalyze economic growth. The Chinese position is supported by a number of successful cases of infrastructure development in China and in Africa during past decades. Yet, this approach also constantly faces challenges in various contexts because it depends on the effective build-up of development synergism. China-Africa collaborations on infrastructure and industrialization are still evolving and their overall impacts on Africa's development need more time to unfold.

[58] Ministry of Finance of People's Republic of China, Debt Sustainability Framework for Participating Countries of the Belt and Road Initiative, April 25, 2019.

4 Agriculture

4.1 Hope and Hardship in the Cotton Fields

In August 2013, after an eight-hour ride through the mountains from Lusaka, I arrived at the headquarters of China-Africa Cotton (CAC) in Chipata, Eastern Province of Zambia. There, I was amazed to see mountains of cotton piled on the ground, dozens of trucks stationed in a large area, and ginning machines roaring in the factories. It was toward the end of the harvest season. Several dusty trucks entered the gate with a full load of packed cotton. Snow-white cotton shreds were scattered along the red dirt road behind them. The general manager of CAC, Shi Jingran, who was about fifty years old and used to be the head of a textile mill in Shandong province, told me that the firm had already become the second largest cotton buyer in Eastern Zambia, with purchases of more than 11,000 metric tons of cotton from the local contracted farmers in 2013. However, the main shareholder of the company, China-Africa Development Fund (CADF), was not satisfied. They set a goal of purchasing 35,000 tons of cotton in the following year. To increase the production of cotton and attract more farmers, CAC installed machines imported from China to delint cotton seeds with diluted sulfuric acid. This process was expected to significantly improve the germination rate of the cotton seeds. In addition, the firm planned to build a spinning mill in the Mozambique port city of Beira the next year. As China had an import quota for cotton from other countries, the managers hoped to facilitate cotton exports to China by processing the lint into textiles.

At that time, a feeling of optimism was clearly expressed on the faces of Shi Jingran and a dozen other Chinese employees at CAC. The company was established in 2003, when a manager of the former Chinese aid project Mulungushi Textiles in Zambia, Ju Wenbin, from Qingdao city, sensed an opportunity in the burgeoning cotton market. He partnered with several private investors to set up the Chipata

Cotton Company in Zambia. The firm grew at a modest pace until 2010, when CADF joined the board. The amount of cotton purchased before 2009 averaged merely 3,000 tons per year. CADF not only brought in huge amounts of capital, but also helped the company get short-term loans from China Development Bank. In the fierce scramble for cotton, the availability of capital played a decisive role in winning contracts with farmers. CAC also set up branches in Malawi, Mozambique, Zimbabwe, and Mali. Especially when Malawi and China reestablished diplomatic ties in 2008 after Malawi cut ties with Taiwan, the investment of CAC there was welcomed as a bilateral project of strategic importance. It had become the largest cotton buyer in Malawi in 2011 and 2012.[1] As of 2013 it had set up six ginneries and two cottonseed oil extraction plants in four southern African countries, purchasing more than 100,000 tons of cotton per year, employing 3,300 local workers, and partnering with more than 200,000 local growers.[2] The firm was celebrated in Chinese and African media; the *People's Daily* called it a "sparkling gem of Sino-African Agricultural Cooperation."[3] China Central Television (CCTV) suggested that the firm's operation impacted the structural transformation of host countries. "Cotton processing has become a pillar industry in Malawi. A large part of the foreign currency is earned from exports of cotton lint, seed oil and other side products."[4]

However, when I visited Chipata again three years later, the optimism of the Chinese managers had largely waned. CAC's annual cotton purchases in Zambia during the period from 2013 to 2016 fluctuated between 7,500 and 12,000 tons. These were not only far behind the previously set goal of 35,000 tons, but also significantly lower than the company's record of 27,650 tons in 2012.[5] Shi

1 Malawi, Ministry of Agriculture, 2012.

2 Company profile, China Africa Cotton Development Ltd., 2013. www.ca-cotton.com/ (accessed September 6, 2013).

3 The Wonders of China-Africa Agricultural Cooperation (*Zhongfei nongye hezuo de qipa*中非农业合作的奇葩), *People's Daily*, November 30, 2011. news.cntv.cn/world/20111130/103436_1.shtml (accessed July 14, 2020).

4 Rediscovering Africa ep2: Growing Cotton: A Way to Wellbeing in Malawi, Reporter: Xu Zhaoqun, CCTV.com, November 10, 2015. english.cntv.cn/2015/11/10/VIDE1447132682320847.shtml (accessed July 8, 2016).

5 Zambia Cotton Board based on data reported by each ginnery, 2016. However, professionals in this sector cautioned that the ginneries were likely to underreport the amount of cotton purchased so that they can pay less fee to the Zambia Cotton Board.

Jingran considered drought a main reason for the decrease in yield in recent years. Total cotton production in Zambia had reached its peak of 500,000 bales in the 2011–2012 season, but production in subsequent seasons stagnated between 192,000 and 240,000 bales.[6] The decrease of cotton purchase at CAC was just part of a more general trend. There were also other explanations for the decline of the cotton sector in Zambia. A local manager of another foreign ginnery Cargill pointed out that the "world market price's distortion" attracted large numbers of Zambian farmers to grow cotton in 2011, when market prices were high, but they were disappointed the following year, when the cotton buying price was almost halved. Some farmers never came back to cotton after the 2011–2012 price plunge. Meanwhile, the Zambian government used incentive schemes to promote other commodities, such as maize. Thus, fierce competition emerged among various crops.[7]

The situation in other countries was even worse. The Malawian government has changed regulations for the cotton contracting system several times over the past five years, first trying to centralize the distribution of seeds and inputs through state agencies, and then having to give up the state monopoly due to lack of capacity. In 2016, Malawian authorities set a fixed purchasing price of 375 kwacha per kilogram of cotton, but as the country's currency surprisingly reversed a trend toward depreciation, this price became too high, especially for the quality of cotton there, which was very low. Consequently, CAC did not purchase any cotton in Malawi that year.[8] In Mozambique, armed conflicts between the ruling FRELIMO party and the opposition, RENAMO, had caused disruption in Sofala province, where the cotton concession of CAC was located, since 2013. This instability greatly affected the cotton production. In the years following these conflicts, CAC acquired only several thousand tons of cotton annually, a significant decrease from more than 18,000 tons it got in its best year. Plans for setting up a spinning mill in Beira had to be cancelled too.[9]

6 United States Department of Agriculture, www.fas.usda.gov/commodities/cotton (accessed July 14, 2020).

7 Emmanuel Mbewe, Project and PR manager of Cargill Zambia, Chipata, August 2016.

8 Shi Jingran, General Manager of CAC and Zhao Xiangjun, Manager of CAC Malawi, Balaka, August 2016.

9 Shi Jingran, August 2014 and August 2016.

Nevertheless, the company's acid-delinted seeds quickly became popular among the local farmers because of their high germination rate. Initially, CAC distributed processed seeds only to its own contracted farmers. Later on, other cotton firms brought their seeds to CAC for delinting, at the expense of fees paid to CAC. Although the farmers overwhelmingly welcomed this new CAC technique, I could not find any evidence of significant improvements in productivity. A historical comparison showed that the average yield of CAC in 2012 was 450 kg/ha, whereas that of CAC in 2015 was 250 kg/ha. Compared with that of Cargill, which did not use acid to delint its seeds, CAC's yield in 2015 was nearly 30 percent less.[10] I asked Shi Jingran why the yields of acid-delinted seeds did not increase significantly in spite of their popularity. He explained that seed is just one of the three key factors to elevate cotton yield; the other two are inputs (including pesticide, fertilizers, herbicide, tools, etc.) and field management. Farmers in Zambia had such limited financial resources that ginneries had to give them seeds and inputs upfront. This kind of outgrower scheme involves high risk for the ginners, as they may not get enough cotton from the contracted farmers to recover their preinvestments. Consequently, CAC was reluctant to invest too much in inputs. In addition, since outgrower schemes do not exist in China, Chinese executives were inexperienced in managing the system. As for field management, there was also a large difference between China and southern Africa. "There are state-owned farms in almost every town in China, therefore technicians can be easily found there. The farmers were able to learn how to grow cotton from the technicians," Shi Jingran noted. In Zambia, by contrast, knowledge of cotton planting had to be disseminated by ginneries. A Zambian manager of CAC said, "The farmers are little educated. They need to be reminded repeatedly how to weed, how to seed, how to use pesticide, when the crop is growing etc. The buyers (of ginneries) need to check the farmers regularly, remind the farmers to visit the field regularly." Zambian CAC staff implemented field management training, while Chinese staff barely did any training in this regard. "The way of growing cotton in China was totally different [from that in Zambia]. We have no idea how to teach them [the Zambian farmers]," a Chinese supervisor commented.

[10] Zambia Cotton Board based on data reported by each ginnery, August 2016.

Figure 4.1 Zambian workers in the China-Africa cotton ginnery, 2016.

Over the past three years, CAC's progress was not as smooth as expected. Shi Jingran still believed that Zambia's cotton sector had room for growth. He recalled: "The productivity of cotton in China has increased several times in the past few decades. Africa looks like China did in the 1980s. It has the potential to develop."[11] CAC will continue focusing on improving the seeds of local cotton varieties. An agricultural technology demonstration center in Malawi, which was a Chinese government aid project and managed by CAC, has been in operation since 2015. A researcher with a PhD in agricultural science from China has been working with the center since April 2016. Shi Jingran hoped that the research capacity of the center would accelerate the development of good seeds. However, he did not have plans for expanding the scale of CAC operations in Zambia and neighboring countries in the near future. A few examples of unsuccessful Chinese investments in Africa's agricultural sectors had warned him of the high risk in this sector. A firm from Shandong province planted cotton in Sudan and reaped a harvest in the first year, but the cotton quality deteriorated dramatically in the second year. In two other cases, Chinese firms invested heavily in Ethiopia and Mozambique, but difficult market

[11] Interview, Shi Jingran, Chipata, Zambia, August 2016.

conditions ultimately led them into financial trouble. "Anyway we've managed to stay profitable these years, even with a small margin." Compared to three years ago, Shi Jingran has less ambitious plans, but he has become more pragmatic and more adapted to the African reality. While remaining hopeful about Africa's long-term development, he has realized that the transformation requires more effort and more time.

4.2 Dilemma of Subsistence Farming and Agricultural Modernization

The story of CAC exemplifies how the Chinese understand and deal with the numerous challenges in Africa's agricultural sector. Chinese agriculturalists who have worked in Africa have an ambivalent view on the development prospect of the sectors. On the one side, vast uncultivated land in Africa has a special attraction to them. On the other side, the low productivity and numerous challenges in the rural area appear daunting for the investors. In Africa, I often heard Chinese experts lament how land there was so abundant, yet so underdeveloped. It is estimated that Africa contains more than half the world's uncultivated arable land.[12] However, agricultural productivity and crop yields in Africa are still at a low level. At present, Africa's crop yield per hectare is less than half of the world average, and the index of per capita agricultural production has increased only from 93.64 in 1961 to 98.86 in 2016.

The geographic and climate conditions in Africa are obviously unfamiliar for Chinese at the beginning, but it just takes a period for the newcomers to know and get adapted to the new natural environment. The Chinese managers of agricultural firms can also have knowledgeable local staff to assist them in this respect. A bigger challenge is the broad political, social, and economic contexts in Africa's rural area that constrain changes of agriculture production there. In particular, the dominance of traditional subsistence farming in sub-Saharan Africa tends to cement an equilibrium of low productivity, harsh investment environment, and difficulty of change.[13] Various obstacles form

[12] African Transformation Report 2017: Agriculture Powering Africa's Economic Transformation, African Center for Economic Transformation (ACET), 2017.

[13] Subsistence farmers may sell surplus production after meeting their household requirements, but their main motivation is not commercial; they do not run their farming operations as a business.

vicious circles and hinder transformation toward agricultural modernization.

First, the underdevelopment of the market in Africa seriously constrains the growth of agricultural sector. Despite policy of market liberalization in many African countries, the markets of farming inputs and agricultural products remain fragmented and unreliable. Subsistence peasants constitute the majority of Africa's farmers. As they are scattered in the backward rural area, the subsistence farmers frequently suffer from deficiency of transport infrastructure, lack of storage, credit shortage, limited information channels, scale-related barriers, and other problems.[14] Consequently, most of them have very few market activities, but mainly grow crops with their own means and consume their own products. The self-relying production manners are accompanied with low productivity and low income. This further leads to underdevelopment of transport infrastructure, financial supports, and market structure, keeping the farmers away from accessing high-value-added markets.

Relatedly, the social behaviors of the subsistence farmers are conservative and difficult to change as a result of being disconnected from the market system. Researchers found that most subsistence farmers are motivated only to produce enough crops to feed their families for the entire year and to have sufficient inputs for the following season.[15] Correspondingly, the subsistence farmers are more risk adverse and more likely to pursue subsistence-oriented activities instead of undertaking more productive and innovative activities.[16] Being vulnerable to health shocks and natural disasters, the farmers hesitate to seek more profitable livelihood opportunities outside of agriculture or refuse to grow crops that have more economic value but need more resources. They are thus trapped into

14 W. Chilowa, The Impact of Agricultural Liberalization on Food Security in Malawi, *Food Policy*, 1998. George Daniel Lulandala, *Analysis of Factors Affecting Agricultural Productivity in Selected Subsistence Farming Villages in Tanzania*, PhD dissertation, University of Maryland College Park, 1994.

15 George Daniel Lulandala, *Analysis of Factors*, p. 158.

16 S. Dercon, Risk, Poverty, and Insurance, 2009. Brief 3 in *Innovations in Insuring the Poor*, edited by R. Vargas Hill and M. Torero. 2020 Vision Focus 17 (Washington, DC: International Food Policy Research Institute); S. Fan and R. Pandya-Lorch, eds., *Reshaping Agriculture for Nutrition and Health* (Washington, DC: International Food Policy Research Institute [IFPRI], 2012).

a vicious circle of vulnerability, low productivity, and slow development.[17] Additionally, many villages have their indigenous knowledge systems of social production, which are different from the modern scientific knowledge and often counterproductive.[18]

Last but not least, Africa's agricultural development is highly politicalized because of the importance of agriculture in the national economy and society. State interventions are common in a broad range of issues from land ownership and seed distribution to food pricing and input and credit subsidies.[19] The fragile status of the small farmers calls for protection by the government, but the politically motivated measures, such as land policy and fixed pricing, deviate from market dynamism and do not help with the elevation of productivity. In the long run, excessive political influences in agriculture actually contribute to the sector's underdevelopment and make the farmers more dependent on state protection rather than on their competitiveness. Another vicious circle of politicization, underdevelopment, and intervention further impedes the transformation toward a modern market economy in Africa's agricultural sector.

All these economic, social, and political challenges are meanwhile interrelated and generate circular constraints at a higher level.[20] The investments in agri-tech modernization won't increase without available labor or appropriate market regulation. A functioning market of land property rights and agricultural products won't be established if millions of farmers still rely on their own land for subsistence and cannot afford any business risk. Moreover, the obstacles mentioned earlier have not yet exhausted all the challenges encountered in the reality. International market volatility, climate change, fragmented

[17] Shenggen Fan, Joanna Brzeska, Michiel Keyzer, and Alex Halsema, From Subsistence to Profit: Transforming Smallholder Farms, Policy Report, July 2013, Washington, DC, IFPRI.

[18] George Daniel Lulandala, *Analysis of Factors*, p. 158.

[19] Ruth Hall, Land Grabbing in Southern Africa: The Many Faces of the Investor Rush, *Review of African Political Economy* (June 2011) 38.128, 193–214; Jane Harrigan, U-Turns and Full Circles: Two Decades of Agricultural Reform in Malawi 1981–2000, *World Development* (2003) 31.5, 847–863.

[20] Hazell, P., C. Poulton, S. Wiggins, and A. Dorward. The Future of Small Farms for Poverty Reduction and Growth. 2020 Discussion Paper 42. Washington, DC: IFPRI; World Bank, 2007. World Development Report 2008: Agriculture for Development. Washington, DC, 2008.

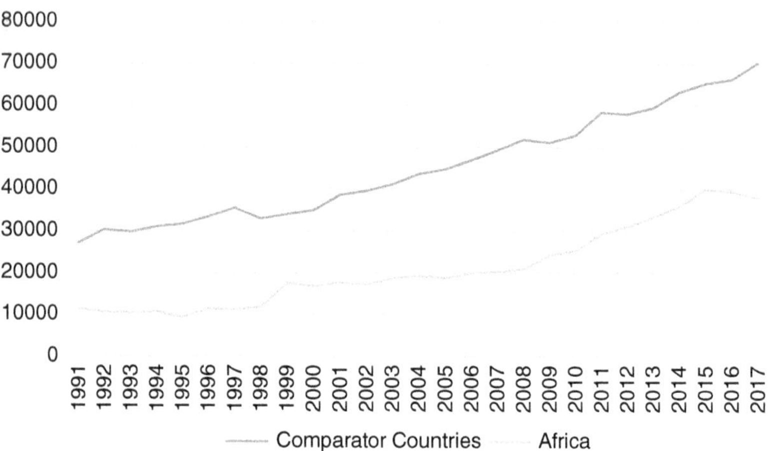

Figure 4.2 Annual agricultural value added per capita in Africa and comparator countries, three-year moving average, 1991–2017. Comparator countries include Brazil, Chile, Indonesia, Malaysia, South Korea, Thailand, and Vietnam.*
Source: World Development Indicators

regional market, and other factors greatly affect the rural development in Africa as well.[21] As a result, although the value-added per capita in Africa's agricultural sector has been increasing most of the time during past decades, its growth rate is significantly slower than that of the comparator countries on other continents (Figure 4.2). This has caused an expanding productivity and income gap between African and other countries.

As in other sectors, the structural adjustment programs, sponsored by the World Bank and International Monetary Fund (IMF), had huge impacts on the development of Africa's agricultural sector in the 1980s and '90s. The programs pressured African countries to minimize the role of the government, liberalize price policies, cut public spending in extension services and infrastructure investment, and privatize state-owned farms and enterprises. The privatization approaches did not work particularly well, as the private sector found it too risky and difficult to invest in the underdeveloped

[21] International Food Policy Research Institute, China-Africa Agricultural Modernization Cooperation: Situation, Challenges, and the Path Ahead, September 27, 2018, pp. 42–43.

markets.[22] Previously, state-funded institutions and services could still offer supports, albeit not always efficient, to overcome constraints in infrastructure, skill training, or social welfare. Since these mechanisms were swept away by rounds of structural adjustments, the vast majority of agricultural producers in Africa were left isolated to face the intertwined challenges. Although some producers, producer organizations, and nongovernmental organizations (NGOs) strive to fill the vacuum and take over the roles formerly played by public institutions, their services can rarely be sustained for a long time and are dependent on the availability of external funding.[23]

The reality of a suffering agricultural sector forced the African countries and the donors to revise their policies of liberalization. In the ensuing period, more nuanced interactions between the state and the market have been developed to address the practical challenges. Policy supports have been reintroduced to overcome nonprice constraints such as timely access to inputs, availability of technology tutoring, marketing information and arrangements, and so forth[24] The state is seen by the World Bank as complementary in supporting markets and liberalization is carried out in a relatively gradualist manner.[25] Nevertheless, owing to the shortage of public funding, lack of economic institutions, and weakness of farmer organizations, the modernization of Africa's agricultural production and market has not yet seen steady and broad progress.[26]

Chinese engagements in Africa's agricultural sector have a long history that can be traced back to the 1950s and '60s. Unlike Western donors, China has never interfered in the policy decisions of African states, but instead concentrates on aid and investment projects. However, the project-based approaches have clear policy implications. As the action plans of the Forum on China-Africa Cooperation

[22] African Center for Economic Transformation (ACET), African Transformation Report 2017: Agriculture Powering Africa's Economic Transformation, pp. 144–189.

[23] African Agriculture, Transformation and Outlook, NEPAD, November 2013.

[24] T. S. Jayne, and S. Jones, Food Marketing and Pricing Policy in Eastern and Southern Africa: A Survey, *World Development* (1997) 25.9; Jane Harrigan, U-Turns and Full Circles, 847–863.

[25] Report on Adjustment Lending II: Policies for the Recovery of Growth, Document R90-99. Washington, DC: World Bank, 1990.

[26] African Agriculture, Transformation and Outlook, NEPAD, November 2013.

(FOCAC) state, China mainly works with the Comprehensive African Agricultural Development Program (CAADP), established by the African Union in 2003, to enhance agricultural growth, transformation, upgrading, and modernization in Africa.[27] The China-Africa agricultural cooperation projects can in general be divided into two categories: official aid and commercial investment. The former is supposed to be free of business interests, whereas the latter aims for profit. Yet, China's own experience of market-oriented reform blurs the line between these two categories. Since China's successful development has been achieved mainly through nurturing of business activities and construction of functioning markets, many Chinese actors believe in a close connection between development and business. Yet, they lay emphasis on incremental changes through real practices and projects rather than on prescription of liberalization policies. What are the effects of this pragmatic method? Can Chinese efforts provide solutions to the dilemma between subsistence farming and agricultural modernization in Africa? The following sections will examine the various practices of Chinese aid and investments in Africa's agricultural sector and their impacts.

4.3 From Aid to Business

Agricultural aid constitutes a very significant portion of China's official aid to Africa. According to statistics, over the half-century from 1960 to 2010, China completed a total of 220 agricultural projects in Africa – roughly one fifth of all turnkey projects.[28] In the 1960s, most of China's agricultural aid projects in Africa were large-scale farms and agricultural technology promotion stations. Through the early 1980s, a total of 87 agricultural projects were built on up to 43,400 hectares of cultivated land. The most famous of these are the Mbarali and Ruvu farms in Tanzania, the Chipemba and Doho farms in Uganda, the Gombe farm in Congo Brazzaville, N'djili experimental farm in Zaire (DRC), Ghana's rice and cotton farms, Mali's sugar cane plantations, and Mpoli farm in Mauritania.[29] However, many of these projects

27 FOCAC action plans 2010–2021. www.focac.org (accessed July 14, 2020).

28 Deborah Brautigam and Tang Xiaoyang, China's Engagement in African Agriculture: "Down to the Countryside," *China Quarterly* (2009) 199, 686.

29 Yun Wenju, The Strategic Choice of China-Africa Cooperative Agricultural Development (*Zhongfei hezuo kaifa nongye de zhanlve xuanze*中非合作开发农

could not sustain operations for very long. Some began to suffer deficits after a period of time, and they gradually fell into disuse, or went bankrupt and had to be sold.[30] Searching for the causes behind this trend, Chinese researchers noted that initially, "there was an over-emphasis on show, on scale, and excessive attention to the function of demonstration, with very little consideration for economic benefit."[31] As a result, if recipient governments had funding shortages, there would not have been enough investment for maintenance, making it difficult to guarantee the long-term sustainable operations of the farms. Moreover, technology promotion stations were small in scope, very expensive, and were not economically self-sufficient. Some agricultural research projects required even larger expenditures, but results manifested rather slowly, leaving aid recipient countries with a heavy financial burden.[32] In addition, the departure of Chinese experts would usually result in an unstable transition period, which could lead to the failure of a project.

To make aid projects more sustainable, the Chinese government considered various ways to allow Chinese technical personnel to remain in Africa over the long term. If they could put roots down locally, instead of creating only short-term surface effects, deeper improvements might be made in recipient countries' agricultural production. One method was to combine aid with market-based mechanisms, by allowing enterprises to execute aid projects. In 1996, when President Conté of Guinea visited China, he made a plea for help with agricultural development, hoping that China would assist Guinea to realize self-sufficiency in grain

业的战略选择), *Chinese Soft Sciences* (*Zhongguo ruan kexue*中国软科学), December 1998, p. 96.

30 Mahmud Duwayri, Dat Van Tran, and Van Nguu Nguyen, Reflections on Yield Gaps in Rice Production: How to Narrow the Gaps, FAO Corporate Document Repository. www.fao.org/docrep/003/x6905e/x6905e05.htm (accessed July 14, 2020); Ma Jianhua, Uganda's Chipemba Farm Is Revived (*Wuganda qibenba nongchang chongxian shengji*乌干达奇奔巴农场重现生机), *International Economic Cooperation* (1992) 12, 38.

31 Li Jiali, The Form and Effectiveness of Economic and Development Cooperation from China to Africa (*Zhongguo duifei jingji canyu fazhan hezuo de xingtai yu chengxiao*中国对非经济参与发展合作的形态与成效), China International Poverty Alleviation Center, May 2010, p. 6.

32 Xue Hong, Agricultural Development and Economic Cooperation from China to Africa (*Zhongguo duifei nognye fazhan yu jingji hezuo*中国对非农业发展与经济合作), China International Poverty Alleviation Center, March 17, 2010, p. 10.

production.[33] The following year, in coordination with the State Council, the Ministry of Agriculture established an African Agricultural Development Center specifically for this purpose. Operating as an enterprise, the center established a joint venture with the Guinean Department of Agriculture, which is named Sino-Guinea Agricultural Cooperation Development Company or Koba farm. The basic line of thinking established by the Ministry of Agriculture for this project was: "Government provides support; businesses manage operations. Be vigorous yet cautious, in tasks small and large. For equality and mutual benefit, pay attention to substantial results. With grain as the priority, diversify the economy."[34] Adhering to these principles, the company constructed a roughly 2,000-hectare farm, where it planted a variety of high-yield hybrid rice. Moreover, in response to market demands, the company set up a breeding farm with 10,000 pairs of chickens and 50,000 chicken coops for commercial egg production. They also established a small-scale livestock feed processing plant with annual production of 5,000 tons, a factory for plastic woven bags, a rice processing plant, and a maintenance plant for agricultural machinery, among other projects.[35]

From the broader perspective of foreign aid, after reforms were instituted in the mid-1990s, the Chinese state vigorously promoted economic aid in the form of low-interest concessional loans and encouraged the integration of aid with investment, trade, and other market activities. Many agricultural enterprises leveraged the support provided by such policies to "go global" (invest overseas). Some built new farms in Africa, while others renovated and revitalized previous aid projects. In 1994, China State Farm Agribusiness Corporation (CSFAC) borrowed US$600,000 in loans to purchase an abandoned farming village of 3,600 hectares in Zambia and built CSFAC Farm. In line with local conditions and the company's own capacities, the farm

33 Xia Zesheng, China-Guinea Cooperative Development Project Under the Care of the President (*Zongtong guanhuai xia de zhongji nongye hezuo kaifa xiangmu*总统关怀下的中几农业合作开发项目), *China Agricultural News*, November 8, 2007.

34 Going to Africa, to Build a Farm: A Visit to China-Guinea Koba Farm, *People's Daily*, January 22, 1998, 9th ed.

35 Guinea Big Companies of the Century (*Jineiya shiji gaoda gongsi*几内亚世纪高大公司), CSFAC official website (*Zhongguo nongken jituan zonggongsi wangzhan*中国农垦集团总公司网站), November 10, 2010. http://a7610815.site.hichina.com/_d270821186.htm (accessed October 12, 2012).

started with a poultry project that had a short cycle and fast returns, gradually building it up, and ultimately using only three to four years to pay off capital and interest on the loan. In 1998, the farm accessed another loan from the Ministry, of US$1.5 million, and expanded its scale of production. By 2010, it possessed 1,200 heads of cattle, more than 1,000 pigs, and 2,000 acres of corn and wheat. It employed 7 Chinese employees and 260 local workers, and its total assets exceeded US$3.5 million. In particular, the eggs from the farm made up 20 percent of market share in the Zambian capital of Lusaka.[36]

In 1996, China Light Industrial Corporation for Foreign Economic and Technical Cooperation (CLETC) established a joint venture with the Malian government to renovate two sugarcane farms built in Mali in the 1960s and '70s. By 2005, the sugar cultivation area had expanded to 5,000 hectares, more than 30,000 tons of sugar produced annually, and close to 10,000 laborers employed during the busy season.[37] In 2006, the sugar plant decided to build an even larger third refinery, and received a 500 million RMB concessional loan to support the project.[38]

These pioneer commercial projects were relatively small and did not engage actively with local small farmers. However, their success prompted the Chinese government to come up with new ideas on how to provide aid to a broader circle of African farmers and to explore business opportunities in the agricultural sector at the same time. At the Beijing Summit in 2006, China promised to build ten agricultural technology demonstration centers (ATDCs) in Africa and later increased the number to fourteen in response to demand from African countries. At the 2009 FOCAC meeting in Sharm el-Sheikh, the

[36] CSFAC: Africa Is the ideal Region for Agricultural Development (*Zhongken jituan: Feizhou shi zuilixiang de nongken qu*中垦集团：非洲是最理想的农垦区), *China Investment*, November 1, 2007. trade.ec.com.cn/channel/print.shtml?/tradehwtz/201011/1105963_1 (accessed July 14 2020); Opening a Farm in Africa (Zai Feizhou kai yige nongchang在非洲开一个农场), *Southern Weekly*, April 8, 2010. www.infzm.com/content/43574 (accessed July 14, 2020).

[37] Mali Sukala SA to build the 3rd sugar refindery (马里上卡拉糖联将建第三糖厂), Commercial Office of Chinese Embassy in Mali (驻马里使馆经商处), March 19, 2006. ml.mofcom.gov.cn/aarticle/jmxw/200603/20060301709328.html (accessed July 14, 2020).

[38] China Exim Bank signed concessional loan agreement with Mali (中国进出口银行与马里签署优惠贷款协议), Commercial Office of Chinese Embassy in Mali (驻马里使馆经商处), November 27, 2008. ml.mofcom.gov.cn/aarticle/jmxw/200811/20081105918517.html (accessed July 14, 2020).

number increased again to a total of twenty, and by November 2016 there were twenty-five such centers across Africa.[39] These demonstration centers have three main functions. First, they use advanced technology and mechanical equipment to demonstrate high-yielding crop production, breeding, and cultivation of various vegetables and livestock. Second, they train technicians and farmers of the host country, providing them with the necessary skills in order to successfully manage the projects. Third, they aim to ensure the sustainable operation of the centers over the long term. The Chinese government provides enough funding to cover building costs for the project (40 million RMB each), as well as aid for the first three years of demonstrations and training (5 million RMB per year). After three years, if the host country desires, the Chinese side can continue to manage the demonstration center, but it will yield leadership to a corporation, which will implement market-oriented management. Thus, the center will be restructured as a commercial farm that can balance income and expenditures or even generate profits. As shown in Table 4.1, demonstration centers in several countries have been overseen by a research center or university. I once asked an official in the Chinese Ministry of Agriculture whether this could negatively affect a project's sustainability. In his response, he noted that the government shares this concern, but asserted that, to a certain extent, the exceptional technological capacities of these research institutions could make up for their deficiencies in market experience. However, they will not receive special consideration, and, just like other enterprises, will have to learn how to compete in the market.[40]

From 2011 to 2018, I visited ATDCs in Zambia, Malawi, Mozambique, Tanzania, Cameroon, and Ethiopia, in order to investigate how the three goals set by the Chinese government had been met. First, the effects of the demonstration at centers that I visited were quite different from the expectations of the Chinese government. Technology demonstrated by Chinese experts frequently did not fit the African contexts in which they were being implemented. For instance, while

39 China has aided 25 agricultural tech demonstration centers in Africa (我国已在非洲援建25个农业技术示范中心), *Farmer Daily* (农民日报), November 23, 2016. finance.china.com.cn/roll/20161123/3999008.shtml (accessed July 14, 2020).

40 Interview with Ministry of Agriculture Cooperation Officer, September 2008, Beijing.

Table 4.1 *Chinese agricultural technology demonstration centers in Africa, 2006–2017*

Country	Operating Enterprise	Status	Surface Area
Mozambique	Hubei Lianfeng Overseas Ag. Dev. Co.	In operation	52 hectares
Sudan	Shandong Academy of Ag. Sci. and Shandong Int'l Ec. & Tech. Coop. Group	In operation	65 hectares
Tanzania	Chongqing Academy of Ag. Sci. & Zhongyi Seed Co.	In operation	62 hectares
Ethiopia	Bagui Agricultural Tech Co. transferred to Liaoning International	In operation	52 hectares
Cameroon	Shaanxi Nongken Group, later transferred to Shaanxi Overseas Inv. & Dev. Co.	In operation	100 hectares
Togo	Jiangxi Huachang Infrastructure Engineering Co.	In operation	10 hectares
Zambia	Jilin Agricultural University	In operation	120 hectares
Liberia	Yuan Longping High-Tech Co.	In operation	(construction area) 26,000 square meters
Benin	China National Agricultural Development Co.	In operation	51.6 hectares
South Africa	China National Agricultural Development Co.	In operation	(construction area) 3,000 square meters
Uganda	Sichuan Huaqiao Fenghuang Group	In operation	(construction area) 3,000 square meters
Rwanda	Fujian Agriculture and Forestry University	In operation	22.6 hectares
Congo Brazzaville	Chinese Academy of Tropical Agricultural Sciences	In operation	59 hectares
Zimbabwe	Chinese Academy of Agricultural Mechanization Sciences	In operation	109 hectares
Angola	Xinjiang Beixin Construction Engineering Group Co.	In operation	54 hectares
Mali	Jiangsu Zijinhua (Bauhinia) Textile Technology Company	Under construction	

Table 4.1 (*cont.*)

Country	Operating Enterprise	Status	Surface Area
DRC	ZTE Energy	In operation	60 hectares
Mauritania (agriculture)	Mudanjiang Yanlin Zhuangyuan Sci. & Tech. Co.	In operation	50 hectares
Mauritania (cattle)	TBD	In operation	
Malawi	China-Africa Cotton Development Co.	In operation	50 hectares
Central African Republic	Shanxi International Economic & Technology Cooperation Co.	Under construction	
Eritrea	TBD	Under construction	
Côte d'Ivoire	TBD	Under construction	
Equatorial Guinea	Jiangxi Ganlian Industrial Co.	In operation	No data
Burundi	STECOL Corporation	Under construction	

Sources: Media reports, company internal reporting, interviews and fieldwork conducted in Africa and Beijing, as of November 2018

Chinese experts proudly presented the high yields of hybrid rice in Tanzania, a local senior official was unenthusiastic about the new varieties. In her view, "(Tanzanian) people like to eat rice, but cannot afford it. Rice was eaten only at ceremonies and Christmas …… Tanzanians do not target such high yields as Chinese do, for this may sacrifice taste. We want to balance yield and taste."[41] The Mozambican center built a sophisticated greenhouse to grow vegetables for demonstration. Chinese experts at the center reported that all the local visitors were impressed by the advanced equipment and technology. Yet a local researcher commented that such demonstrations hardly generate real results for local farmers, as the technology is too expensive and complicated for them to imitate.[42] This perspective was echoed by a Mozambican farmer, who was quoted in another report, "I learned

41 Sophia Kaduma, Deputy Permanent Secretary of MOA, September 2011.
42 Sergio Chichava, August 2014.

some things but at the end everything goes into the garbage because we don't have the means to implement what we've learned."[43] However, the Mozambican center did make adaptations to the local environment. Taking advantage of the good climate in southern Mozambique and avoiding the burdensome process of seed certification, the center did not use hybrid rice, but instead demonstrated how to plant local rice varieties.[44]

When it came to training, the implementation process likewise involved numerous unexpected challenges. The Tanzanian center, located in Dakawa, Morogoro Region, is more than 300 kilometers away from Dar es Salaam. The training budget of 5 million RMB per year, provided by the Chinese government, covered the costs of accommodation and courses at the center. Tanzanian partners were supposed to finance transportation to and from the center. However, the Tanzanian government did not allocate sufficient funds for transportation in their budget. Thus, trainees from other regions could not come to the center, and the center was able to train farmers only in nearby regions. The Zambian center, operated by Jilin Agriculture University, partnered with University of Zambia to offer training courses to students, teachers, and extension workers. Understandably, this partnership with the University of Zambia helped the Chinese begin their training, but it also limited the coverage of their training.[45] An official in the Zambian Ministry of Agriculture told me that he did not fully understand the function of the demonstration center. He stressed, "In order to reach farmers, they (the center) should work with the ministry because the Ministry of Agriculture knows farmers."[46] The center in Mozambique had the Ministry of Science and Technology as its local partner while the Ministry of Agriculture did not take part in the center's operation and training. According to a Mozambican researcher, various ministries fought to partner with the Chinese, for they believed that connections with the Chinese could benefit their ministries.[47] But this power struggle hindered the center's ability to effectively reach farmers.

43 Sergio Chichava et al. (2013). Brazil and China in Mozambican agriculture: Emerging insights from the field. IDS Bulletin, 44(4), 101–115.

44 Liu Housheng, director of Agritech demonstration center, August 2014.

45 See also Deborah Brautigam, *Will Africa Feed China?* (Oxford: Oxford University Press, 2015), p. 163.

46 Malumo Nawa, Chief field crops agronomist, Zambia Ministry of Agriculture, August 2013.

47 Sergio Chichava, Maputo, August 2014.

Facing various financial and administrative constraints, Chinese partners also adjusted their approaches to training. Instead of waiting for farmers to come to the centers, the Chinese government began to encourage Chinese experts to go to the fields. According to an official in Chinese Ministry of Agriculture, this method was drawn from the experience of the center in Benin and then promoted in other countries. The Chinese experts carried small generators to the villages and showed slides to several hundred farmers at one time. They also demonstrated various techniques in the field itself. In this way, they were also able to overcome language barriers, by teaching through demonstration.[48]

The third goal was to keep the centers running sustainably through market mechanisms. As the first ATDCs had been in operation only for a few years at the time, it is too early to evaluate their sustainability. Still, progress at that time indicated that this target would not be easily reached. The centers in Tanzania and Cameroon are located in remote regions and the Chinese manager had not been able to find good business opportunities. In Ethiopia, local laws forbid foreign aid projects from conducting any commercial activities and thus make it impossible for the center to implement its original business plan. In comparison, the center in Malawi is in a good position to achieve commercial sustainability. CAC uses the center not only to train their own contract farmers, but also to provide training for other farmers and agri-technicians as part of their corporate social responsibility activities. In addition, CAC plans to develop new seed varieties with the laboratory facilities at the center. CAC managers do not intend to limit seed development to cotton, but instead intent to expand their business to selling food crops and vegetable seeds as well.[49] The training and demonstration activities of the center have strategic importance for the operation and growth of CAC, which in turn continues to invest in the center. This win–win combination of business and aid was what the Chinese government always hoped to achieve with the ATDCs. However, not many centers were actually able to implement these practices. Without abundant capital, excellent location, or favorable policies, most enterprises found it too difficult to start a profitable business with the centers.

[48] Qin Lu, director of International Cooperation Center, Chinese Ministry of Agriculture, March 2013.

[49] Mou Zhengang, director of ATDC, Selima Malawi, August 2016.

Nonetheless, the ATDCs yielded benefits through cooperation with other Chinese investors. Hubei Lianfeng Co. arrived in Mozambique in 2007 to set up a rice farm, and one year later it was commissioned to build a demonstration center. Owing to capital shortage and corporate strategy, the firm was not able to expand its investment. Still, this experimental project drew the attention of the Hubei branch of China Development Bank. The bank wrote a report about the great potential of agriculture in Mozambique and attracted several Chinese investors from Hubei province to investigate the Mozambican agricultural sector. Among them, three firms, Wanbao, Hefeng, and Yumixiang, decided to invest in the country by 2014. The center helped these companies survey the market and prepare for investment. For this reason, the center was praised by the Chinese government. It was ranked number one among the fifteen existing agri-tech demonstration centers in Africa by the Chinese Ministry of Commerce (MOFCOM) and the Ministry of Agriculture in 2014.[50] MOFCOM also created a new requirement, mandating that all the centers serve as platforms for facilitating future Chinese investment in the African agriculture sector. The centers in Tanzania, Cameroon, and Zambia as well assisted Chinese investors in their respective countries through collaboration on training or plantation experiments.

The transformation of agricultural aid to Africa over the past fifty-plus years provides much food for thought. From the "monumental" projects that took no cost into consideration to the more recent emphasis on profit and sustainability; aid and commerce seem to have moved ever closer together. As stated earlier, this change, on the one hand, originates from the demand for aid itself. The previous experience demonstrated that if aid projects are to survive over the long term and generate meaningful impacts, they must abide by economic principles and align their operations with the market. On the other hand, the evolution of aid corresponds to China's own deepening understanding of the market economy. From early rejection of the market, to the gradual formation of a market concept and the maturing and perfecting of market operations in the post-reform period, up to the recent internationalization, diversification, and integration of business

[50] A Brief Account of the Development of Hubei Agricultural Reclamation (*Hubei nongken "zouchuqu" fazhan jilve*湖北农垦"走出去"发展纪略), January 19, 2014, *Hubei Daily* (湖北日报).

activities, the rapid changes in Chinese society have deeply influenced aid modalities. However, these market-oriented changes have so far failed to reach the goal of sustainable productivity growth. Apart from aid, a number of Chinese firms also directly invest in Africa's agricultural sector. Can the pure commercial projects achieve better results?

4.4 Earthbound Entrepreneurs

Just as the history of agricultural aid to Africa has been full of trials and tribulations, the expansion of Chinese agricultural enterprises in Africa has been far from smooth. An economic counselor for the PRC in Tanzania once said, "The risks in agricultural production are huge; it is very difficult to achieve 'win–win.'"[51] Apart from the difficult circumstances in Africa's rural area, agricultural investments tend to have long return period. The profit margin is limited and the operation is vulnerable to unexpected changes in climate, policy, and other aspects. Thus, most Chinese investors see this path as a dangerous one. Only a small number of Chinese enterprises in Africa are involved in agriculture. The investment in farming, forestry, and fisheries amounted to only 2.5 percent of total Chinese direct investment in Africa.[52] The numerous media reports about Chinese agricultural investments and land grabs in Africa are mostly proven to be untrue.[53]

CSFAC was the leading firm investing in Africa's agricultural sector in the early years. Since the 1990s, it has established a handful of farming projects in Zambia, Tanzania, Guinea, Mali, Mauritania, and other countries.[54] Because Africa is sparsely populated, and its purchasing power is generally relatively weak, the Chinese managers paid special attention to controlling the scale of operations and avoiding hasty investments in expensive equipment.[55] During the initial establishment of the CSFAC farm in Zambia, husband and wife managers Wang Chi and Li Li brought only 200 chicks, and without any chicken coops, raised them in a bedroom. It was only later, with the

[51] Deborah Brautigam and Tang Xiaoyang, Chinese agricultural and rural engagement in Tanzania, IFPRI Discussion Paper 01214, October 2012.

[52] China and Africa Trade Cooperation 2013, State Council Information Office, August 29, 2013.

[53] Brautigam, *Will Africa Feed China?*, pp. 76–80.

[54] Deborah A. Bräutigam and Tang Xiaoyang, China's Engagement in African Agriculture, *The China Quarterly* (September 2009) 199, 686–706.

[55] Africa is the ideal region for agricultural development, CSFAC.

gradual expansion of production and sales, that they installed electrical wiring, built a large-scale modern chicken farm, and imported numerous farm implements.[56]

Similarly, in a sisal farm of CSFAC in Tanzania, Chinese staff had cleared an open space in the midst of a jungle full of brambles and thorns. With their own hands, they had built a single brick house, and without any division of rank, the five or six of them slept and ate together, all under one roof. The Chinese managers even planted a vegetable garden behind their living quarters, where they raised a few chickens, saving labor and the cost of traveling to the nearest town to purchase food. In a developed country, the boss of a company with several thousand employees would have no need to concern himself with basic life necessities; through the market, he could conveniently purchase any kind of good or service. But in the uncultivated wilderness, market supplies are difficult to come by. Pioneering enterprisers must not only attend to the activities of specialized, modern production, but they must also sustain a traditional life of self-subsistent farming.

As China enhances business ties with Africa, the amount of investment in Chinese agricultural projects in Africa also increases. Section 4.3 mentioned how Hubei Lianfeng Co. was not able to expand its pilot farm in Mozambique due to lack of capital. In 2012, Wanbao Grain and Oil Investment Ltd., a company from Hubei province that had an annual turnover totaling 2 billion RMB, decided to take over the Lianfeng farm, which is located in the Xai-xai region, and invest in expansion. Seeing that Mozambique imports hundreds of thousands of tons of rice ever year, Wanbao was confident of the prospects of a rice plantation in the country. Within three years, Wanbao spent a whopping 800 million RMB (more than US$120 million) to develop more than 10,000 hectares of land and build warehousing and processing facilities.[57] They planned to eventually extend the plantation area

56 Planting in a Foreign Land and Harvesting Hope: The Story of a Chinese Farm Manager in Zambia (*Gengyun yixiang shouhuo xiwang: Zanbiya huaren nongchang jingyingzhe de gushi*耕耘异乡收获希望 赞比亚华人农场经营者的故事), *Xinhua Net*, October 18, 2006. www.gqb.gov.cn/news/2006/1019/1/3323.shtml (accessed July 14, 2020).

57 Cai Yong, country manager of Wanbao, August 2014. See also XiangyangWanbao Co. Agricultural Development Project in Mozambiqueapproved (襄阳万宝粮油公司莫桑比克农业开发项目获批), Xiangyang Commerce Administration, April 23, 2012. www.mofcom.gov.cn/aarticle/resume/n/201204/20120408084422.html (accessed July 14, 2020).

to 20,000 hectares and have local out-growers grow rice in another 100,000-hectare area.[58] In 2013, CADF signed an agreement to join the project, taking 49 percent of the total shares. This further enhanced the financial position of the firm.

As an important part of its business plan, Wanbao designed three steps to cooperate with local farmers. First, they launched a training program to teach local farmers how to grow rice. The trained farmers are expected to become out-growers to cultivate a 100,000-hectare rice field. Second, after two years of training, some farmers would become "demonstration farmers" and manage their land independently. Each demonstration farmer would get four to five hectares land to grow rice. They would need to invest in seed, tools, herbicide, and labor on their own. Wanbao planned to give them a loan to cover 50 percent of the investment amount as a loan, but they needed to get another 50 percent from local bank loans. Lastly, Wanbao would welcome local individual farmers and enterprises to become out-growers and supply rice. Wanbao was willing to provide seeds, technology, and machinery services for the out-growers. As a gesture of support, Gaza governor's wife became one of the local partner farmers and started to grow and supply rice to Wanbao.

To support the plan of cooperation, Wanbao is also building up a complete machinery and technology service system. They charge a fee for all the services provided. Wanbao acknowledged that the price tag of its service offered is higher than that of the existing service system in Mozambique, which is provided by local government. Wanbao's country manager Luo Haoping commented on the existing system: "Although it charges little, the service is bad." As the local government cannot guarantee maintenance and reparation of equipment, the farmers cannot get sufficient technical support and have very low production. This forms a vicious circle. By comparison, Luo Haoping talked about Wanbao's vision, "We charge a higher fee to start a virtuous circle. Likewise, we sell our seeds for higher price. Only when we are profitable, we will invest. The key is to raise farmers' income and production."[59]

58 Wanbao's Overseas Farming Aims to Build the Largest Farm in Mozambique (*Wanbao gongsi haiwai zhongdi dazao mosangbike zuida nongchang*万宝公司海外种地 打造莫桑比克最大农场), CRI Online, June 20, 2014. www.nongcun5.com/news/20140620/31420.html (accessed July 14, 2020).

59 Luo Haoping, Xaixai, August 2014.

However, the expected virtuous circle of high-input and high-outcome rice production was not realized. First, two consecutive years of flooding from upstream of Limpopo devastated the farms. Wanbao harvested nothing in 2012 and saved only 1,800 hectares out of the 8,800 hectares cultivated from the inundation in 2013. The cooperating farmers were seriously hit as well. In 2012, all twenty-five local households, who were selected to be part of the tutoring program, suffered from the flooding and yielded nothing. In 2013, sixty-eight households were chosen to receive training in an area of seventy hectares. Although they did not lose the entire harvest, lack of communication and information caused the trainees to become indebted. For example, after farmer trainees sold their grains to Wanbao, they suffered a net loss because the training and service provided during the year were added to the total annual fee, which the farmers were unaware of.[60] In addition, local credit provider Fundo Desenvolvemento Agricole (FDA) was concerned about Wanbao's capacity to support the farmer trainees and was reluctant to provide loans to the farmers. In the end, only a handful of selected farmers and partners, including the local governor's wife, earned a profit during the first two years of the project. Owing to the influences of natural disaster, knowledge deficiency, and financial constraints, most of the farmers, particularly the less educated and the financially vulnerable ones, lost money during the cooperation with Wanbao. This unfortunate experience discouraged them from continuing the experiment.

Even the Wanbao enterprise itself also fell into a vicious circle. After the second flooding, the company had to build a long wall around the vast experimental area to protect the fields. As Mozambique lacks infrastructure and material supply, Wanbao has to take care of many things along the value chain of rice production. Not only do they need to develop land and grow rice, they also need to build warehouses and processing plants. To construct these facilities, they set up a small steel plant and a brick factory. New houses were built to accommodate hundreds of Chinese and local workers. Three processing areas in Xai-xai region were undergoing construction. Luo Haoping said, "Wanbao has been dragged to a very long value chain. Everything needs to be done by ourselves. This requires huge investment."[61] Eventually the

[60] Sergio Chichava, Maputo, August 2014.
[61] Luo Haoping, Xaixai, August 2014.

heavy financial burden forced Wanbao to stop further investment in 2015, as it faced several debt lawsuits within China. September 2015 CADF had to take over the management of the project. As an equity investor, CADF does not specialize in operating agricultural business. By April 2017, CADF management had just managed to maintain a very low level of activity at the Xai-xai project while they waited for a new investor to revive the project.[62]

The director of the ATDC in Mozambique saw how the Xai-xai project was managed by Lianfeng and Wanbao. He acknowledged that the firms had done a lot of feasibility studies and preparation before the investment, but the risk of agricultural projects remained immense. "It's impossible not to have natural disasters and other kinds of unpredictable incidents in the agricultural business … Risks in industrial production is controllable, but in agricultural production they are uncontrollable."[63] The Wanbao case proves that the "high input–high outcome" business model can hardly work in the African rural area where the vicious circle of vulnerability, low productivity, and slow development prevails.

Actually, the survival of Chinese agricultural projects frequently depends on the managers' perseverance rather than on commercial calculation. In 2005, the manager of Zambia CSFAC farm, Wang Chi unfortunately passed away in a car accident, and his widow Li Li had to take up the heavy task of managing the farm on her own. Every day, she worked eighteen hours and endured several car accidents, robberies, fires, and other life-threatening disasters. She admits that many people have asked her why she went to Africa and stayed for twenty years, whether it was really worth it. She has often asked herself the same question. Without giving a clear answer, she says only, "I really have no regrets! All this time, no matter what has happened, really, I have nothing to regret. All these days, I think I have lived to the fullest, including the most difficult ones."[64] Likewise, a few dogged agriculturalists kept the sisal farm in Tanzania alive. Former director Jia

62 Briefing on the Wanbao Mozambique Agricultural Park Project (*Guanyu wanbao mosang nongyeyuan xiangmu de qingkuang jieshao*关于万宝莫桑农业园项目的情况介绍), Sichuan Agricultural University, April 1, 2017. jdxy .sicau.edu.cn/info/1076/6086.htm (accessed July 14, 2020).

63 Liu Dehou, director of ATDC in Mozambique, August 2014.

64 "Li Li, the woman who moved Africa." ["感动非洲的李莉"], *China Agricultural Development News* [中国农发报], May 17, 2012. www .cnadc.com.cn/xwdt/2012/5/6905dn0v25.htm (accessed May 24, 2012).

Qingquan, nearing his sixties, cannot forget the many years of struggle he spent farming in Africa. Sighing with emotion, he said, "African soil is just too attractive. When I see a piece of fertile land, still uncultivated, I start to drool with desire. I simply love to plant on new land."[65] Director Jia recalled how in 2002, when the bank stopped granting loans, in order to concentrate their limited funds and put them to good use, the farm delayed payment of salaries for Chinese managers for more than five years – the total amount added up to over US$100,000. Although these managers suffered economic losses, they continued their diligent work for the sake of the sisal project's success. It was only when the harvest season came that the farm finally secured its local footing.[66]

The bumpy experiences of these pilot projects suggested that Chinese firms in general have not yet found effective approaches to invest in Africa's agricultural sector. As with foreign aid, Chinese investors have kept searching for suitable models for this sector in gradualist and experimental manners. Whether in regard to aid or investment, the Chinese government and other enterprises have consistently emphasized the role of the market and promoted projects that were commercially sustainable.[67] We can see that pragmatism continues to guide Chinese engagements in agricultural sector, albeit with more challenges and less success. Chinese actors not only adapt their practices to suit Africa's reality, but also borrow business models from Africa and other countries. As noted in the CAC case, China did not use a contract farming model to grow cotton at home; rather, Chinese firms learned from local market practices to develop their own out-grower schemes. Owing to its challenging conditions, agriculture demands a much steeper learning curve for foreign investors. From a development perspective, the transition toward market economy and modern production in rural areas requires extensive changes for many people who still largely

65 Jia Qingquan, Comments on the 30th Anniversary of Graduation from August 1st Agricultural University (*Baiyi nongda biye sanshizhounian yougan* 八一农大毕业三十周年有感), Netease Blog, August 20, 2009. nj1976j.blog.163.com/blog/static/17387637420097220584410З/ (accessed November 12, 2012).

66 Ibid.

67 It is groundless to assume that Chinese agricultural investments in Africa are sponsored by the government for the purpose of land grabbing and transporting food crops back to China. See Brautigam, *Will Africa Feed China?*, pp. 151–158.

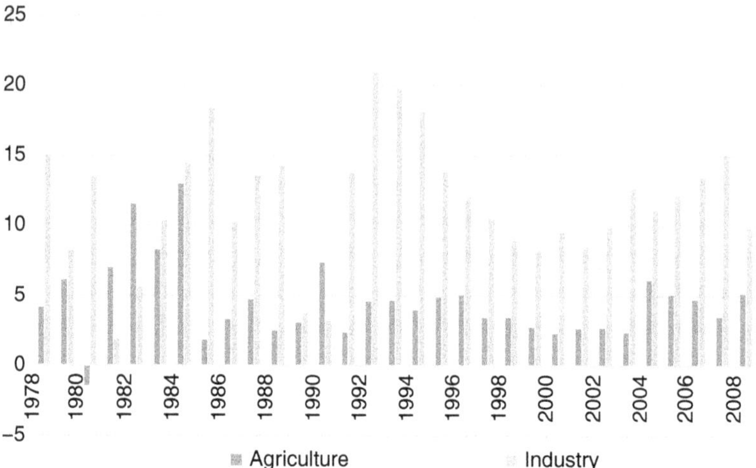

Figure 4.3 Agricultural and industrial value added in China, 1978–2008 (annual growth percent).
Source: World Bank

maintain traditional modes of livelihood and production. A few foreign investors alone can hardly generate the necessary transformation.

During China's own development process, agriculture and rural areas were also the number one challenge for reformers for a long period. It is true that China's market-oriented reform started in rural areas in the late 1970s and agriculture enjoyed rapid growth until 1984, but after mid-1980s, the agricultural sector lost steam. It grew on an average of just 2–4 percent per year for the next two decades, whereas the industrial sector grew on an average more than 11 percent annually (see Figure 4.3). As industries boomed, millions of farmers left the land and flowed into in cities and towns. Even in rural area, the rising stars were not farmers, but township and village enterprises, which engaged with agri-product processing as well as low-level manufacturing. These enterprises experienced explosive growth and created numerous employment opportunities for the rural population and expanded the market of agricultural products. In addition, they made it possible for specialized farmers to bring the land together by leasing it from those who worked in the factories and cities. Mechanized large-scale farming can be gradually implemented to raise the productivity of agriculture. This process corresponds to a fundamental model in development economics that suggests that the solution to the low-productivity subsistence farming does not come within the agricultural sector itself, but is provided by the broad transition from agriculture to industrialization and urbanization.[68]

Indeed, policymakers in both China and Africa have increasingly laid emphasis on cross-sector collaboration in the bilateral agricultural cooperation. The FOCAC plan for 2010–2012 talked merely about a "growth-oriented agricultural agenda," which includes cooperation in grain production, technology transfer, processing and storage of agricultural products, and so forth. Nine years later, the FOCAC plan for 2019–2021 had a much more comprehensive vision on Africa's agricultural modernization. China pledged to "help Africa upgrade the industry and agricultural infrastructure, increase agricultural productivity and the value added of agro-products, improve Africa's ability to ensure food security, invest in testing and adaptation of machines to African conditions, establish African dealerships capable of after-sale support and service, support township and village industries' development, promote inclusive growth and shared prosperity." By integrating both China's own experience of rural transformation and the lessons learned from previous projects in Africa's agriculture, the new document clearly indicated establishment of functioning market mechanism and industrialization as the key directions for cooperation to develop agriculture. Accordingly, the following chapters will examine Chinese engagements in Africa's industrial sectors so that we can understand the coevolution of various sectors and the trend of structural transformation in depth.

[68] Shenggen Fan, et al., *From Subsistence to Profit*, p. 3.

5 *Manufacturing*

5.1 A Beacon in the Wilderness

Near the town of Dukem, more than 30 kilometers away from the Ethiopian capital, Addis Ababa, lies a newly flourishing industrial zone. Six rows of alternating yellow and green factory buildings have been planted in lines across the smooth and expansive earth – especially eye-catching in the midst of the farmland that surrounds them in all directions. This Eastern Industrial Zone, built and run by Chinese enterprises, has already acquired some fame in Ethiopia. In June 2012, when I visited the Eastern Industrial Zone, I saw long lines forming outside the main gate. Numerous young people, leaning on the railings, stood on tiptoe or stretched their necks, trying to catch a glimpse inside; their anxious expressions betrayed intense anticipation and desire. They had all come to apply for jobs after reading recruitment advertisements. Some were residents of villages and towns within a 10-kilometer radius of the industrial zone, while others came from Addis Ababa, more than 30 kilometers away, specifically looking for work. There were even recent graduates who had come from remote areas hundreds of kilometers away, searching for opportunities around the capital. Their shared target was a shoe manufacturer from Dongguan in Guangdong Province: Huajian Group.

In November 2011, Huajian had just decided to invest in building a local factory. They not only rented an entire row of factory buildings in the industrial zone, but they also selected nearly a hundred Ethiopian employees to receive two months of training at their factory in China. This kind of large-scale, one-time overseas training program was unprecedented among Chinese enterprises in Ethiopia, as well as among foreign investors in manufacturing across the African continent. Because of this, the Huajian factory attracted broad attention from local and Chinese media, as well as American business periodicals, the BBC, and other Western news organizations.

After only half a year, Huajian's factories were already full of busy people and roaring machines. The person responsible for overseeing the Ethiopia project, Ms. Hai Yu (Helen), vice president of the Huajian Group, was in her thirties but had already spent more than ten years studying and working in the United Kingdom and Switzerland. She had earned four master's degrees and had served as chief actuary and vice president at a Swiss bank. Still, in 2011 she accepted Huajian's invitation to come to Ethiopia and take on the responsibility of constructing the company's first overseas factory. She noted that Huajian began investing in Ethiopia after Ethiopian prime minister Meles Zenawi visited China in August 2011. There, he met with President Zhang Huarong of the Huajian Group, whom he invited to Ethiopia to explore investment opportunities. A month later, Huajian executives visited Ethiopia and were very impressed by the investment climate. First, they noticed that the local labor was extremely low, about a tenth of the cost of labor in coastal regions of China. Second, Ethiopia had arguably the largest stores of livestock of any African country, meaning that there would be sufficient leather supplies to guarantee raw materials for a shoe manufacturing business. Third, the political situation in Ethiopia was stable, with a government that actively promoted market-based economic reforms. Thus, in October of 2011, the Board of Directors of Huajian made a decision to invest. The company began preparation immediately. With substantial support from local government, and the assistance of facilities at the Eastern Industrial Zone, it took only three months to register, construct factory buildings, install machinery, recruit employees, and send them to China for training. On January 5, 2012, the trial period officially began. The speed with which this foreign investor built their facilities and started production caused quite a sensation in the local community.[1]

However, the path to success is destined to be rocky, especially in a country like Ethiopia, with a weak industrial base and underdeveloped economy. Every detail had to be carefully considered if a large-scale factory was to keep running properly. For instance, when I visited Huajian, it was importing nearly all of its machinery and a large portion of its raw materials. According to Ethiopian government policies, these imports should all have been duty free. However, in practice, local customs officials were unclear about which regulations to

[1] Hai Yu, July 2012, Addis Ababa.

enforce, and they continued to levy taxes on imports. In response, Hai Yu went in person to the Customs Authority, found a diagram of the organizational structure, and spent a full six hours communicating one by one with relevant staff, until she finally clarified the customs process and resolved the problem. Another time, a rumor circulated among Chinese companies that the Ethiopian government had banned sending profits back to China. To clarify this critical question, Hai Yu made thorough inquiries to the relevant administrative bodies, analyzing written regulations sentence-by-sentence and word-by-word, to verify that there were no limits on profit repatriation, as long as a company had proper documentation. In addition to the time and energy spent dealing with the government, logistical supply issues can also be significant. From big problems with electricity and water shortages to small issues like an insufficient number of showerheads, these can all substantially impact factory production and worker efficiency. Hai Yu sighed, in order to run a factory in Ethiopia, one must do all kinds of small jobs – only by thoroughly communicating with all parties, by understanding every detail, can one guarantee successful implementation of a plan.

At dawn the next morning, I made my way to the factory to observe a day in the lives of workers from two different countries on the same production line. By 7:30 a.m., a large group of local workers began to pour through the gates of the industrial zone, while an equally imposing crowd assembled outside the gates – job seekers looking for open positions. A palpable jealousy could be seen in the gaze of those waiting outside, while those walking through the gates bore expressions of pride. At 7:40 a.m., despite the drizzling rain, the entire Chinese and Ethiopian staff, dressed in work uniforms, stepped in line to the tune of "March of the Athletes" and assembled on a patch of ground in front of the factory to do their morning exercises. I counted roughly 800 Ethiopian workers and 200 Chinese staff – apart from a small number of managers, the others were all young men and women in their twenties. After a few rounds of synchronized exercise, Assistant Manager Ye gave a brief report on the work of the previous week and awarded a team whose performance had been outstanding with bonuses and a silk pennant.

As the clock approached 8 a.m., the workers all assumed their proper places. Each workstation on the assembly line was brightly lit by fluorescent lights up above, and the large machines slowly started up, emitting a low growl. Supervisors, dressed in black, stood in front of their production lines, hands clasped behind them, making their final inspections before work began. With the shrill blow of a whistle, the factory floor erupted in activity: cutting, peeling, sewing, molding, and packaging – each task allocated to a specific group. Every production team was made up of fifteen to twenty-five workers, and among these workers there was both a clear division of labor and meticulous coordination. For example, on the sewing team, ordinary workers, dressed in green, prepared materials, worked the sewing machines, or hammered the edges with small hammers. Wearing yellow were the quality inspectors, who sat at the end, calculating inventory and checking for quality. The team leaders, in red, ran from the front to the back of the line, supervising workers and resolving their questions, while also making sure that materials to be processed were brought over and finished materials were sent to the next station.

There were always three to five Chinese workers mixed into each group, working side by side with their Ethiopian colleagues and shouldering similar tasks. One of these workers told me that when production first started, the proportion of Chinese workers at the factory had been even higher, more than 300 in total. After six months of demonstrations and adjustments, the technical capacity of the Ethiopian workers had greatly improved. Now, the roughly 200 Chinese workers who remained at the factory served primarily as operators of sewing machines or other equipment requiring higher technical skill, to maintain efficiency and quality. He estimated that in a few months, even more Chinese workers would be replaced by local staff. Localization was swiftly spreading, not only on the factory floor but also at the management level. At the time of my visit, each team was led by two team leaders: one Chinese and one Ethiopian. I saw an Ethiopian young woman in a red uniform work for an entire morning without sitting down once; instead, she stood beside various work stations, bending over to assist her team members. I went over to ask her, "Aren't you tired? Why don't you sit down?" She lifted her head and looked at me. Without stopping her work, she answered, "Because I'm the team leader."

I took advantage of the midday break to strike up a conversation with some local workers. They were all either recent college graduates or undergraduate students, some at technical schools. They had majored in subjects ranging from biology to geography, journalism, or architecture, but had discovered that work was hard to find.[2] Now, they were starting from scratch, learning how to make shoes. Among them, a small group had gone to China for training, but the majority learned their craft through the practical work of production. They found that the company did not grant any special treatment for employees who had more formal education. On the production line, one had only to demonstrate outstanding performance, abide by regulations, and be willing to work hard to be promoted to the status of team leader. However, once in such a position, their responsibilities would increase; apart from supervising production, they would also have to participate in additional training. From Monday through Saturday, they slept at the same dormitories as the Chinese supervisors. Every morning at 7 a.m., all the Chinese and Ethiopian managers would run for thirty minutes to their factory workplace – an activity that elicited complaints even from the Ethiopians, whose country is known around the world for producing long-distance runners. On the other hand, they were very interested in the Chinese classes they attended twice a week. One young woman admitted that before she had known nothing about China, but now she keenly anticipated traveling there in the near future.

Just as we were speaking, the faint sound of a whistle could be heard from inside the factory. The workers hurriedly took their leave, and I followed them back to the workshop. In front of the production line, each team was lining up in formation, and several Ethiopian team leaders in-training could already use Chinese to command the ensemble: "One, two, one! One, two one!" "Turn left! Look right!" Once the teams were standing still, the Chinese and Ethiopian team leaders summarized the morning's work and indicated areas for improvement. One Chinese supervisor on the molding team told me, even though shoemaking is a traditional craft, the production process is even more complicated than manufacturing computers. Production lines for computers are already completely mechanized and automated, whereas shoemaking still requires a great deal of manual work. In the process of shoe production, there are always questions – for example, about the amount of adhesive to use, about how to arrange shoes on the assembly

[2] According to an official sample survey, from 2009 to 2011, the unemployment rate in the Addis Ababa region was greater than 25 percent, and even higher for youth aged fifteen to twenty-nine. Key Findings on the 2011 Urban Employment Unemployment Survey, Ethiopia Central Statistical Agency.

line to maximize efficiency, whether to adjust the temperature of machines according to the materials used, and so forth. Therefore, the Huajian factory holds two or three team meetings every day to promptly report and resolve problems. The supervisor pointed out a young Ethiopian man speaking to the team: "That's my apprentice. He's very smart, and learns quickly."

I noticed a large board hanging in a conspicuous part of the room. On top was displayed the projected output for that day, while the blank space at the bottom was filled in with the actual output for every hour. Every other hour, a statistician from the Logistics Department would write down the latest calculations. During breaks, the team leaders and a few workers would go up to the board to examine how much their own team had completed in terms of the plan and compared their progress with that of other teams. Those in the lead would naturally cry out with joy, while the teams that had fallen behind would hurry back in search of problems, rushing to catch up.

The base salary for Ethiopian staff on the production line was only 600 birrs per month (around US$35), so any additional income had great appeal. Apart from bonuses for outstanding work performance, workers could receive full-attendance awards for lack of absences and tardiness, and they were paid overtime for working evenings or weekends. Of course, in spite of all these gains, employees' monetary income was still very low in local terms. Huajian was aware of this shortcoming, and Hai Yu admitted that, because the Ethiopian factory had still not been able to break even, from a financial perspective, it would be difficult to raise salaries immediately. However, she emphasized that there will always be hardship in the beginning stages of a business; everyone must be patient and look toward long-term development.

At 7:30 in the evening, the Chinese and Ethiopian workers had stayed to work overtime at the factory, while the Ethiopian team leaders in-training sat in the canteen with their teacher, studying Chinese, one character at a time. I left the factory alone. In the car, as I turned to look back at the Industrial Zone, the surrounding area was pitch black, and the only lights came from the Huajian factory, which continued to run without any sign of exhaustion. On this vast ancient and tranquil land, it was like a beacon, symbolizing the latest footsteps in African modernization and industrialization. But would it be a single light, blazing in the wilderness, or a vanguard followed by thousands of others? What kinds of effects would the arrival of Chinese factories bring to long-term local development? The sections to follow provide a comprehensive review of the activities of Chinese enterprises in African manufacturing, as well as an analysis of the most recent changes and trends.

5.2 The Rocky Path of Manufacturing

Over the past half-century, manufacturing industries on the African continent have traveled a bumpy road to development. In the 1960s and '70s, many newly independent countries, having thrown off the shackles of colonial rule, began to support indigenous factories, especially those that manufactured consumer goods for daily use. They did so to reduce the historical dependence on imported goods as well as in the hope that these factories could provide a basis for the gradual industrialization and modernization overall. However, such "import substitution" policies stimulated rapid growth in manufacturing for only a short initial period (see Figure 5.1). Factories receiving support were inefficient and lacked competitiveness. Moreover, large amounts of precious foreign currency were spent on imports of factory equipment, energy resources, and supplies of raw materials. Add to this the devastating effects of the oil crisis, and it becomes apparent why many African countries fell into serious predicaments with foreign debt, leaving their original industrialization models with little chance of survival.[3]

Subsequently, Western donor countries urged African countries to implement "structural adjustment," cancelling protections and subsidies for national manufacturing industries, privatizing state-owned enterprises, and liberalizing the market. The hope was that by means of the market itself, through survival of the fittest, truly competitive businesses would develop. However, results went contrary to expectations. In the 1980s and '90s, with the exception of a small number of countries such as Mauritius, Lesotho, and Swaziland, African manufacturing stagnated, and there were even cases of recession. According to statistics from the World Bank, in sub-Saharan Africa the share of manufacturing value added amounted to 16.53 percent of GDP in 1982, but by the year 2000 it was only 12.62 percent (see Figure 5.2). As researchers have noted, after market liberalization, African

[3] Economic Development Report in Africa Report 2011, UNIDO and UNCTAD, pp. 10–11.

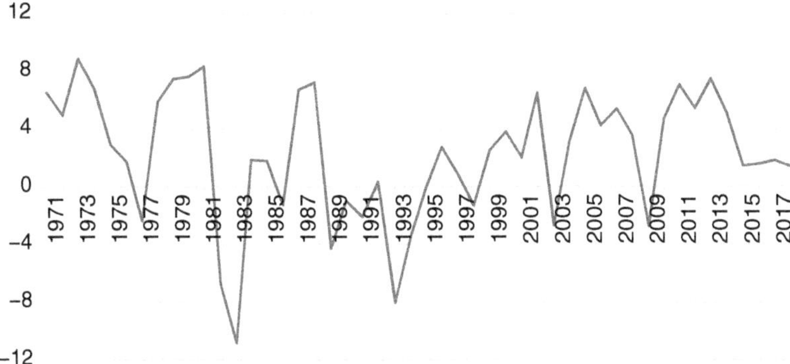

Figure 5.1 Annual growth rate for manufacturing value added in sub-Saharan Africa, 1971–2018 (percent).
Source: World Development Indicators

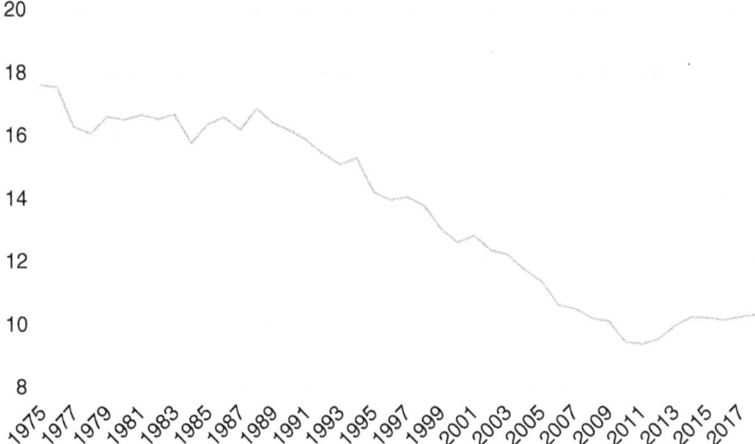

Figure 5.2 Manufacturing value added in sub-Saharan Africa as a percentage of GDP, 1975–2018.
Source: World Development Indicators

manufacturing was doubly attacked by fierce competition from other regions, and reductions in government support only further weakened local industrial bases.[4]

4 Economic Development Report in Africa Report 2011, UNIDO and UNCTAD, pp. 2, 12.

In the twenty-first century, African countries once again marked out a path to industrialization. The primary goals for development of manufacturing industries became: diversify the economy, export processed goods to increase foreign currency income, and reduce excessive reliance on primary sector exports such as agricultural products and minerals. However, the effectiveness of these new strategies and approaches is unclear. Although over the past decade the absolute output of Africa's manufacturing sector has maintained growth in most years, the growth rate is slow, and the sector's proportion of GDP had actually declined until 2011 (see Figure 5.2). In comparison with other regions, one can see how far behind it is on a global scale. In the year 2000, sub-Saharan Africa made up 4 percent of manufacturing output among all developing countries, but by 2010 it dropped to only 2 percent before rebounding to 3 percent by 2017. By contrast, the proportion held by China over the same period jumped from 34 percent in 2000 to 47 percent in 2010 and 58 percent in 2017 (see Figure 5.3).

As early as the 1960s and '70s, in line with African governments' development of national industries and the demands of import substitution, China began to provide manufacturing-related aid to African countries. By 1987, China had built fifty to sixty factories in countries like Guinea, Mali, Somalia, Tanzania, Uganda, Rwanda, Zaire, Mauritania, Madagascar, Ethiopia, Niger, and Sierra Leone, for production of cigarettes and matches, bricks, tiles, furniture, clothing, leather, and processed agricultural products. Textile mills constituted the largest proportion of these projects, with a total of thirteen African countries receiving aid in this form.[5] One reason for this was that China's own textile industry had developed much earlier, so its technologies were relatively mature by that time. Moreover, textiles constitute a basic industrial commodity that every country needs.

However, given the broader conditions of stagnation in African manufacturing at the time, none of the factories built with Chinese aid performed particularly well. Initially, the Chinese government emphasized "turnkey projects." It pushed for technical training to be completed as soon as possible after a factory had been built, so that factory operations and management could be completely handed over to local African employees. Aid-receiving countries had only to "turn

[5] W. Bartke, *The Economic Aid of the PR China to Developing and Socialist Countries*, 2nd ed. (Munich: K. G. Saur, 1989), pp. 25–28.

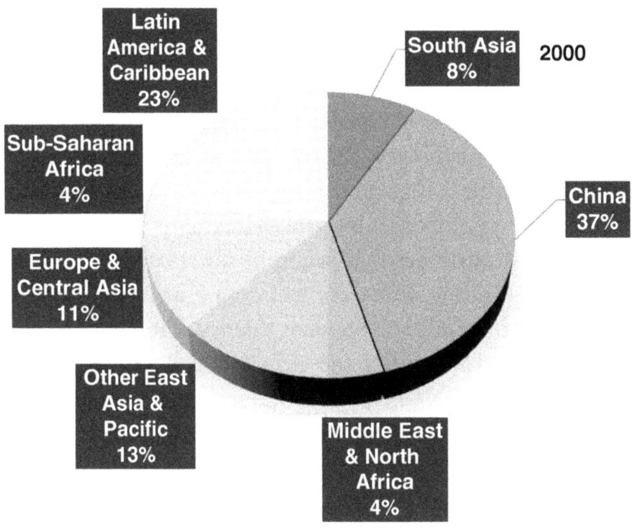

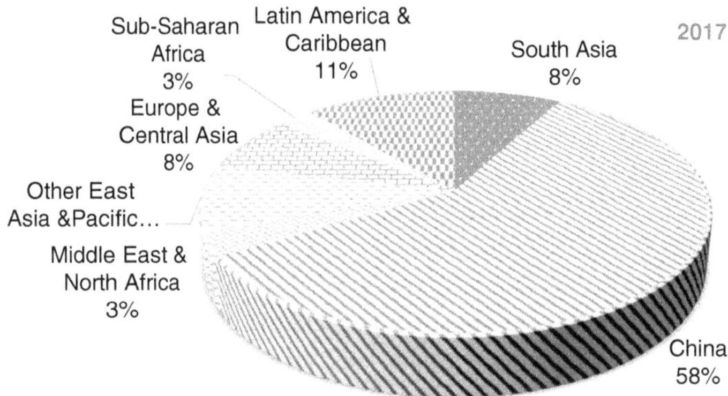

Figure 5.3 Comparison of manufacturing value added among developing countries, 2000–2017.
Source: World Development Indicators

the key" in order to begin production.[6] Unfortunately, it was frequently the case that, shortly after Chinese staff left, management of

[6] Shi Lin, ed. *Contemporary Chinese Overseas Economic Cooperation* (*Dangdai zhongguo de duiwai jingji hezuo*当代中国的对外经济合作) (Beijing: China Social Sciences Press, 1989), p. 42.

the factory began to slacken; either local officials demanded exorbitant amounts of products as gifts, or employees and neighbors willfully pilfered equipment and materials.[7] Even if the factory could just barely continue functioning, unreliable electricity and water supplies, as well as aged and deteriorating machinery, contributed to serious losses.

After reforms of the Chinese foreign trade system began in 1987, the Chinese government once again examined these ineffective forms of aid and experimented with new modes that might be more successful. One method was to use contracting and technical cooperation to provide necessary technical support and management talent for manufacturing projects in Africa. For example, after the aid-funded Benin Industrial and Textile Company (SITEX) began formal production in 1987, China Foreign Textile Corporation immediately established an eight-year management contract and a six-year period of technical cooperation. In Ethiopia in 1999, textile companies from Wuxi, Tangshan, and Dalian each signed agreements with local textile factories in Hawassa, Kombolcha, and Adama to undertake management over a five-year period.[8] Another method followed the trend toward privatization in African countries by converting projects into joint ventures. In 1995, when then vice premier Zhu Rongji visited Tanzania and Zambia, he suggested that Chinese enterprises insert themselves into former aid projects by establishing joint ventures to rescue deteriorating factories. The Changzhou bureau of textile manufacturing agreed to purchase shares in Tanzania's Urafiki (Friendship) Textile Factory, and Qingdao Textile Corporation also took over organization of Mulungushi Textiles, two joint ventures were established.

The Chinese enterprises cooperating with African governments had just gone through the "Enlightenment" of transition to a market economy in their own country, and they hoped to bring the lessons and strategies they had learned to Africa at the same time that they used cooperation opportunities to open up international markets. However, in the process of experimenting with cooperation, many companies discovered situations on the ground that differed sharply from their expectations. A former manager of the Kombolcha textile factory management cooperation project gave this example: the Ethiopian

[7] Brautigam, *The Dragon's Gift*, pp. 195–196.

[8] Interview with Tangshan Huaxin Textile Group Employee, Addis Ababa, September 2011.

government pushes the company to export in order to earn foreign currency, even when this may cause a loss for the company. Chinese managers asked whether profits or exports were more important to local government. After considering the question for a moment, the Ethiopian official still chose to prioritize exports. Although the Chinese partners respected this decision, on completion of their five-year contract they refused to extend the partnership. As a business, profit had to be their first priority. There was no way for the two partners' interests to be aligned, and this kind of cooperation "cannot benefit both sides," the Chinese manager said.[9]

Joint venture projects also encountered enormous challenges. As Wu Bin, president of the Urafiki Textile Company, explained to me, when the company was established in 1997, it relied on a commercial loan of US$100 million from China Exim Bank as starting funds for upgrading equipment and making staff adjustments. Thus, it was able to bring factory production and operations back on track, leading to excellent sales on the local market. This success served to buoy what was at that time a bleak Tanzanian textile industry. However, as the Tanzanian textile industry gradually resuscitated, competition became increasingly intense, and flaws in the structure of the Urafiki Company began to appear. The joint venture had to retain 1,900 workers from the old factory – an excessive number of staff. Moreover, around half of them were hired under a lifelong tenure system and could not be dismissed. These permanent employees exploited their seniority, avoided working overtime, and worked inefficiently.

Another problem emerged through divergences in business philosophy. Many competitive enterprises engaged in diversified production, for example by extending business to the upstream or downstream of the cotton industry chain to effectively control raw materials and markets. Chinese management at the Urafiki Company had proposed such an expansion of the business model, but their Tanzanian partners were not interested. Wu Bin thought that this was because the government-appointed Tanzanian managers only cared about resolving unemployment and passing on tax revenue to local government. They did not worry about the competitiveness or development of the company itself, because they believed that their Chinese partners would

[9] Interview with Tangshan Huaxin Textile Group Employee, Addis Ababa, September 2011.

continue to provide assistance indefinitely to this historical aid project, which is dubbed as "child of Chairman Mao and Nyerere (Tanzania's founding president)." Qingdao Textile Corporation likewise encountered severe labor issues with its Zambian joint venture, Mulungushi Textiles. After ten years of struggling to keep the business afloat, facing abolition of the Multi-Fiber Arrangement (MFA), and under pressure from both increasing international competition and rising salaries in Zambia, the company finally had no choice but to shut down in 2006.[10] Similarly, in Brautigam's research on Chinese joint ventures during the late 1990s in countries like Côte d'Ivoire, Ghana, and Namibia, she found that all had performed rather poorly.[11]

In the course of its own development, China had learned that companies must continuously improve productivity in order to achieve the goals of capital appreciation and profit, thereby paving ground for development in a competitive market. However, due to the particular political and social needs, African collaborators did not prioritize the economic performance of aid projects. They would rather sacrifice profit and production in exchange for benefits in areas such as employment, tax revenue, and foreign currency. The problem is that if a company fails to survive amidst competition, these kinds of benefits will also disappear. Therefore, neglecting profit and the market while paying exclusive attention to political and social benefits is like "killing a chicken to get the eggs." Managed in this fashion, aid projects cannot sustain productivity growth or keep operations in the long run. To be fair, African governments do understand the laws of market. Still, they have failed to use market economy measures with Chinese aid projects, instead placing their hopes on the ability of the Chinese side to take a political perspective and afford preferential treatment that would transcend market rules. However, China has already departed from an exclusively political focus in regard to aid and the enterprises that participate in aid projects are also primarily concerned with economic benefits. Owing to conflicting aims, the aid projects are in general underperforming and their role in advancing Africa's manufacturing sector is limited.

[10] Andrew Brooks, Spinning and Weaving Discontent: Labour Relations and the Production of Meaning at Zambia-China Mulungushi Textiles, *Journal of Southern African Studies* (2010) 36.1, 113–132.

[11] Brautigam, *The Dragon's Gift*, pp. 201–204.

5.3 Dilemma of the Value Chain

Apart from the government aid projects, Chinese investment in Africa's manufacturing sector is a quite recent phenomenon. Raphael Kaplinsky still wrote in 2008 that "there is no evidence that Chinese firms will begin to use sub-Saharan Africa as a manufacturing base."[12] G. A. Donovan and Mike McGovern also asserted that "scarcely any Chinese manufacturing firms have set up plants employing local workers."[13] Statistics show that a small number of manufacturing investments from mainland China started to arrive in Africa from the 1990s to early 2000s, particularly in South Africa.[14] Since 2009, the growth of Chinese manufacturing investments in many sub-Saharan African countries has accelerated.[15] According to a Chinese Ministry of Commerce database, 1,418 out of the 3,049 Chinese enterprises that had registered their outward investments to Africa by January 2015 were engaged in the manufacturing sector; that is to say, nearly half of the Chinese investments in Africa were involved in manufacturing.[16]

What are the reasons for these investments? Some scholars have observed that Chinese manufacturing investments in Africa aim to take advantage of local market and substitute imports. Song Hong found several Shanghai and Hong Kong business families investing in Nigeria over four decades and currently holding dominant positions in

[12] Raphael Kaplinsky, What Does the Rise of China Do for Industrialization in Sub-Saharan Africa? *Review of African Political Economy* (March 2008) 35.1, 20.

[13] G. A. Donovan and Mike McGovern, Africa: Risky Business, *China Economic Quarterly* (2007) Q2, 24.

[14] M. Y. Wang, The Motivations Behind China's Government-Initiated Industrial Investment Overseas, *Pacific Affairs* (2002) 75.2, 187–206; Asian Foreign Direct Investment in Africa: Towards a New Era of Cooperation Among Developing Countries (Geneva: UNCTAD, 2007).

[15] Shen, Xiaofang, Private Chinese Investment in Africa: Myths and Realities, World Bank Policy Research Working Paper 6311, January 2013; Wenjie Chen, David Dollar, and Heiwai Tang, Why Is China Investing in Africa? Evidence from the Firm level. CESifo Working Paper Series No. 5940, June 13, 2016. https://ssrn.com/abstract=2805863 (accessed July 15, 2020).

[16] Tang Xiaoyang and Irene Sun, Social Responsibility or Development Responsibility? *Cornell International Law Journal* (2016) 49.1, 69–99. However, the MOFCOM database does not cover all the Chinese investments overseas on the ground. Investments under US$100 million (before 2014 April) or US$1 billion (after 2014 April) are not required to register with MOFCOM but can do it on a voluntary basis. On the other side, some firms on the list may not actually invest or have stopped the operation.

the production of enamelware, plastic sandals, and building materials in Nigeria's domestic market. In the twenty-first century, more Chinese investors from light and textile industries came to Nigeria to enjoy a market with less fierce competition and establish a head start in the Nigerian market.[17] Gu Jin's survey showed that most private Chinese investors began in trading and gradually moved to set up factories for manufacturing. The most common reasons mentioned by the surveyed Chinese investors was the attraction of African markets as well as being pushed out by a competitive and evolving Chinese market.[18] The Chinese government also encouraged investors to set up manufacturing bases in Africa to reduce the negative impact of overwhelming Chinese imports on local industry.[19]

Researchers have also found that a number of Chinese investors set up factories in Africa for the purpose of getting better access to raw materials. Gu Jin documented that large Chinese manufacturing projects in Africa in the late 1990s and early 2000s often involved linkages to resource-based and infrastructure investments.[20] For instance, China Nonferrous Metal Mining Co. set up an industrial zone in Chambishi, Zambia, focusing mainly on the smelting of copper and cobalt or related metallurgy industries. More recently Chinese enterprises were reported to set up tanneries in Ethiopia and build weaving mills in Tanzania in order to secure supplies of leather and cotton, respectively.[21]

Another important aim of Chinese investors is to use the preferential treaty that African countries have to export to European and American markets. UNCTAD (United Nations Conference on Trade and Development) statistics indicate that Chinese clothing manufacturers

[17] H. Song, Chinese Private Direct Investment and Overseas Chinese Network in Africa, *China & World Economy* (2011) 19.4, 109–126.

[18] J. Gu, China's Private Enterprises in Africa and the Implications for African Development, *European Journal of Development Research* (2009) 21.4, 570–587 (pp. 575–577).

[19] R. Kaplinsky, What Does the Rise of China Do for Industrialisation in Sub-Saharan Africa? *Review of African Political Economy* (2008) 35.115, 7–22 (pp. 11–13).

[20] J. Gu, China's Private Enterprises, p. 572.

[21] Deborah Brautigam, Margaret McMillan, and Xiaoyang Tang, The Role of Foreign Investment in Ethiopia's Leather Value Chain, PEDL Research Note – ERG project 106, June 2014; Tang Xiaoyang, The Impact of Asian Investment on Africa's Textile Industries, Carnegie-Tsinghua Center for Global Policy, August 2014.

invested in Africa even before 2000, to take advantage of quota access through the MFA.[22] After 2001, the African Growth and Opportunities Act (AGOA), which give African products preferential access to US markets, further incentivized manufacturers to invest in Africa.[23] However, such investments are known to be "footloose." As the preferential treaties or financial incentives of African countries change, foreign investors may leave quickly. For instance, when the MFA expired after 2005, most export-oriented clothing factories in southern Africa, whose owners were mainly from China and other Asian countries, stopped operation. Some moved away from Africa and others shifted their focus from the export market to Africa's domestic and regional markets.[24]

Since 2011, a new wave of Chinese manufacturing investments aimed at exporting to global markets have arrived in several East African countries. Huajian is an example of this new group of investors. Justin Yifu Lin and Wang Yan suggest that such investments are driven by structural economic factors rather than preferential trade in Africa. As labor costs in China rise, Chinese manufacturers are ready to shift their production bases to Africa and may serve as "leading dragons" to drive the development of manufacturing sectors in Africa.[25] Lin's and Wang's convictions are based on the "flying geese" model, which posits that countries tend to be leaders or followers in producing for global value chains, depending on their comparative advantages.[26]

However, tax incentives and cost advantages of African countries are largely offset by a rather unfavorable business environment. Instable security situations, arbitrary policies, fragmented regional markets, and deficient infrastructure in Africa constitute external challenges to the manufacturing sector, whereas poor worker skills, inexperienced

22 Asian Foreign Direct Investment in Africa: Towards a New Era of Cooperation Among Developing Countries (Geneva: UNCTAD, 2007).

23 R. Kaplinsky, and M. Morris, Do the Asian Drivers Undermine Export-Oriented Industrialisation in SSA? *World Development Special Issue on Asian Drivers and Their Impact on Developing Countries* (2008) 36.2, 254–273.

24 Tang Xiaoyang, The Impact of Asian Investment on Africa's Textile Industries, Carnegie-Tsinghua Center for Global Policy, 2014. http://carnegietsinghua.org/publications/?fa=56320 (accessed July 15, 2020).

25 Justin Yifu Lin and Wang Yan, *Going Beyond Aid: Development Cooperation for Structural Transformation* (Cambridge: Cambridge University Press, 2017), pp. 45–51.

26 K. Akamatsu, A Historical Pattern of Economic Growth in Developing Countries, *Journal of Developing Economies* (March–August 1962) 1.1, 3–25.

management, and scarcity of upstream and downstream support are intraindustry barriers. As Nicolas Kaldo observed, all these extrasector and intrasector factors have circular causal relationship with the development of manufacturing sector.[27] Chapter 2 discussed how government regulations may affect market activities and how economic growth may improve government capacity. In Chapter 3, we saw the interrelated linkage between infrastructure construction and industrial development. As these extrasector factors are conditioned by the broad contexts, they won't be discussed in this chapter.

Among the intrasector factors, the management and worker training issues will be discussed in Chapter 7. This chapter focuses on the chicken-and-egg dilemma along the value chain in Africa's manufacturing sectors. As noted earlier, an increasing number of Chinese investors have been attracted to Africa to establish factories by the continent's abundant resources, immense potential, favorable tariff, and cheap labor. Yet, many of them encountered numerous challenges in real operations to find upstream supplies or downstream clients. The lack of supporting industries greatly constrains the growth of manufacturing investments. But as the number and scale of the existing manufacturers are small, they can hardly persuade the upstream and downstream enterprises to move to Africa with them together. In the text that follows, I will use some real cases of Chinese manufacturing investments in Africa to illustrate the conundrum concretely.

5.3.1 Downstream Constraints

A few Chinese manufacturing projects process primary agricultural products, such as cotton, leather, and sisal, and export them to China and other countries for further manufacturing. They are actually willing to expand the processing activities in Africa to take advantage of favorable policies and low costs, but the constraint of the value chain often prevents them from upgrading the production. For example, the Ethiopian government twice, in 2008 and 2011, imposed a punitive export tax, on semiprocessed leather (wet blue) and

[27] Nicholas Kaldor, *Causes of the Slow Rate of Economic Growth in the United Kingdom* (Cambridge: Cambridge University Press, 1966). Reprinted in Nicholas Kaldor, *Further Essays on Economic Theory* (Teaneck, NJ: Holmes and Meier Publishers, 1978), pp. 110–112.

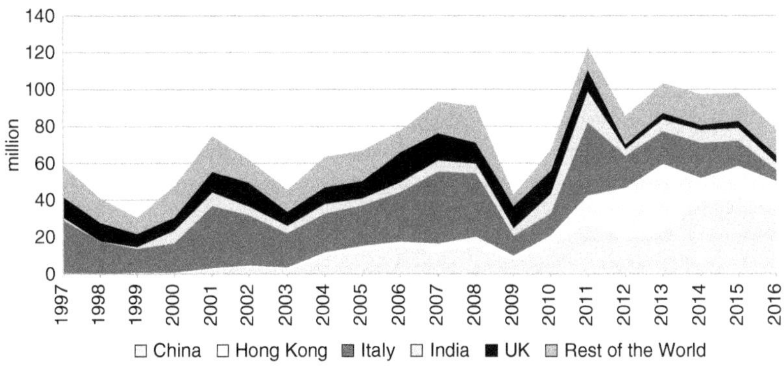

Figure 5.4 Ethiopia's leather exports to major countries, 1997–2016 (in US$).
Source: UN Comtrade

unfinished leather (crust) to encourage tanneries to process leather within the country and export only finished leather with higher value added. Other incentives, such as tax exemption for machine imports and free training for scaling up, were offered as well. Chinese investors responded positively to these policies. Six companies from mainland China, along with one from Taiwan and one from Hong Kong, had set up tanneries in Ethiopia by 2018, making China by far the largest investing country in this sector, followed by two firms from India and one from the United Kingdom. Statistics shows that leather exports from Ethiopia to China increased rapidly after the arrival of Chinese investors (see Figure 5.4).

However, the lack of downstream leather producers in Ethiopia constitutes a serious bottleneck for the tanneries to build sophisticated processing capacity. Manufacturers of leather products need to follow the latest fashion. Therefore, the manufacturers of leather products require their leather suppliers to make quick responses and adjustments according to the market demands. Since finished leather from Ethiopia takes months to arrive in the hands of manufacturers in China, the supplies may no longer meet the demands for latest products. Zhang Jianxin, a tannery owner said, "The risk is high (for exporting finished leather from Ethiopia), because it is not connected to the market. It takes too much time for finished leather to go to the market. The color and style of skins do not match. For example, there are many kinds of brown leather, and a small difference can make it unsellable. Production must be flexible and connected to the market."[28] Therefore, the color and style of the finished leather exported to China need to be further adjusted by the tanneries there to meet the demands of the customers.[29] Similarly, cotton products are exported out of Africa usually as simply ginned lint or at best as yarn, because further weaving, dyeing, and processing of textile require close interaction with the garment making sector, which is very small on the continent.

5.3.2 Upstream Constraints

An incomplete and weak supply chain is one of the most critical disadvantages for Africa to compete in the international market. For instance, South Africa used to offer generous subsidies and tax breaks to attract many garment makers from Hong Kong and Taiwan before the 1990s. When the preferential policy stopped, many of these investors moved out of the country. One important reason is that South Africa has only a small number of textile mills. The variety of fabrics produced by them is very limited because the capacity of garment makers in South Africa is too small to attract textile suppliers to invest and produce locally. A large amount of the fabrics used by the garment makers must be imported from Asia. The dependence on imported supply increases the costs of production in the region and hinders growth of the sector. By contrast, China and other Asian countries have a complete value chain, a vast number of mills, and plenty of accessory suppliers. Even though the labor costs in China have continued to rise since 2000, the competitiveness of the Chinese garment sector has not been much affected. South African manufacturers have not only been outcompeted in the export market to countries such as the United States, but have also lost their own domestic market to Chinese imports (see Figure 5.5).

Both the scale of industry and the quality of production hinder the formation of a complete supply chain in Africa. Although Chinese and other foreign investors started to manufacture footwear, gloves, and garments in Africa recently, they source few supplies from local producers apart from some generic leather and fabric. Almost all other supplies and accessories, from high-quality special leather and fabric

[28] Zhang Jianxin, owner of Koka Addis tannery, Modjo, January 2015.
[29] Jiang Lele, deputy GM of Pelle tannery, August 2018.

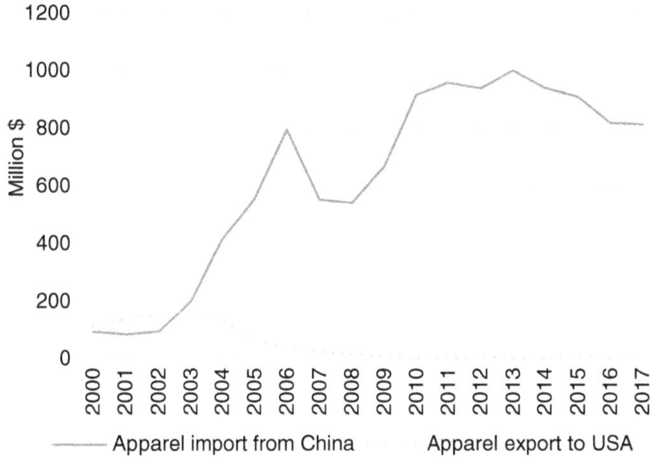

Figure 5.5 South Africa's apparel trade with China and the United States, 2000–2017 (in US$).
Source: UN Comtrade

to buttons, strings and zippers and even packaging materials, come from China or other industrialized countries. Even when imports significantly increase costs and complexity of production, Chinese managers stress that it is a must. Quality assurance is the top priority for the manufacturers in international market. "If one component does not meet European or American standards, the whole container (of finished products) will be disqualified and returned," said a Chinese manager.[30]

5.3.3 Intertwined Obstacles

The aforementioned problems often result from intertwined challenges in various stages of the supply chain. The complex of obstacles contains circular causations and cannot be improved easily by one-sided measures. The following case study of the value chain of leather and leather products in Ethiopia demonstrates such an interlocked complexity. At the stage of raw material supply, the tanneries complained about deteriorating quality and shortage of sheep skins and cow hides in spite of the government's initiative to develop leather processing sector. The problems of skin and hide supply were mainly caused by

[30] Billy Young, production director of Pittards, Addis Ababa, January 2015.

inappropriate ways of raising cattle, slaughtering animals, and collecting and preserving hides available for leather processing. Since cattle raising and slaughtering are under the responsibility of the Ministry of Agriculture, the industrial policymakers, namely Ministry of Industry and Leather Industry Development Institute (LIDI), do not have much influence on these issues.

At the stage of leather processing. Ethiopia has to import almost all the chemicals needed for leather processing. Yet, the varieties of chemicals available are still limited, Owing to complicated and costly transportation, small amounts of special chemicals cannot be imported and the delivery of chemicals requires a long time. Therefore, the tanneries often cannot get needed chemicals to do sophisticated processing.[31] The deficiency of raw materials and chemicals seriously limits the growth space for the tanneries in Ethiopia. When the manufacturers of leather products like Huajian shoe factory source leather from local tanneries, they can only find ordinary generic leather. The tanneries are unable to process leather with special colors or patterns. In addition, tanneries often cannot deliver their leather supply in time because of delayed imports of chemicals. Machinery repair can be another factor in delay. For instance, when a bearing of a processing machine was broken in Ethiopia, it had to be sent to China or Italy for one month to repair. Lack of supporting industries contributes to the inefficiency and low productivity of the tanneries as much as the lack of skills and experience.

The weakness of leather processing further hinders the development of the leather product sector. The Chinese investors in footwear and glove manufacturing report that their factories in Ethiopia produce only for the orders that have relatively flexible delivery schedules and relatively low technical requirements. Otherwise, they will face severe penalties if the production cannot meet the delivery dates or quality standards. Accessory supply is another constraint. Accessories as simple as the thread, glue, and cartons used by the manufacturers must be imported because some accessories are not produced locally and some locally made inputs, for example, cartons, do not meet international standards. Import of accessories costs again much time and money. Consequently, the scale of manufacturing cannot expand quickly. Between 2011 and 2018 merely three shoe factories (including Huajian) and three glove factories were established by foreign

[31] Zhang Naizhi, East Africa tannery, June 2016.

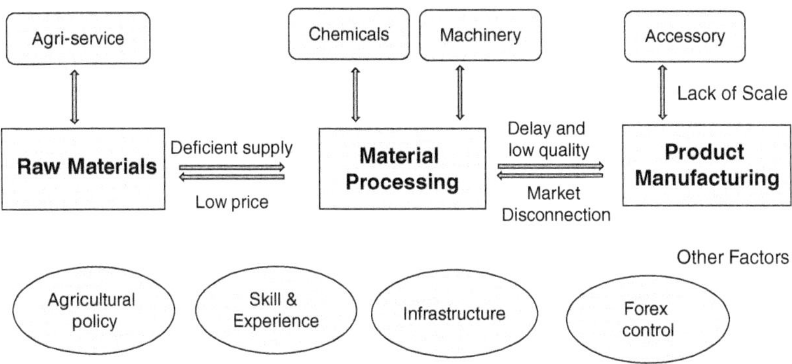

Figure 5.6 Intertwined challenges in the value chain of leather and leather product sector in Ethiopia.
Source: Author

investors. As of July 2018, the employees of these six projects combined were just over 11,000, whereas one factory of Huajian in China had more than 20,000 workers.[32]

Conversely, the stagnation of footwear and glove manufacturing affects the upgrading of the leather processing sector also. As mentioned earlier, the tanneries are so distanced from the manufacturers that they cannot supply finished leather to meet the market demands in a timely way. The tanneries that are stuck with generic low value-added leather processing in turn can only pay a very low price to the suppliers of raw materials. The farmers who just receive meagre income from selling skins and hides have little motive and means for better practices of cattle-raising and skin preservation. Additionally, the shortages of supporting branches, including production of accessory and chemicals, machinery repair, and agricultural services, impose constraints on the leather and leather product sector, whereas an underdeveloped leather sector cannot attract more investments in these supporting businesses. The value chain of leather-related processing and manufacturing in Ethiopia thus falls into multiple vicious circles (see Figure 5.6).

32 Author's survey, July 2018. It's interesting that all these six projects are related to China. Four factories (Huajian, New Wing, George, LYU) belong to Chinese owners. The German glove factory Ottokessler has a factory in China and uses Chinese technicians to train Ethiopian workers. The British glove maker Pittards uses a Chinese partner to train Ethiopian workers and supply the accessories.

The vicious circle of value chain exemplified by Ethiopia's leather and leather product sector is a common phenomenon in Africa's industrialization. Many African countries are merely capable of primary processing of raw materials, but have to export the semifinished materials, such as lint and leather, to other countries for advanced processing. Meanwhile, when the African countries attract foreign investors to build garment and shoemaking factories, they have to import almost all the processed materials for product manufacturing. Although Africa has the comparative advantages of abundant resources and cheap labor, the deficiency of the material processing stage and supporting industries hinders the formation of a continuous supply chain in Africa. The missing linkage of industrial processing adds immense costs of time and transportation to other manufacturing operations in Africa and seriously constrains the entire industrial development. Can Chinese investors find a solution to tackle this critical challenge?

5.4 Building Local Linkages

For the purpose of strengthening the supply chain in Africa, it is critical to establish a development synergism among all the related sectors and stakeholders of manufacturing. Moreover, the synergism apparently cannot depend on a few foreign/Chinese investors, but ought to involve more and more local producers so that the growth of manufacturing and supportive industries can be sustained. Although some researchers doubt that Chinese investors are willing to help local enterprises grow, the need of industrial development requires the foreign and African enterprises to work together so that all of them can benefit.[33] A survey of seventy-three Chinese manufacturers in Ethiopia in 2017 revealed that nearly two-thirds of them have local suppliers. Even Chinese and Ethiopian competitors may work well on some occasions. For example, the tanneries and shoe factories often share chemicals and accessory supplies with each other when transportation delay happens. They also lobby the

[33] Raphael Kaplinsky, Dorothy McCormick, and Mike Morris, The Impact of China on Sub-Saharan Africa, Working Paper, Funded by DFID China Office, February 2007, p. 22; K. Kamoche and L. Q. Siebers, Chinese Management Practices in Kenya: Toward a Post-colonial Critique, *International Journal of Human Resource Management* (2015) 26.21, 2718–2743, DOI: 10.1080/09585192.2014.968185.

Ethiopian authorities together for better industrial policies.[34] A Chinese manager said that the manufacturing sector in Africa is still in its nascent phase and all the firms should collaborate to "make the cake bigger," namely to help the entire sector grow.[35]

However, the effects of synergism building vary greatly. I conducted field research on Chinese manufacturing investments in South Africa, Botswana, Tanzania, Zambia, Ethiopia, Ghana, Kenya, Malawi, and Nigeria during 2012–2019. The study of the practices on the ground suggest that some investment projects have difficulty in integrating local enterprises into the supply chain, failing to overcome the bottleneck of industrial processing, whereas a number of other projects are able to gradually increase their supplies from African countries and build synergism with local producers. The key difference between these two types of investments is the markets served by them. The former targets high-standard international markets, whose stringent requirements on delivery time and quality are daunting for local enterprises. The latter sells mostly to customers in Africa's markets, which has low standards and small volume. But the inclusion of more and more local producers into the manufacturing supply chain benefits the sector's sustainable growth in the long run. Below I will expound the dynamism and impact of these two kinds of projects with real cases collected from the field.

5.4.1 Export Processing

The arrival of large Chinese manufacturers that aim to export is welcomed by local authority and public, as they can bring foreign exchange and thousands of jobs. Yet, these manufacturers have limited interactions with the local producers. To secure the quality and time of supplies, the exporting manufacturers prefer to build their own upstream and downstream supply chain. Two out of three Chinese shoe factories in Ethiopia have built their own tanneries, whereas a Chinese tannery and a British tannery add lines to produce leather gloves for export. US-based PVH Group brought a Chinese textile mill

34 Tang Xiaoyang, Chinese Manufacturing Investments and Knowledge Transfer: A Report from Ethiopia, Working Paper No. 2019/3, China Africa Research Initiative, School of Advanced International Studies, Johns Hopkins University, Washington, DC.

35 Helen Hai, Dukem, July 2012.

to Ethiopia to supply PVH and its partners' garment factories in Hawassa Industrial Park. Dahong group and China-Africa Cotton built spinning mills in Tanzania and Malawi, respectively to further process the cotton collected in Africa. China Nonferrous Metal Mining Co. (CNMC) set up a dozen smelters, chemical plants, cable manufacturing factories, and precious metal recycling facilities in Zambia to process copper and cobalt before exporting them. Of course, the extension of a high-quality supply chain is beneficial for Africa's industrial development, but the local enterprises are rarely involved in such advanced manufacturing activities.

Moreover, few local manufacturers are able to follow the examples of the foreign investors to take part in the exporting business. The scale of the export processing sector therefore tends to shrink after the policy "big push" to attract foreign direct investment (FDI). For instance, the export processing sector experienced a boom in southern Africa as a result of local government incentives and the quota system under the MFA. Yet, after both conditions terminated, a large number of investors from Asia left the region. Few local apparel factories are interested in taking over the exporting market from the Asian investors, shying away from the complex challenges of guaranteeing delivery time and quality in Africa's circumstances.[36]

Since 2010, several East African countries have adopted the industrial policy to encourage export processing too. Indigenous enterprises were initially eager to learn from the foreign investors to manufacture for export. Nonetheless, the learning path proves much harder than they thought. Using Ethiopia's footwear manufacturing again as an example, indigenous firms there had a relatively long tradition of shoemaking and they were already able to venture into the export market during the mid-2000s.[37] Yet, when Huajian and other foreign shoe factories arrived, the local shoe firms were astonished to see a very different business model. Ethiopian firms used to export only seasonally for small quantity. The manager of a local shoe factory told me his experience, "When I visited Huajian, I saw their massive operation,

[36] Tang Xiaoyang, The Impact of Asian Investment on Africa's Textile Industries, 2014, Carnegie-Tsinghua Center for Global Policy, p. 18. http://carnegietsinghua.org/publications/?fa=56320 (accessed July 15, 2020).

[37] Girum Abebe and Florian Schaefer, High Hopes and Limited Successes: Experimenting with Industrial Polices in the Leather Industry in Ethiopia, EDRI Working Paper 011, December 2013.

I was shocked. It was an army of people. Everybody was chikchikking (sewing and working), that's crazy! Ethiopians were not used to that. We could not do that. It was the first time that we saw this."[38] Seeing the gap of management and productivity, his firm decided to buy machines from Italy and hire five Italians to train their workers 2014. The manager believed that his workers would be able to catch up with Huajian's workers in two years. The firm fortunately got a test order from a US buyer soon and was confident of its prospect of export business at that time.

However, when I revisited the firm two years later, the manager told me that the firm did not get any more orders for export. The key problem encountered in the test order was the supply of accessories. There are no qualified manufacturers of shoe accessories in Ethiopia. The US buyer connected its certified accessory suppliers in China with the Ethiopian firm. However, the Chinese suppliers required a down-payment before shipment. As the firm already took out loans to buy equipment, it could not purchase a large number of accessories at once and had to import accessories in several batches. The shipments were often delayed and production was disrupted. When the US buyer sent experts to inspect, the factory happened to suspend production due to shortage of accessories. The buyers never came back again. Likewise, other Ethiopian shoe factories did not succeed in expanding the export business either because of various constraints such as capital, supply chain, marketing, and so forth. The local firms rather turned their attention to domestic and African regional markets.

With a few exceptions such as Mauritius, the export processing sector in Africa is dominated by foreign investors.[39] They have far superior production and management skills than local manufacturers, as they need to compete in the global market, but this prevents them from building synergism with the local industries. They are only interested in natural resources, cheaper labor, and fiscal incentives in Africa. Hence, the foreign investors tend to move away when these elements are no longer available.

[38] Girma Ayalew, deputy manager Fontanina, Addis, February 2015.

[39] D. Brautigam, Close Encounters: Chinese Business Networks as Industrial Catalysts in Sub-Saharan Africa, *African Affairs: The Journal of the Royal African Society* (2003) 102.408, 447–467.

5.4.2 Targeting at African Market

By contrast, when foreign investors aim to tap the emerging markets in African countries, they have many more interconnections with the local industries. The growth of this genre of foreign investors actually depends on their coevolution with the local economy.

The number of Chinese investments targeting the domestic and regional markets in African countries is much larger than that of the export processing companies. In a survey of SAIS CARI 2014–2016 in four African countries, only twelve Chinese projects were found to focus on exporting to global market, while seventy-seven Chinese manufacturers produced mainly for Africa's local markets.[40] The local market-seeking firms are also more widely distributed in terms of both geography and sector. In every African country I conducted research, I can identify at least a handful of such companies. Their products include plastics, steel, cement, home appliances, vehicle assembly, garment, footwear, tableware, paper, food, furniture, and other kinds of industrial and consumer products. In comparison, Chinese export processing factories, concentrated in apparel, footwear, and resource-related sectors, were not found in important countries like Ghana and Nigeria. The local market-seeking producers have smaller size on average, ranging from a dozen of employees to hundreds. Merely several steel mills have more than 1,000 workers. The exporting garment and shoe factories have at least several hundred workers and Huajian had more than 7,000 workers as of July 2018.

The existence of numerous small manufacturers leads to the formation of industrial clusters that are easy to join and expand. When a factory is established in one country, its success may attract a number of other Chinese to invest in the same sector. The entire sector will therefore grow quickly and require more supplies. Since the production for local markets has lower thresholds of technology and capital, indigenous enterprises can also become part of the clusters, as suppliers or as competitors. For instance, in 2005, six Chinese businessmen set up a joint venture, Ohuade, to recycle the used water sachets into shopping bags in Ghana. As the factory rapidly became

[40] Deborah Brautigam, Tang Xiaoyang, and Ying Xia, What Kinds of Chinese "Geese" Are Flying to Africa? Evidence from Chinese Manufacturing Firms, *Journal of African Economies* (August 2018) 27. Suppl 1, i29–i51. https://doi.org/10.1093/jae/ejy013.

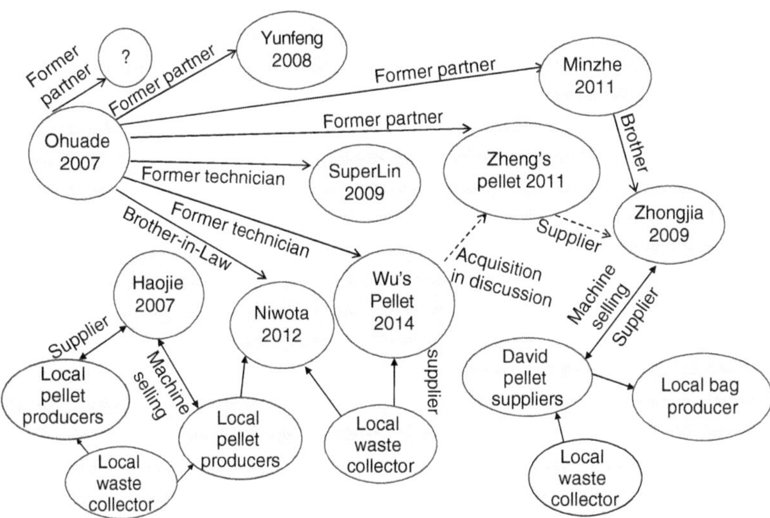

Figure 5.7 Cluster of Chinese plastic recycling factories in Ghana, 2014.
Source: Author's own illustration according to interviews

profitable, the minority shareholders and several former Chinese technicians quit to open their own recycling factories. They also brought their brothers, uncles, and friends from China to Ghana to open factories. As of 2014, it was estimated that about twenty Chinese recycling factories were operating in the country.[41] Seeing the success of Chinese firms in the plastic recycling sector, a couple of Ghanaian businessmen also bought plastic recycling machines, which cost just several thousand US dollars, to start their own business (see Figure 5.7).

Some Chinese manufacturers actively support Ghanaian companies as their suppliers. At the beginning, Chinese firms had to do everything from waste collection to plastic crushing to finished products. As the sector grew, more and more local people started to collect waste for the recycling firms. In small cars, they went around to all the small trash collection stations every day. Realizing the incomparable advantages that local collectors had, Chinese firms quickly exited the waste collecting business and focused on the processing of finished goods. A Chinese recycler first subcontracted several local collectors to supply waste to him. Later, he

[41] Tang Xiaoyang, Geese Flying to Ghana? A Case Study of the Impact of Chinese Investments on Africa's Manufacturing Sector, *Journal of Contemporary China* (2018) 27, 114, 924–941.

also sold crushing machines to his suppliers so that they could supply crushed plastics. In this manner, he not merely secured supply, but also earned additional profit from selling crushing machines.[42] Another Chinese recycler imported printing machines and pellet-making machines from China to sell to Ghanaian sachet water makers and pellet suppliers, respectively. This helped both sachet water and recycling businesses to grow as well as secured abundant high-quality waste sachets for his own factory.[43] According to a coordinator of the Ghana Plastic Manufacturers Association, there were around fifty large local sachet collectors with crushing machines as of 2014. Among them, a handful of local waste collectors climbed up the value chain to produce pellets.

Spin-offs created by former employees of the companies are common in such small-scale manufacturing businesses, a phenomenon that has never been seen in the capital-intensive resource-seeking manufacturing or the highly competitive export processing sector. David, a Ghanaian in his thirties, learned how to operate machines for the first time when he worked at a Chinese plastic products company, Fanpack, in Accra. Later, he decided to start his own waste collection and pellet production business. David bought three pellet-making machines from Chinese recycling factory owners for 13,000 Cedi (approximately US$7000 as of 2012) and as of 2014 he had hired ten workers. That said, examples of African workers transitioning into investment are few, mainly because of capital constraints. Most of the spin-offs are established by former Chinese supervisors or technicians, as witnessed in Ghana's plastic sectors and southern Africa's garment sector.[44]

Last but not least, there are more joint ventures between Chinese and Africans among the manufacturing projects that target local markets, and this constitutes an important channel for interaction between both sides. In the nine countries investigated, I did not find any Sino-African joint ventures among export processing or resource processing investments except for several mining projects that need local partners for licensing purpose. Among local market-seeking investments, about a dozen of joint-ventures were identified, counting 7–8 percent of the firms researched. Although the proportion is

42 Chen Zhong Wei, Haojie Waste Plastic Recycle Accra, July 2014.
43 Jin, Yunfeng, manager of Yun Feng Plastic Production CO, Kumasi, July 2014.
44 Tang Xiaoyang, The Impact of Asian Investment on Africa's Textile Industries, 2014. Carnegie-Tsinghua Center for Global Policy, http://carnegietsinghua.org/publications/?fa=56320 (accessed July 15, 2020).

still small, these joint ventures have more comprehensive and in-depth collaboration. Usually, the role of local managers in the Chinese factories is confined to production and human resources, but in the joint-ventures, local partners are seen to be in charge of sales, finance, procurement and strategic management, occupying more critical positions. As a result, the joint ventures have more knowledge of the host country's socioeconomic system and are more integrated into its market.

To have a close look at the dynamism within the joint-ventures, I use Sino-Ethiopian Associate Plc. as a case study. The Ethiopian partner, Zaf Tsadik, was originally a sales agent for a Chinese pharmaceutical trading company in East Africa since 1991. Sensing opportunity in Africa's market, the Chinese company decided to build a capsule factory in Ethiopia in 2001. Two Chinese investors have 70 percent of the shares, whereas Zaf took a 30 percent share of the joint venture. Zaf was appointed as the general manager to take care of the entire business in Africa. She recalled that she was surprised and moved by the trust given to her by the two Chinese shareholders when she saw the appointment letter presented by the attorney's office.[45] As of 2015, the firm had a total investment of 140 million birr (about US$10 million considering fluctuations in exchange rate) and employed 170 staff, of which only two were Chinese: an engineer and a production manager. Six Ethiopian employees were sent to China for month-long training during past decade and they gradually replaced the Chinese managers and technicians after returning home. Deputy general manager Shegaw Aderaw claimed "technology is fully transferred."[46] Ethiopian staff were very motivated to run the company. It is said to be the first and only capsule maker in sub-Saharan Africa and has acquired a Good Manufacturing Practices (GMP) certificate. Its products sell not only in Ethiopia, but also to Kenya, DRC, Sudan, Zimbabwe, and Yemen. The Chinese shareholders are satisfied to see the progress and have decided to expand the investment. In 2015 two new lines were added to the previous three lines, doubling the production capacity. Such positive synergism between Chinese and African partners is built upon decades-long good collaboration and

45 Zaf Tsadik, general manager, July 2012.

46 Zaf Tsadik, general manager, and Shegaw Aderaw, deputy general manager, Liu Engineer, Sino-Ethiop Associates Plc., January 2015.

Figure 5.8 A Chinese plastic recycling plant in Accra, Ghana, 2014.

mutual trust. Other joint ventures may not be as successful yet, but they are facilitating the in-depth interaction as well.

5.5 Coevolution Between Industry and Market

The local market-seeking production are often labeled as "import substitution" by development economists.[47] Examining the behaviors of Chinese investors and their impacts on African markets more closely, I find this notion problematic. Many of the products manufactured by the Chinese investors in Africa cannot be imported or have significant difference from the imported products. For instance, the plastic recycling business in Ghana can only be done locally. The apparel makers in southern Africa today mainly work on the fast fashion business model, which has recently been adopted by local retailers. The model requires fast feedback and reaction within one week and can only rely on local manufacturers. Likewise, textile mills in Tanzania like Urafiki produce traditional woven fabrics

[47] Ana Mendes, Mario Bertella, and Rudolph Teixeira, Industrialization in Sub-Saharan Africa and Import Substitution Policy, *Brazilian Journal of Political Economy* (January–March 2014) 34.1, 120–138.

such as Kanga and Kitenge to serve local and regional consumers. Imports of Kanga and Kitenge are few, as huge modern mills in industrialized countries do not pay attention to the relatively small markets. The food processing sector also needs adaptation to meet local consumers' tastes. A Chinese company Viju Milk started with importing yoghurt and beverage to Nigeria, and later set up a factory to produce a special kind of yoghurt drink for the Nigerian market only. The tailored product has become so popular that a handful of other Chinese businessmen have built factories in Nigeria to produce similar drinks too.

Certain products, such as cement, ceramics, steel pipes, and other construction materials, are too costly and inconvenient to be imported to Africa through long-distance transportation. Local production replacing imports of these products is a natural consequence of market development and has little to do with "import substitution," which has a negative connotation relating to protectionism and state intervention. For most of other products, the tariff protection in African countries is in general modest too. In plastic products, for example, Ghana and Nigeria have a 20 percent import duty, Tanzania 25 percent, and Ethiopia 35 percent as of 2018. Although producers within these countries take slight advantage of the protection, the government policies do not seriously distort the market competition and are not the decisive factor for the Chinese investments.[48]

Many of the local market-seeking manufacturers had traded with Africa for an extended period before deciding to invest. The main reason for them to shift to investment is not to compete with the imported goods, but the discovery of "vacuums" in African markets. In other words, they found local market demands that are not yet satisfied by existing products. A Chinese manager in Ghana said, "The market here is empty. Only a few products are produced here. We don't want to follow others and make similar things. We can easily come up with a few products that nobody has made here yet."[49] The new products can have a new function, a new design, or a new grade according to the market needs. Therefore, the local market-seeking manufacturers from China do not just substitute imported goods, but

[48] Deborah Brautigam, Tang Xiaoyang, and Ying Xia, What Kinds of Chinese "Geese," August 2018.
[49] Oxen Zhang, manager, Shifa Plastic, Accra, July 2014.

rather stimulate the growth of local markets by increasing varieties and filling the niches.

The immense and comprehensive manufacturing system in China gives Chinese investors in Africa an incomparable strength of industrial support, which enables them to build production capacity with ease and speed to address the local market demands. Often the Chinese investors do not know the production technologies, but as soon as they identify market opportunities for investment, they can find machinery and technicians back in China. Weng Licheng, a businessman from Fujian province, shifted from operating a shopping mall to manufacturing plastic slippers in Tanzania several years ago. He said, "Technology and machinery (for plastic shoe making) are mature in China. Anybody can easily buy a machine and put it into operation. Machine suppliers provide technicians to install and test their products. They can even help buyers hire Chinese technicians (to work in Africa)." The low-cost machines made in China help these small and flexible ventures too, as they significantly reduce the amount of initial investments. For example, a machine of ethylene vinyl acetate (EVA) processing costs 2–3 million RMB in Italy, and approximately 1.5 million RMB in Taiwan, but only 700,000–800,000 RMB in China. Moreover, the molds supplied by factories from China are also much cheaper than from any other countries; thus the Chinese manufacturers in Africa can update product models more frequently.[50]

The Chinese investments have another characteristic of rapid scaling up and clustering. As noted in the case study of recycling sector in Ghana (see Figure 5.7), the kin and social networks among Chinese businessmen can facilitate their investments in Africa and shorten the period of observation and preparation. After a factory is established in one country, its success may attract a number of other Chinese to invest in the same sector. The plastic slipper sector in Tanzania had similar growth trajectory. Weng Licheng's first shoe factory 2005 was a success. Then his sister, brother, a friend of his cousin, and the aunt of his son-in-law gradually came and invested in the same sector. Meantime, when they ordered batches of shoemaking machines from home, several neighbors immediately sensed the opportunities and

[50] Weng Licheng, owner of Zhongfu International Co. Dar es Salaam, August 2014.

came to Tanzanian market as well.[51] The quick growth of Chinese investments in a sector intensifies the competition, but also increases the scale of the industry. This may attract suppliers and support industries to invest too. The clustering of small Chinese manufacturers is a common phenomenon in the sectors of garment, plastic, and construction materials in various African countries.[52]

The numerous small projects and the low thresholds for capital and technology open up opportunities for the indigenous businesses, ranging from supply chain connections to spin-offs and competition. As analyzed in Section 5.4, the local market-seeking investments, in comparison to the export processing ones, have more intertwined engagements with the local companies. Different degrees of local linkage indicate different coevolution dynamisms between manufacturing FDI and local markets. While export processing projects primarily deal with international market and have little connection with Africa's local markets, the growth of local market-seeking investors depends on the development and expansion of local markets. It's true that the volume of Africa's local market is much smaller than that of the global market. However, the arrival and growth of local market-seeking investments stimulate the local market to expand. As noted, this kind of investment does not simply replace the existing products, but also discovers neglected demands, creates new markets, and increases sales by offering products with much lower prices and many more varieties. Conversely, the growing market attracts more investors to supply and to provide related supports and services. The industrial environment thus becomes more convenient for further investments.

The circular cumulative dynamics between industrial and market growth has been discussed by Nicholas Kaldor and other scholars in the context of industrialization in the West.[53] A strong level of domestic demand is viewed as boosting business confidence and stimulating investment. Investment can generate productivity increases through economies of scale, learning by doing, spatial agglomeration,

[51] Ibid.

[52] Deborah Brautigam, Tang Xiaoyang, and Ying Xia, What Kinds of Chinese "Geese," August 2018.

[53] Nicholas Kaldor, *Causes of Growth and Stagnation in the World Economy* (Cambridge: Cambridge University Press, 2007); Eatwell, John, The Principle of Cumulative Causation, in John Eatwell, *Whatever Happened to Britain? The Economics of Decline* (London: Duckworth, 1982).

infrastructure construction, and innovation. According to the original Kaldorian model, increasing investments and productivity can stabilize international finance systems and expand global exports. This in turn spurs further domestic demand and investment, successive upswing of innovation and productivity, and so on ad infinitum.[54]

In Africa's context, when FDIs build factories to meet the growing domestic demands, they not only improve the balance of international trade of the African countries, but also have transformative effects on the local socioeconomic structure. As many of the domestic demands were neglected by international manufacturers and the market is underdeveloped, a large part of the African population still relies on traditional handwork, by family members or local small workshops, to stitch dresses, make shoes, process food, carve furniture, and build houses. The productivity is extremely low and the business can hardly go beyond the local neighborhood. The Chinese factories bring changes to both production and consumption manners in the related sectors. Specialized machine manufacturing and professional workers replace manual labor and craftsmen. Large numbers of industrial products stimulate market network to expand toward every corner of the country. As the Chinese investors state, Africa's market is "empty"; namely there is still much untapped market potential. The industrial production itself requires and promotes intense market activities, from collection and supply of raw materials to distribution and sales of products. The change of production and consumption manners intrinsically generate more market demands, which further attract more investments in production (see Figure 5.9).

To be sure, the effects of structural transformation driven by the Chinese investments are currently still very limited and need further research to measure, because it's just a recent phenomenon. However, the case studies of the emergence and local linkage of Chinese manufacturers in this chapter suggest that they are not just following the footprints of other investors, but also creating new industrial models and clusters in Africa. Meanwhile, their numbers increase rapidly, making socioeconomic change in a relatively broad circle possible. In Ethiopia, for example, Chinese manufacturing projects registered as "in

[54] Phillip Anthony O'Hara, Principle of Circular and Cumulative Causation: Fusing Myrdalian and Kaldorian Growth and Development Dynamics, *Journal of Economic Issues* (June 2008) XLII.2, 384.

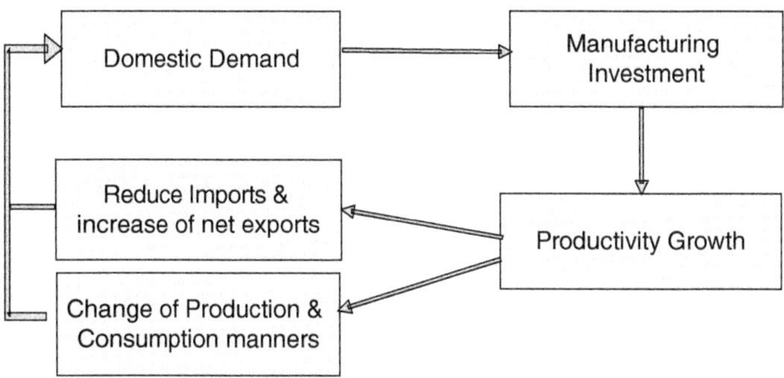

Figure 5.9 Coevolution between domestic markets and industrial investment.
Source: Author

operation" as of August 2017 totaled 482, among which 451 arrived after 2005. India and the United States ranked the second and third largest sources of manufacturing FDI in operation, with 202 and 73 projects, respectively.[55] Tanzania Investment Center reported 348 registered manufacturing investments from China during 1990–2014, followed by India with 191 registrations.[56] Ghana had 183 registrations of Chinese manufacturing projects during 2004–2014.[57] According to the database of the Chinese Ministry of Commerce (MOFCOM), only 16 approved outward direct investments aimed at Africa's manufacturing sector until 2004, whereas between January 2005 and January 2015, the number rose to 1,401.[58] As noted, an overwhelming majority of these investment projects target Africa's domestic and regional markets so that they stimulate the formation and development of Africa's market. Given a stable sociopolitical environment, the cumulative circle between industrial production and market economy will keep attracting more investments and promoting structural transformation in African countries.

55 Ethiopia Investment Commission, List of licensed foreign investment projects, August 2017.
56 Tanzanian Investment Center, Investments with Chinese Interest from 1990 to June 2014. But the registered projects may not be all implemented.
57 Tang Xiaoyang, Geese Flying to Ghana? A Case Study of the Impact of Chinese Investments on Africa's Manufacturing Sector, *Journal of Contemporary China* (2018) 27, 114, 924–941.
58 To understand the meanings and relationship of these different statistic figures, please see Deborah Brautigam, Tang Xiaoyang, and Ying Xia, What Kinds of Chinese "Geese," August 2018.

By comparison, the export processing investments have little interaction with local markets. Even in the global market, the factories in Africa serve clients in relatively simple and passive manners, mainly relying on cost advantages such as labor, resources, and policy incentives without knowing the market trends and needs in detail. In fact, the African branches receive their orders usually through headquarters in Asia or international agents from Asia. Marketing, sales, design, and customer services are all controlled from outside Africa. Consequently, the relationship between the export processing FDI and local development is one dimensional. The host countries merely receive a number of low-pay and low-skill production jobs, which are also easy to float away because of cost changes. A few export processing investments alone cannot sustain long-term and extensive industrialization.

The importance of market in the industrialization is also supported by other studies on foreign investments in general. Deborah Winker's research based on survey data from Chile, Ghana, Kenya, Lesotho, Mozambique, Swaziland, and Vietnam shows that market-seeking FDI has a much more positive relationship with the share of sales to the host country as well as the probability of supplier assistance than cost- and resource-seeking FDI.[59] Gary Gereffi argues that the simple participation in export processing business would not help the poor countries develop the institutions, the know-how, or the consumer markets[60] Moreover, evidence from the apparel sector in China, Turkey, India, and Europe shows that the growth and upgrading of export processing factories needs a developed domestic market. To produce higher-value and more complex garments for exporting markets, the firms usually need to build up their capability of design, branding, and service in their home markets first.[61] As noted in Chapter 1, industrialization and the formation of market economy requires comprehensive socioeconomic transformation. Isolated factors, such as cheap labor cost, industrial

59 Deborah Winkler, Determining the Nature and Extent of Spillovers: Empirical Assessment, in Thomas Farole and Deborah Winkler, eds., *Making Foreign Direct Investment Work for Sub-Saharan Africa: Local Spillovers and Competitiveness in Global Value Chains* (Washington, DC: World Bank, 2014), pp. 87–114.

60 Gary Gereffi, *Global Value Chains and Development* (Cambridge: Cambridge University Press, 2018), p. 408.

61 Cornelia Staritz, Gary Gereffi, and Olivier Cattaneo (ed.), Shifting End Markets and Upgrading Prospects in Global Value Chains, *International Journal of Technological Learning, Innovation and Development* (2011) 4.1/2/3, 73–75.

policy or preferential tariff, may influence the transformation, but without an inclusive synergism to mobilize various aspects of the society, the "big push" is set to encounter numerous obstacles. Justin Yifu Lin's New Structural Economics, focusing on solely comparative advantages in international competition, can explain neither the growth stagnation of export processing FDI in Africa nor the prosperity or diversity of local market-seeking manufacturers. Believing that market functions are constrained by just a few exogenous binding factors, Lin's theory fails to realize that the markets and industrial activities have endogenous relationship and must coevolve together.[62]

To summarize, over the past decade Chinese investments in Africa's manufacturing sector have increased rapidly. Unlike previous aid projects, the new investors, most of whom are private firms, are driven primarily by economic considerations. The major business interests include securing natural resources, using cheaper labor and seeking local markets. All these types of investments contribute to the industrialization of host countries, but their development synergisms with the local economy are not the same. While resource- and export-processing projects create many employments and revenues immediately, their growth is seriously constrained in Africa's current socioeconomic conditions and the prospects of their businesses depend on the availability of resources and policy incentives. The competitiveness of these types of manufacturers lies solely in the supply side. The distance from the market hinders them to expand or upgrade. The local market-seeking investments, on the contrary, discover and meet the market demands within Africa with corresponding production capacity and technology. Starting with low thresholds, they are able to involve many more stakeholders in various parts of African society to grow together, ranging from suppliers and business partners to competitors and consumers. Chinese businessmen's extensive network accelerates the formation of industrial clusters. China's unique strength as the world's manufacturing powerhouse facilitates the investments in Africa by providing machinery, accessory, and other supplies and services. Hence, it's the local market-seeking manufacturers that are fostering the most dynamic and sustaining coevolution between Chinese investment and

[62] Justin Lin, From Flying Geese to Leading Dragons, Policy Research Working Paper 5702, World Bank, June 2011, pp. 24–30.

Africa's structural transformation. The increasing presence of factories have already led to significant changes in some aspects of Africa's socioeconomic life. The following chapter will use special economic zones as examples to depict the comprehensive impacts of Chinese industrial investments on Africa.

6 *Special Economic Zones*

6.1 From a Desert to a City

In June 2009, I set off from Egypt's capital, Cairo, traveling eastward for approximately 100 kilometers to Suez, a city located at the junction between Asia and Africa, adjacent to the Suez Canal, and connecting the Mediterranean and Indian Oceans. China had established an economic and trade cooperation zone (ETCZ) there: The China-Egypt Suez ETCZ (hereafter referred to as "the cooperation zone"). The cooperation zone is not located in Suez city, but near the Ain Sokhana Port, approximately 30 kilometers from the urban center. Not long after my van left the city, I found myself surrounded by endless desert sands, a sight characteristic of the Middle East. Wherever the van went, dust flew into the air. Only when I approached the port did I notice industrial plants scattered throughout the barren desert. After stepping out of the van, I had to walk for approximately twenty minutes to reach the cooperation zone. Exposed to the scorching 40°C heat, I felt like all the moisture in my body was rapidly evaporating into the dry air. Fortunately, the buildings of the cooperation zone stood out in the emptiness. The office of the cooperation zone was a small, pale yellow, two-story building with several rows of flat houses at the rear, giving the appearance of factories surrounded by a few construction sites. One of the construction projects was a five-story building that was taking shape as the future investment service center of the cooperation zone. The other buildings were factories still under construction, covering a considerable area.

The general manager of the cooperation zone, Liu Aimin, was roughly forty years old. He was gentle in appearance, but responsive and orderly in his words and actions. He originally worked at the Tianjin Economic and Technological Development Area (TEDA) before being sent to Egypt the previous year to manage development of the cooperation zone. He explained that the history of the Suez cooperation zone could be traced back to 1994. When former Egyptian president Muhammad Hosni Mubarak visited TEDA while in China, he invited TEDA to Egypt to cooperate and share its experience in developing and managing development zones. Under a negotiation agreement between the corresponding governments of both parties, TEDA and four Egyptian companies formed the Egypt-China Investment Company to jointly develop land beside the Ain Sokhana Port, covering an area of more than 20 square kilometers. TEDA accounted for 10 percent of the shares. However, establishing the cooperation project was not a smooth process. TEDA could not execute its plans because it lacked decision-making power. In addition, corruption in local bureaucracy severely hampered normal operations. Funds remitted from China even disappeared from company accounts. In 2003, the Egypt-China Investment Company suspended development and returned most of the land to the local government. However, TEDA was determined to stay in Egypt and develop on its own. Therefore, TEDA established another wholly owned company, purchasing a piece of land near the original sector to establish a small and medium-sized enterprise (SME) industrial park. The park was built to attract Chinese enterprises investing in Egypt. After a few years of operations, approximately ten enterprises had settled in the park. In 2007, TEDA considered opportunities for Egyptian market redevelopment to have matured. TEDA applied to the Chinese Ministry of Commerce (MOFCOM) to spearhead an overseas ETCZ project and was successful. Subsequently, in March 2009, the Egyptian government launched a new special economic zone (SEZ) project, opening bidding to international developers for its first SEZ. Given its experience in the Egyptian market, TEDA won the bid, out of more than thirty competitors from other countries. The China-Africa Development Fund (CADF) also invested in the cooperation zone, accounting for 30 percent of overall shares. Learning from past lessons, Chinese has become majority shareholder of the new project, controlling 80 percent of total shares. Benefiting from the preferential policies promoted by both Chinese and Egyptian governments, and aware of the corresponding responsibilities entrusted to the company, TEDA sent additional elite staff members to the Suez cooperation zone to initiate an ambitious project.

At this point in Mr. Liu's narrative, an employee knocked on the door, announcing that it was lunchtime. Liu invited me to join him in the canteen, which was located in the basement of the office building. The basement contained seven or eight long tables and twelve benches arranged in a simple manner. Everyone who ate in the canteen was Chinese, and several dozen people were already seated, filling the room. Liu explained that in addition to serving the managerial staff at the cooperation zone, the canteen also served the Chinese employees of all companies in the zone. Egyptian employees, by contrast, generally brought their own lunches. The lunch was a standard meal – water bamboo shoots with sliced meat, cucumbers, bean sprouts, rice, and a bowl of clear soup – that cost approximately EGP $5 (slightly more than US$1). The canteen was run by a contracted restaurant from Tianjin, and the Tianjin Municipal Government provided every first-year Chinese employee with a food allowance of RMB 10,000 (US$1,600).

During lunchtime, an employee rushed over to speak with Liu. Water supply in the park was low, he reported, and the newly planted flowers and grass had nearly withered. Liu grumbled in discontent, "How can the Egyptian government brag about developing an SEZ if they cannot even ensure basic supply of water and electricity? Problems like these never end!" Liu quickly gulped down a few mouthfuls of rice as he spoke, before asking the deputy general manager of the cooperation zone to take over my tour, after which he gathered a few pertinent staff members and left hastily to negotiate with local authorities.

The deputy general manager, Mr. Fu, had been in Egypt for three years. He said that building an industrial park required a considerable amount of time and effort; even in China, developing a considerable industrial scale would take twelve to fifteen years. Considering the characteristics of the Egyptian economy, four types of industries were selected as the pillar industries of the park: light industries, such as textiles and clothing; oil equipment; automobile assembly; and low-voltage electrical appliances. By mid-2009, sixteen companies had settled in the park, including Egypt CTMC Nonwovens Co., Ltd. and Changjin Egypt Stainless Steel Products Co., Ltd., which were larger companies that separately hired approximately 100 Chinese and Egyptian employees. In addition, Honghua Petroleum Equipment Co., Ltd., a joint venture between China and Egypt, enabled Egypt to break the production deadlock that had plagued local manufacturers of drilling equipment. Moreover, in order to provide essential commercial services to manufacturing firms, the park invited firms in the service sector, such as a banks, restaurants, and logistics firms with customs clearance services.

The tour ended back at the office, where I continued to discuss development of the ETCZ with Mr. Fu. He told me that initial costs for developing the park area were substantially high. TEDA could not rely solely on rental income to recover the costs. The developers' commercial objective was to raise the value of a large area of land through construction and management, thereby reaping the rewards of land sales and rentals. He optimistically estimated that after two years, the SME industrial park would be full, housing fifty firms and creating thousands of jobs for local people. In three to five years, the expanded park could begin to yield profits. However, TEDA was never content with garnering short-term commercial profits. Mr. Fu pointed at the vast desert outside the window and spoke with confidence: "The ultimate objective of the cooperation zone is to achieve urbanization, to transform the desert into a modern city, like Binhai New Area in Tianjin."

After leaving the cooperation zone office, I was immediately surrounded once again by suffocating, hot air. As I walked along the empty highway, hoping to find a minibus and gazing at the endless desert of yellow sand that extended to the horizon, I could not help but doubt the grand blueprint Mr. Fu had proposed: transforming this barren desert that had remained the same for thousands of years into a modern city was an unusually challenging task. Was TEDA's plan a pure fantasy? Could this plan be realized?

I could not understand why TEDA had come up with such an astonishing idea until two years later, in 2011, when I visited Binhai New Area. Binhai New Area was just as modern as any city in the world. Convenient rail traffic, wide and clean roads, clusters of skyscrapers, simple and orderly urban planning, and a large-scale industrial park combined to form a thriving organic entity. In the Binhai New Area library, I found historical files on TEDA (the former administrative institution of Binhai New Area). Looking through the pages, I saw pictures taken in 1984, when the development of the area first started. I suddenly realized why Mr. Fu had uttered those words years ago. The picture showed that the location of the area was originally a piece of grassless saline land. The first cement foundations were simply driven into the cracked land. Another picture taken later showed a few factories that had been built in the area, with only an asphalt road extending to connect it to the outside world. Comparing the hardship and poverty of the past with the current development and prosperity that I saw outside the library window, I could hardly suppress my shock that such a vast transformation from a barren land into a modern city had been achieved within less than thirty years. When TEDA staff worked laboriously on this piece of saline land in the early 1980s, they probably did not expect that their efforts would lead to such distinct changes and achievements. What made TEDA staff even more admirable was that they did not gloat over their remarkable achievements. Soon, they received an even more difficult task, going to Egypt to reproduce the success they had achieved in Tianjin, China, in the deserts of Egypt. Such courage and confidence were unique to the administrators and developers who had miraculously transformed terrain over the past thirty years. These qualities would accompany them in continuing to write new chapters in the progression of modern industrialization.

6.2 Attempts to "Go Global"

As early as the 1990s, Chinese developers started to set up a few small industrial zones in Vietnam, Pakistan, and Egypt to help Chinese enterprises to invest and produce in these countries. In 2002 Henan Guoji Group went to Sierra Leone, originally intending to develop real estate (villas and hotels), but was persuaded by Sierra Leone's government to invest in a joint venture industrial park near the port. In 2003 China Nonferrous Metal Mining Co. (CNMC) began developing an industrial area for mineral smelting and processing at Chambishi Copper Mine in Zambia, which it had previously purchased.[1] Shandong Yahe Textile Ltd. also developed the seventeen-hectare Linyi Industrial Park in Guinea, accommodating textiles, pharmaceuticals, rubber, and timber factories. In 2005, sales revenues reached up to US$20 million.[2] Launched by individual enterprises, these early experiments of Chinese zones in Africa were scattered and relatively small.

1 D. Brautigam and X. Tang, African Shenzhen: China's Special Economic Zones in Africa, *The Journal of Modern African Studies* (2011) 49.1, 27–54.

2 Linyi (Guinea) Industrial Park. Jiuzheng Construction Materials Networks (九正建材网), November 14, 2006. news.jc001.cn/detail/283474.html (accessed July 16, 2020).

As the Chinese government increasingly encouraged Chinese enterprises to "go global," namely to invest and operate in foreign countries, MOFCOM called for more Chinese firms to set up economic and trade cooperation zones overseas. Between 2006 and 2007, MOFCOM organized two rounds of open bidding to select the best plans and most qualified developers to develop overseas cooperation zones. In total nineteen proposals were selected out of 120 project applications. Seven of these selected projects were located in Africa: Egypt Suez ETCZ, Mauritius Tianli ETCZ (currently Jinfei ETCZ), Nigeria Ogun-Guangdong Free Trade Zone (FTZ), Nigeria Lekki FTZ, Zambia-China ETCZ, Ethiopia Eastern Industrial Zone, and Algeria-China Jiangling ETCZ. Subsequently, following major revisions to investment laws in Algeria, which required the Algerian party to hold most of the equity, the Jiangling ETCZ was not developed. The other six zones have been implemented since then and have seen various degrees of progress.

Meanwhile, many of the African countries that host these ETCZs have their own zone programs too and the ETCZs are integrated into their national strategies of development. As noted, the Suez ETCZ was originally initiated by the Egyptian government and 2009 won the tender to become the country's first SEZ. The Zambian government announced its Multi-facility Economic Zones (MFEZ) program in 2005 and the Zambia-China cooperation zones, which have two locations in Chambishi and Lusaka, became the first two MFEZs in the country too. Mauritius has a long and successful experience of developing export processing zones. The government assigned public land to the Chinese zone project in the hope of further attracting foreign direct investment (FDI) and upgrading economic structure. Likewise, Nigeria already has more than twenty free trade zones, which are developed either by private firms or by public sector. The two Chinese-invested cooperation zones are new additions to them. In comparison, the Eastern zone in Ethiopia was the first industrial park in the country, which did not have a well-defined industrial park program until 2012.[3] Yet, the Ethiopian government has quickly discovered the value of the industrial parks from the example of the Eastern zone. Not only did it announce an ambitious plan to build a dozen state-owned industrial

[3] Arkebe Oqubay, *Made in Africa: Industrial Policy in Ethiopia* (Oxford: Oxford University Press, 2015).

parks, but also offered incentives for more private investors to develop zones in Ethiopia. Consequently, a few more Chinese firms set up new industrial zones alongside the Eastern zone.

The number of Chinese-invested industrial zones has been growing across the whole continent. From Kenya, Tanzania, Uganda, and Djibouti to Guinea, Ghana, Congo Brazzaville, and Botswana, private and state-owned Chinese firms have been actively proposing to construct industrial zones in African countries during the past decade and most African governments are enthusiastic with the cooperation zone projects. Usually the Chinese developers undertake all or most of the development costs, whereas the African partners offer preferential policies and supporting infrastructure.

Although the China-Africa cooperation zones have become a remarkable form of industrial zone development in the continent, the outcome and impact of this form of cooperation have not yet been appropriately examined. A few scholars investigated the motivation and genesis of the cooperation zones.[4] Several researchers studied the performance of individual zones.[5] However, there is no systematic analysis of the model of cooperation zones as a whole. Based on a decade-long tracking of the growth trajectory of the cooperation zones, this chapter aims to provide a comprehensive investigation on what the zones have achieved so far and what they have not, particularly on how these zones may bring China's experience of industrialization and facilitate structural transformation in African countries. The six ETCZs selected by the MOFCOM bidding are the main objects of this research, because they have comparable size and owner structure, and have been in operation for a certain period. I have visited all these ETCZs multiple times since 2009. For each zone, I interviewed the Chinese and African managers of the

[4] M. J. Davies, Special Economic Zones: China's Developmental Model Comes to Africa, 2008, in R. I. Rotberg, ed., *China into Africa: Trade, Aid and Influence* (Baltimore, MD: Brookings Institution Press), pp. 137–154; P. Dannenberg, Y. Kim, and D. Schiller, Chinese Special Economic Zones in Africa: A New Species of Globalization, *African East-Asian Affairs* (2013) 2, 4–14.

[5] G. Mthembu-Salter, Chinese Investment in African Free Trade Zones: Lessons from the Nigerian Experience, South Africa Institute of International Affairs, Policy Briefing 10, 2009; Fei, Ding, Work, Employment and Training Through Africa-China Cooperation Zones: Evidence from the Eastern Industrial Zone in Ethiopia, China Africa Research Initiative, SAIS, Johns Hopkins University, Working Paper 19, September 2018.

zones, the investors residing within the zones, the African officials who administrate the zone programs, the employees working in the zones, as well as enterprises having business linkages with the zones. In the text that follows are the profiles of other five cooperation zones beside the Suez ETCZ.

6.2.1 Zambia-China Economic and Trade Cooperation Zone

Chambishi is a mining area 420 kilometers north of landlocked Zambia's capital, Lusaka, home to a major copper mine complex operated by CNMC since 1998. In 2003, CNMC began planning an adjacent industrial processing zone, comprising a smelter and ancillary factories. The foundation stone was laid in 2004. The Chambishi MFEZ comprises 11.49 square kilometers in Chambishi, including the Chambishi copper mine. CNMC also undertook to build a 5.7 square kilometer subzone near the Lusaka international airport. Firms in the zones will have a 25 percent customs duty on imported equipment waived and will not have to pay Zambia's 16.5 percent value added tax, among other incentives. They are not exempted from the Zambian labor or environmental codes and must invest at least $500,000 to be able to take advantage of these incentives.

The zone developers highlighted an intention to attract investors who would form an industry chain covering mining, smelting, and processing mineral resources such as copper and cobalt. By August 2016, more than thirty companies had settled in the Chambishi zone, including CNMC affiliates such as a copper smelting company, hydrometallurgy company, Sulphur acid plant, and foundry, as well as several private Chinese and local companies providing support services such as machine repairs and logistics. In total, this project created almost 8,000 local jobs.[6] However, the remote location of Chambishi rendered the location unsuitable for developing other industries.

[6] Zan Baosen, CEO of ZCCZ, August 2016. Warm Celebration of 10th Anniversary of the Establishment of Zambia-China Economic and Trade Cooperation Zone (*Relie qingzhu zanbiya-zhongguo jingjimaoyi hezuoqu chengli shizhounian*热烈庆祝赞比亚-中国经济贸易合作区成立十周年), February 24, 2017. zccz.cnmc.com.cn/detailtem.jsp?column_no=070401&article_millseconds=1486732392343 (accessed July 16, 2020).

The Lusaka branch of the zone is intended to host diverse industries involved in areas like manufacturing and logistics.[7] This subzone faces more challenges with infrastructure construction than the Chambishi branch, because building costs were high and investors' demands were low. Manufacturers don't find the business environment of the landlocked Zambia very appealing. Development of the zone started in 2009. The delay and deficiency of power supply added difficulty for the zone to attract investors. By 2017, there were only several firms in operation, including a brewery, a mushroom processing facility, a pharmaceutical company, and a plastic slipper factory.

6.2.2 *Ethiopia Eastern Industrial Zone*

Eastern Industrial Zone in landlocked Ethiopia is located 32 kilometers away from the capital Addis Ababa, near the town of Dukem, on the main road linking Addis Abba to the port of Djibouti, about 550 kilometers away (see Figure 6.1). The major developer, Qiyuan Group, was originally a private pipe-making company based in the Zhangjiagang Trade Zone of Jiangsu Province, near Shanghai. When the chair of Qiyuan Group, Lu Qiyuan, visited Ethiopia in 2006, he was attracted by what appeared to be multiple manufacturing opportunities, and appreciated the political stability, security, comfortable climate, and "the strong desire" of the Ethiopian government "to get out of poverty." He brought in other three private companies from Zhangjiagang to coinvest in the zone and competed successfully in MOFCOM's 2007 tender. Zhangjiagang Free Trade Zone provided technical assistance for zone management, under a contractual arrangement.

The 2008 financial crisis affected the steel market in China as well as the Ethiopian economy. According to the developers, shortages of foreign exchange, inadequate electrical capacity (low voltage), and the slow pace of bureaucratic approvals have seriously affected the zone's growth, but the developers managed to slowly advance the project. The 2011 establishment of Huajian shoe factory at the zone could be seen as a turning point. Since then, media and government agencies from various countries have paid greater attention to the

[7] Lusaka East MFEZ, December 17, 2012. http://zccz.cnmc.com.cn/detailentem.jsp?column_no=071005&article_millseconds=1355729183406 (accessed July 16, 2020).

Figure 6.1 Local job searchers waiting in front of the Eastern Industrial Zone, 2012.

Eastern Zone and the factories within the zone. This has significantly helped the zone to attract investors. As of 2011, only twelve firms signed rental contracts with the zone and six of them were operational, providing 1,600 jobs to local workers. By the end of 2018, 82 firms had signed contracts to settle in the zone and more than 50 were already operating, mostly in the sectors of building materials, electric assembly, textiles, garments, footwear, food, and pharmaceuticals. The zone had created more than 13,000 jobs for Ethiopians by this point.

6.2.3 Mauritius Jinfei Economic and Trade Cooperation Zone

JinFei Economic and Trade Cooperation Zone is located in Riche Terre, an undeveloped tract of public land 3 kilometers northwest of Port Louis, near the Free Port. The sole original developer was the Tianli Group, a provincial level, state-owned enterprise active in trade, construction, real estate, and textiles. Tianli arrived in Mauritius in 2001, establishing a state-of-the-art spinning mill, which has since expanded several times. Tianli's plant supplied much of the demand for cotton and synthetic thread in the Mauritius textile industry, as well as exports to other countries.

Tianli's proposal for an overseas zone was one of the winners of the first MOFCOM tender in 2006. The zone was expected to be the smallest of the Chinese zones, with a total proposed area of 211 hectares. In the original proposal, Tianli sought to utilize local natural conditions to construct the zone as a regional managerial headquarters for Chinese companies in Africa. However, resettling farmers who had been leasing the land from the government caused delays in launching the zone, and the zone ran into further difficulties after the developer was hit by the global economic slowdown. After a request from the Mauritian government to assist the zone, the Chinese central government instructed Shanxi province to coordinate capital restructuring of the Tianli zone. Two much bigger partners, Shanxi Coking Coal Group and Taiyuan Iron and Steel Company, joined Tianli to create a consortium. The new developers did not effectively move the project forward either, mainly due to lack of business interests. Another state-owned enterprise, Shanxi Investment Group, took over the ownership 2014 and decided to turn the project into a mixed-use economic and cultural zone, which includes a financial cluster, cultural center, five-star hotel, shopping center, restaurants, reception and wedding hall, shops, and gardens.

6.2.4 *Nigeria Ogun-Guangdong Free Trade Zone*

Nigeria Ogun-Guangdong Free Trade Zone is located in the Igbessa Region of Ogun State, 30 kilometers from the international airport serving Nigeria's commercial center, Lagos. Ogun State Government held 18 percent of the shares in the zone, but it did not directly participate in daily management and operations. Xinguang International Group, a state-owned enterprise from Guangdong Province, China, was the original developer.[8] However, the headquarters of Xinguang Group suffered tremendous losses amidst the 2008 global financial crisis, totaling in the billions of RMB. In early 2012, Ogun State Government terminated cooperation with Xinguang because of its funding shortages and poor management of the zone. Later that year,

[8] Zhiyue Zhong, deputy general manager of Xinguang International Group China–Africa Investment Company, June 2010.

Ogun State Government invited a tenant to the zone – Zhuhai Zhongfu Co., a listed company and leading business in China's packaging industry – to take over the cooperation zone.[9] Zhongfu signed a new joint venture agreement with the Ogun State Government to develop the zone in September 2013. By May 2016, the firm had invested US$60 million in the zone and had increased the number of tenants from five to more than forty.[10]

However, the former developer, state-owned Xinguang Group, now restructured as a part of the New South Group, did not give up efforts to resume its control of the zone. With the help of the Guangdong provincial government, it repeatedly negotiated with the Ogun State Government. Ultimately, Ogun State Government terminated the partnership with Zhongfu in May 2016.[11] In September 2016, the zone was handed over back to New South Group's management team.[12] These abrupt changes by Chinese developers not only caused confusion within the management of the cooperation zone, but would also leave complicated legal disputes looming around the zone in coming years.

6.2.5 *China-Nigeria Economic and Trade Cooperation Zone*

The Lekki Free Trade Zone (LFTZ) is located 60 kilometers east of Lagos on the Lekki peninsula, alongside a planned deep water port. The project had its origin in 2003 with discussions held by China Civil Engineering Construction Corporation (CCECC), which had been operating in Nigeria for more than a decade, and the governor of Lagos State, about transferring the Chinese zone model to Nigeria. In May 2006, CCECC brought three other Chinese firms to partner with the Lagos State Government to establish LFTZ. The government of Lagos State provided 30 square kilometers of land (3,000 ha) to the development company as part of its share. The Nigerian party in total accounted for 40 percent of equity, which was shared with the Lagos

9 Han Jianxin, managing director, Xue Zhen, Chief Operation Officer, Ogun, Nigeria, December 2012.

10 Foreign investor to President Buhari: Please Intervene, Ogun Govt Seeking to Appropriate Our Investment, September 3, 2016, *Premium Times*; and personal correspondence with a Zhongfu manager, October 2016.

11 Ibid.

12 Ogun Guangdong Free Trade Zone Turns a New Page (*Aogong Guangdong ziyoumaoyiqu fankai xinde yiye*奥贡广东自由贸易区翻开新的一页), 2016. www.gdxnf.com/NewsView-339.aspx (accessed July 16, 2020).

Table 6.1 *Progress of China-Africa ETCZs, 2019*

	Establishment Year	First Phase Area (hectares)	Planned Investment (US$ million)	Actual Investment (US$ million)	Number of Resident Companies (operational)	Actual Investment by Resident Companies (US$ million)	Number of Chinese Employees	Number of African Employees
Egypt Suez[a]	2000	334	280	149	70	1,000	1,600	3,500
Zambia Lusaka + Chambishi[b]	2004	1719	410	197	36	1,500	1,372	7,973
Nigeria Lekki[c]	2007	1176	392	205	51	150	120	1,000
Mauritius Jinfei[d]	2009	211	60	50	28	n/a	n/a	2,500
Nigeria Ogun-Guangdong[e]	2009	250	220	180	30	n/a	200	5,000
Ethiopia Eastern[f]	2010	233	101	180	82	450	1,000	14,000

Sources:

[a] Author's interviews, 2009–2019.

www.jwbos.com/channel/tedasuez/. One of the cases of overseas cooperation zones: production and processing type – Sino-Egyptian cooperation zone: modern industrial new city (*Jingwai hezuoqu anli zhiyi: shengchan jiagong xing – zhongai hezuoqu: xiandaihua gongye xincheng*境外合作区案例之一：生产加工型 – 中埃合作区：现代化工业新城), *China Investment* (2015) Volume 13.

[b] 关于赞比亚中国经济贸易合作区发展情况的汇报2014/5/30; Interview with Chambishi Zone, June 1, 2013; Huang Yupei, China-Africa Economic and Trade Cooperation Zone Construction (*Zhongfei jingmao hezuoqu jianshe*中非经贸合作区建设), *China International Studies* (2018) Issue 4.

[c] www.calekki.com/news_detail/newsId=1276.html.

[d] intl.ce.cn/zhuanti/2015/jwjm/fz/201511/26/t20151126_7144784.shtml.

[e] Ogun State Customs Commissioner visits Free Trade Zone (*Aogongzhou haiguan guanzhang laifang zimaoqu*奥贡州海关关长来访自贸区). www.wenji8.com/p/1c2D8dn.html. Speech in Forum on SEZs and Globalization, Tsinghua University, December 2015.

[f] One Belt and One Road Campus Alliance Special Issue 2017, survey of all firms in EIZ, Eastern Industrial Zone, July–August 2017. www.e-eiz.com/news.php.

State Government and the Lekki FTZ Development Co., an affiliate company. In November 2007, the Lekki Zone proposal won support in the second MOFCOM tender. The CADF later became an investor.

The development of the 3,000 hectares on Lekki Peninsula was planned as a three-phase operation. The first phase (1,176 ha) had a target of hosting some 200 companies. Construction began in October 2007 and although it was originally expected to last three years, it was still ongoing as of August 2019. The developers planned to divide the zone into six sections: transportation equipment, textiles and light industry, home appliances and communication technologies, warehousing, export processing, and living quarters and commercial areas.

6.3 Dilemma Between Special Economic Zones and National Structural Transformation

Special economic zones are not new for Africa. Some African countries do have notable, market-driven "bottom-up" clusters of industries such as the footwear cluster in Aba and the vehicle parts cluster in Nnewi in Nigeria.[13] Yet these spontaneous clusters have significant weaknesses, notably weak linkages to modern sources of innovation and technology, and a general absence of government support. Egypt, Senegal, Mauritius, and Liberia launched their export processing zones as early as 1970s. As of 2012, more than thirty African countries have implemented various forms of special economic zone (SEZs), including export processing zones (EPZs), free trade zones (FTZs), and industrial parks.[14] However, with a few exceptions, the general outcome of SEZs in Africa, especially in sub-Saharan Africa, has been lackluster. In some countries, zones are only partially functioning; some have even been abandoned. Some of the major obstacles facing African industrial zones are inadequate infrastructure, excessive bureaucracy,

13 D. Brautigam, Substituting for the State: Institutions and Industrialization in Eastern Nigeria, *World Development* (1997) 25.7, 1063–1080; K. Meagher, *Identity Networks: Social Networks & the Informal Economy in Nigeria* (New York: Boydell & Brewer, 2010); D. Z. Zeng, ed. *Knowledge, Technology and Cluster-based Growth in Africa* (Washington, DC: World Bank, 2008).

14 Foreign Investment Advisory Service (FIAS), *Special Economic Zones: Performance, Lessons, Learning, and Implications for Zone Development* (Washington, DC: World Bank, 2008), pp. 66, 69–70.

inappropriate zone locations, uncompetitive policies, lack of incentive, as well as poor zone development practices.[15]

By comparison, the importance of various industrial zones and special economic zones in China's structural transformation cannot be overemphasized. Using the first four comprehensive SEZs as an example (see Table 6.2), in 2009, the total land upon which these four zones stand accounted for approximately 0.07 percent of China's territory, and the total population accounted for approximately 1 percent of the national population. However, the total production value accounted for approximately 3.5 percent of national GDP, and total imports and exports accounted for more than 16 percent of national imports and exports.

In addition to these comprehensive SEZs, in 1984, fourteen national economic and technological development zones were established in Tianjin, Shanghai, Dalian, Guangzhou, and other coastal cities, where regulations on examinations and approvals for foreign investment were lax, similar to those implemented in SEZs. As of February 2017, China hosted more than 500 national level zones of multiple varieties: free trade, economic and technological development, export processing and high-tech zones.[16] Shenzhen, in particular, grew

Table 6.2 *Overview of first four Chinese SEZs, 2009*

	Shenzhen	Zhuhai	Shantou	Xiamen
Area (km^2)	1,953	1,701	2,064	1,565
Resident population (thousand people)	891	148	506	249
Gross local output (RMB 100 million)	8,201	1,038	1,036	1,623
Gross imports and exports (US$100 million)	2,701	374	60	433

Source: 2009 Statistical Bulletin of Shenzhen, Zhuhai, Shantou, and Xiamen

15 FIAS, Special Economic Zones, pp. 48–51; Cling, J.-P. and G. Letilly, Export Processing Zones: A Threatened Instrument for Global Economy Insertion? 2001. DIAL/Unite de Recherche CIPRE Document de Travail DT/2001/17.

16 China Association of Development Zones, www.cadz.org.cn (accessed July 16, 2020).

from a fishing village to an industrialized metropolis within a generation. African officials have often mentioned how, after seeing Shenzhen as it is today and hearing the story behind its development, they were deeply impressed and eagerly hoped that similar SEZs could be established in their countries by replicating the Shenzhen model in Africa.[17] However, the bumpy experiences of all of the Sino-African cooperation zones show how difficult it is to transfer China's SEZ model to Africa. What is the reason for this situation?

While SEZs offer a way for countries that cannot yet provide sufficient infrastructure or enact favorable policies on a national level to cluster manufacturing investors together for quick start-off, researchers find that the long-term sustainable success of SEZs are closely interconnected with the broad development of the region and the nation. Since SEZs enjoy generous fiscal incentives and special government support, they should not end up with being enclaves of low-cost and low-wage production, but should instead become catalysts for regional and national development.[18] On the other hand, if there is no significant transformation of the macro socioeconomic environment, temporary preferential measures cannot help SEZs sustain growth. SEZs may stagnate or even shrink when these measures stop.[19] More concretely, the micro and macro coevolution can be seen in the following aspects.

1. Coordinate SEZ construction with national infrastructure planning. By concentrating necessary and critical facilities in relatively small areas, SEZs can be a cost-effective means of building infrastructure to meet the needs of national industrial development. Yet, poor coordination between SEZs and general planning may lead to wasteful or ineffective infrastructure construction.

[17] D. Brautigam and Tang Xiaoyang, African Shenzhen: China's Special Economic Zones in Africa, *Journal of Modern African Studies* (2011) 49:1, 27–54.

[18] D. Brautigam and Tang Xiaoyang, Going Global in Groups: Structural Transformation and China's Special Economic Zones Overseas, *World Development* (2014) 63, 78–91.

[19] For example, In the Dominican Republic (DR), employment in the Free Zones reached 200,000 at the turn of the century, but then declined to 120,000 over the decade [J.-M. Burgaud and T. Farole, When Trade Preferences and Tax Breaks Are No Longer Enough: The Challenge of Adjustment in the Dominican Republic's Free Zones. In T. Farole and G., eds., *Special Economic Zones* (Washington, DC: World Bank, 2011)].

2. Establish linkage between local industries and the investors in the zones. The boundary of SEZs should not hinder business interactions. The SEZs need to build forward or backward linkages with external firms and converge with national industrial development trends.
3. Demonstrate and transfer technical and management skills. The SEZs should generate knowledge spillover to the broad economy. Employment and training of numerous local workers and managers can generate spillover effects. Other kinds of sharing business ideas and experiences between foreign and local stakeholders are helpful too. As Deng Xiaoping stated: "The special zone is a window to technology, management capacity, and knowledge."[20]
4. Stimulate sector upgrading and incubate emerging industries. SEZs have advantages in attracting enterprises with sophisticated technologies. Through appropriate support, they can play a strategic role in fostering emergence of new sectors in the economy and help domestic industries climb the value chain.[21]
5. Test new policies and prepare national reform. The special policies given to the SEZs should not be merely confined within the zones, for such exceptional treatment may slow down the nationwide reform. Instead, if successful policies and practices within the SEZs can be applied to the rest of the economy, they will have positive impacts on a much larger scale.[22]
6. Facilitate urbanization. Industrial concentration within the SEZs is accompanied with labor and business concentration. The SEZs can therefore evolve into comprehensive metropolitan areas, such as Shenzhen, Tianjin, and Suzhou Industrial Park (see Table 6.3). The lack of living and commercial support may cause labor shortages and stagnation.

Accordingly, when infrastructural conditions were still generally deficient in China, the SEZs and development zones built

[20] *Selected Works of Deng Xiaoping*, Vol. 3 (Beijing: People's Publishing House, 1993), pp. 51–52.

[21] Justine White, Fostering Innovation in Developing Economies Through SEZs. In T. Farole and G. Akinci, eds., *Special Economic Zones* (Washington, DC: World Bank, 2011), pp. 191–192; K. Omar and W. A. Stoever, The Role of Technology and Human Capital in the EPZ Life-Cycle, *Transnational Corporations* (April 2008), 17.1, 149–150.

[22] Export Processing Zones, Policy and Research Series, Vol. 20, Industry Development Division, World Bank, March 1992, p. 3.

Table 6.3 *Expansion of Chinese SEZs into metropolitan areas*

	Shenzhen SEZ	Tianjin ETDZ	Guangzhou ETDZ	Qingdao ETDZ	Suzhou Industrial Park
Initial area planned/ developed (km^2) [a]	327.5/ 2.14	33/3	9.6	15	6.18
First expansion (km^2)	395	45	38.6	220	40
Second expansion (km^2)	—	100	217	225	115
Area 2009 (km^2)	1,953	100	393.22	274.1	288
Residents 2009 (thousand)	891	168.7	182.67	315.7	315

[a] Suzhou Industrial Park was established 1994. Tianjin, Guanzhou, and Qingdao were set up 1984. The initial area of Shenzhen 1979 referred to the size of the village.
Source: Feng Zhaoyi 2007; *Statistical Bulletin of ETDZs 2009*

standardized infrastructure to make industrial production possible, including "three availabilities and one leveling" (three availabilities refers to the provision of roads, electricity, and piped water; one leveling refers to ground leveling), "five availabilities and one leveling" (adding the provision of drainage and communications infrastructure), and even "seven availabilities and one leveling" (adding the provision of gas and heating infrastructure). These standardized sets of facilities were quick to construct and easy to use and connect. The ready-to-use infrastructure greatly helped the zones attract foreign investors and guarantee smooth production.

Chinese zone developers were very conscious of linking the factories within the zone with local suppliers outside in order to generate spillover effects. Domestic companies and foreign investors in the zones were brought into contact regularly through symposiums. Foreign technology companies were also encouraged to invest jointly with Chinese partners to strengthen connections and facilitate technology transfer.[23] In addition, some zone developers adopted the strategy of

[23] Jianming Wang and Ming Hu, *From County-Level to State-Level Special Economic Zone: The Case of the Kunshan Economic and Technological Development Zone*, in Douglas Zhihua Zeng, ed., *Building Engines for Growth*

introducing a whole industry chain to zones and their neighboring areas so that production could proceed entirely in-zone or in-country.[24] This strategy enabled the development zones to upgrade from assembling isolated components to forming dynamic, self-sufficient industrial systems, providing a fundamental base for China to transform into a global factory.

More importantly, the zones were tasked with the mission of systematically testing China's economic reforms. In the words of Deng Xiaoping, the objective of SEZs zones was "to hew a path" for establishing a market economy in China.[25] During his famous southern tour of 1992, Deng demanded that within SEZs, "the reform and opening up should be conducted with a more daring spirit, instead of being executed with over-prudence …… when goals are set, experiment audaciously and explore boldly."[26] When the reforms tested in Shenzhen, Zhuhai, and other sites achieved preliminary results, the country established additional, larger special zones. In addition, the government gradually disseminated these experiences of activating the economy across the nation, by opening up China's markets to foreign capital. Subsequently, several measures piloted at SEZs, such as land lease and stock market, became national policies. Furthermore, in the early reform period, numerous preferential conditions aimed at attracting investors were first piloted at SEZs before gradually being promoted in other regions.[27] The SEZ experience successfully proliferated and was replicated to the extent that, by the mid-1990s, policies and regulations implemented in most regions in China did not differ substantially from those at SEZs. In other words, the SEZs were no longer "special."[28]

and Competitiveness in China: Experience with Special Economic Zones and Industrial Clusters (Washington, DC: World Bank, 2010), p. 128.

24 Jianming Wang and Ming Hu, From County-Level to State-Level, p. 143.

25 Deng Xiaoping, A speech at the Working Conference of the CPC Central Committee in April 1979.

26 Key Points of the Talks in Wuchang, Shenzhen, Zhuhai, Shanghai, and Other Places, January 18–February 21, 1992.

27 Deputy Director of the Development and Reform Commission Peng Sen: Special Zones Remain the Experimental Field of Reform and Innovation, September 1, 2010, Xinhua. www.gov.cn/jrzg/2010-09/01/content_1693174.htm (accessed July 16, 2020).

28 Yeung, Yue-man, J. Lee, and G. Kee, China's Special Economic Zones at 30, *Eurasian Geography and Economics* (2009) 50.2, 225.

Finally, new urban areas emerged near the zones. The planning of special and development zones in China has invariably involved constructing residential areas. In addition to providing staff accommodation for resident companies, these areas attract more people to live in and around the zones. As business districts and other residential support facilities are gradually completed, the investment environment of a zone improves, thereby attracting more manufacturing companies. These emerging urban areas serve as major drivers of regional development and new homes for millions of people from all over China, specifically from rural areas. The SEZs play a key role in a country's transformation from a rural society to an urban one.

In this way, SEZs in China have been generally successful in that they have synergized with the nation's broad structural transformation. When we look at individual zones in China, not all of them achieved expected growth. For example, in the first wave of special zones, Shantou developed much more slowly than the other three zones did (see Table 6.2).[29] Although the development speed varies among zones, the establishment of the SEZ scheme has effectively promoted China's industrialization in many aspects. One of the greatest contributions of cities like Shenzhen, Pudong, Suzhou, and Tianjian is how they guided neighboring areas and even the entire nation through a process of economic liberalization and industrial development. The amazing achievements of the SEZs are just an iconic example of the comprehensive national prosperity. Therefore, the most essential takeaway from China's SEZ experience is to link the development of the SEZs with that of the entire nation. However, why cannot the SEZ success be replicated in Africa? Can the China-Africa cooperation zones help spread the experience of zone development?

6.4 Challenges for the China-Africa Cooperation Zones

In contrast to the impressive zone development in China, the cooperation zones between China and Africa have not advanced smoothly.

[29] Researchers suggest different reasons for the failed zones, such as inappropriate geographic location, bad management, lack of entrepreneurial culture and modern societal structure, etc.; Li Erping, What Kind of SAR Will Fail in China? Commemoration of 30th anniversary of Shantou Special Economic Zone (*Zai zhongguo shenmeyang de tequ hui shibai? Jinian Shantou jingjitequ 30 zhounian*在中国什么样的特区会失败？纪念汕头经济特区30周年), October 25, 2011. www.douban.com/group/topic/23112635/ (accessed July 16, 2020).

Various challenges, such as infrastructure deficiency, financial constraints, and political stability, seriously slow down the progress. Particularly the departing views of Chinese and African stakeholders and the failure to build a development synergism between the zones and the broad economy contribute to the delay and limit the impact of the zones. [30] Corresponding to the aforementioned six channels of synergism, the challenges for the cooperation zones lie mainly in infrastructure, operation management, and linkage with local business and policies. Sector upgrading and urbanization are not yet significant due to the short periods of the zone development. Thus, they are treated together as divergence on policy and strategy.

6.4.1 *Infrastructure*

One common problem deals with the coordination of infrastructure construction. In general, infrastructure in the cooperation zones can be categorized into two types: infrastructure where developers build facilities inside the parks and infrastructure where local governments connect external facilities (e.g., water, electricity, gas, and roads) to the parks. Separate administration by both parties inevitably caused conflicts and inconsistencies between plans and actions. For instance, the Lusaka branch of the Zambia-China ETCZ was not able to get connected with the national power grid for three years. Even when the line was finally connected, the power supply provided by local authorities was instable, and there were frequent outages during the day. But a transformation station would require an investment of tens of millions of US dollars. The managers of the zone developer CNMC claimed to have already invested US$30 million by mid-2016 to conduct a range of activities including leveling ground, digging wells, paving roads, and building houses. Since investors had little interest in the zone, CNMC was reluctant to spend more money to build expensive infrastructure.[31]

Similarly, the Nigeria Lekki FTZ originally planned to use natural gas from the national gas pipelines to generate power. However, the developer encountered obstacles when connecting gas pipelines outside

[30] Tang Xiaoyang, Chinese Economic and Trade Cooperation Zones in Africa, in Arkebe Oqubay and Justin Yifu Lin, eds., *The Oxford Handbook of Industrial Hubs and Economic Development* (Oxford: Oxford University Press, 2020).

[31] Zan Baosen, CEO of ZCCZ, August 2016.

of the park, and the power generation method was eventually replaced with compressed natural gas. The power problem caused essentially high costs and delayed the construction schedule by two to three years. Moreover, a new airport, deep-water port, and coastal highways in Lagos, which were significant to developing the FTZ, were not realized, regardless of the number of years of planning. These uncertainties severely hampered the FTZ's appeal in attracting resident companies.

In some cases, Chinese companies also failed to fulfill their responsibilities. For example, all Mauritian government departments were fully prepared for the infrastructure that was to be developed in the cooperation zone, with plans to invest more than 400 million rupees (approximately more than US$14 million) into building water pipes, underground thermal power plants, waste treatment facilities, and laying communication cables around the park – even building a highway connecting the park with the port.[32] Yet, the Chinese developers acted slowly after experiencing a financial crisis and capital reorganization.

6.4.2 *Administration and Management*

The zones are supposed to facilitate FDI attraction. Although African countries attempted to streamline administrative process and make new policies in this respect, there are still large discrepancies between the government expectation and the investors' real demands. Several countries have adopted the idea of a "one-stop service," integrating the approval procedures of several departments into one lobby or even one service window to enhance efficiency. However, the follow-through on these measures has been less than satisfactory. For example, in Ethiopia, the establishment of a one-stop service for investment registration in the Eastern zone does not accelerate the process. The documents collected in the zone by the Ethiopian officials need to be forwarded to the headquarters in Addis Ababa. Since the officials cannot make decisions on site, the whole process of registration takes even more time than the original process. In Egypt, although a seventy-two-hour one-stop registration service system was installed, long

[32] Jin Fei: Les investissements des agences de services publics intéressent Alan Ganoo, Jean-Yves Chavrimootoo, L'express, December 13, 2010. www.lexpress.mu/article/jin-fei-les-investissements-des-agences-de-services-publics-int%C3%A9ressent-alan-ganoo (accessed July 16, 2020).

delays persisted because no time limit was prescribed for issuing land and business licenses. In countries such as Nigeria and Zambia, the issuance of labor licenses was often seriously delayed.

The management structure of the cooperation zones, no matter joint venture or solely owned by Chinese, often faces challenges of coordination and may seriously hinder the progress of the zones. The Nigeria Lekki FTZ is a joint venture of Chinese and Nigerian parties. It took a quite long period of time for teams from both countries to learn how to work together. As the Nigerian Deputy General Manager of Lekki FTZ, Adeyemo Thompson, recalled, "The communication between Chinese and Nigerian colleagues were poor at the beginning. Chinese only reported to Chinese managers, Nigerians only reported to Nigerian managers. It looked like two companies." This situation improved significantly only after several years of cooperation.[33]

Other five cooperation zones in Africa are almost exclusively owned by Chinese firms. Exclusive management by the Chinese party is in general considered to be more efficient and straightforward, as it involves less cross-cultural communication and coordination. But these zones may form relatively independent "states within a state." The African managers and officials can learn little about the operation manners of the zones. The knowledge spillover effect is thus reduced. Joint administration may strengthen connections between Chinese and African stakeholders after overcoming the initial barriers of communication.

6.4.3 Linkage with Local Industries

Another key criterion for the spillover effect is whether a park has connection with local industries and assist them to grow together instead of developing into an isolated industrial enclave. In Africa, the limited varieties and exorbitant prices of local supplies often constrain the possibility of cooperation. A procurement manager of the Ethiopia Eastern Zone provided an example: "A plasterer's float costs over 10 USD in local markets (6–7 times higher than in China). Although materials are available in the market, using local materials is overwhelmingly expensive." Therefore, in addition to purchasing industrial equipment from China, the Eastern industrial zone also

[33] Adeyemo Thompson, deputy general manager of Lekki FTZ, Lagos, June 2010.

imported various goods to Ethiopia in large quantities, including cement mixers, generators, household appliances, screwdrivers, nails, overalls, and even blankets, mosquito nets, and instant noodles. The import was thus figuratively called "ant migration."[34]

The situation has been gradually improved after the zone began operation, but the linkage remains weak. In a survey of Chinese manufacturers in Ethiopia August 2017, ten out of twenty-three surveyed factories that were located in the Eastern Zone reported to have local suppliers, equivalent to 43.5 percent of the surveyed firms in the zone.[35] Yet, in the entire country, forty-eight out of seventy-three surveyed Chinese investors, namely 65.8 percent, had local suppliers. The local suppliers provided mainly raw materials such as limestones, minerals, wood, leather, as well as cartons, label printing, and other accessories. The firms in the Eastern industrial zone that did not source locally were mainly garment making factories and machinery/vehicle producers. They could not find necessary fabrics or machine parts in Ethiopia and had to import them, primarily from China. As noted in Chapter 5, in general merely the generic materials can be sourced in Ethiopia. Supplies that require sophisticated processing cannot yet be found locally. This is also the case in other China-Africa cooperation zones.

The lack of industrial enterprises in Africa also affects other possibilities of engagement between Chinese investors and the local economy. High-ranking officials of the Chinese and African governments reached consensus to actively use the cooperation zones to help local companies. The action plan of the 2009 China-Africa Cooperation Forum in Sharm el-Sheikh stated that the cooperation zones "should provide convenience for African SMEs to settle and develop in the zones" (4.2.4). However, the realization of this guideline policy is not easy. For instance, The Zambia-China ETCZ in Chambishi specifically reserved spots for local companies, but could not find suitable investors for many years because of the threshold requirements (minimal investment amount US$500,000). In July 2011, the Deputy Minister of the Ministry of Industry and Trade, Zambia, even appealed to local companies on media, encouraging them to establish in the park to enjoy

34 Wan Sen, Wu Yabo, and Shi Xiangjun, African Roadmap of the Oriental Industrial Park in Conducting the "Ants' Move," *China Inspection and Quarantine Times*, April 27, 2011, p. 5.

35 Survey by the author, Dukem, Ethiopia, August 2017.

excellent conditions there.[36] In 2012, the park finally received its first Zambian investor, a company manufacturing plastic products. Other cooperation zones combined had just a handful of local investors as of 2018, most of whom were actually service providers rather than manufacturers. The developers of the zones stated that they treated investors from China, Africa, and other countries equally, hoping to have more diversity in the zones. But the weak industrial basis in Africa hinders the establishment of effective synergism.

6.4.4 *Policy and Strategy*

Harmonization of zone-related policies and development strategies is the most challenging part. African and Chinese stakeholders obviously have different interests and visions regarding the development of the zones and their roles in the broad economies. Although both parties can find mutual benefits in the cooperation in general, there are numerous divergences and conflicts in the real practice. Especially for the cooperation zones that are also at the front of reform experiments in the host countries, namely those in Ethiopia, Zambia, and Egypt, obstacles are enormous in the way of exploration. Chairman Lu Qiyuan of the Eastern Industrial Zone used a Chinese saying to describe the zone as "the first person to eat crab," because it introduced a new model of industrialization to Ethiopia and had to change the conventional thinking of local governments. The efforts to make changes are not completely ineffective, but the zone developers as foreigners have merely limited capacity to influence the policies and strategies of the host countries.

First, lots of policy discussion focused on preferential policies. Either through a special zone act in the host country or the commitment of local governments to negotiations, every cooperation zone received preferential treatment to encourage investment and facilitate trading, which mainly included tax reductions, relaxed foreign exchange control measures, accelerated customs clearance and registration procedures, and flexible controls on enterprise ownership and foreign worker licenses. However, many Chinese zone developers believed that these measures were inadequate in coverage. From one perspective, the

[36] Zambia: "Apply for MFEZ Plots," *Times of Zambia*, July 19, 2011. allafrica .com/stories/201107190862.html. (accessed July 16, 2020).

government surrendered too little of the profits. Chairman Lu Qiyuan stated that, at the beginning, the Ethiopian government considered the Eastern Industrial Zone only as a private property project and refused to provide any preferential policies. Although, after further explanation and persuasion, the officials changed their position, they granted only a limited amount of tax reduction. Lu stated that according to the experience of Chinese development zones, when the investing companies received a 30 percent refund on business tax, "the zone developed in an explosive manner."[37] Therefore, he actively invited Ethiopian officials to China, hoping that through visiting the Chinese development zones, the officials would further adjust their position on tax refunds.

Another perspective is that the preferential policies were not fully implemented. According to a Chinese managerial staff member at the Lekki FTZ, the related legal documents were indeed signed by the Nigerian Federal Government and Lagos State Government, which established the legal status of the FTZ and approved the preferential policies. However, during the policy implementation, the company encountered difficulty communicating and negotiating with the Nigerian government on major problems because both parties were nonequivalent in status. The major developer CCECC as an enterprise does not have many opportunities to talk to the senior policymakers, neither does it have much capacity of influencing the policy implementation. Furthermore, the departments of the Nigerian government differed in how they interpreted these policy documents, rendering the execution of the policies and agreements difficult.[38] In addition, the developers indicated that the Chinese government was slow in fulfilling its commitment to support policies and inefficient in negotiating with the local government.[39] In Zambia, the tax holidays prescribed by the Zambia Development Agency were shortened after the opposition party won an election in 2011. Criticizing the old law for giving too many advantages to foreign investors, the new law counted the tax holiday from the year of commencing operations instead of from the year of making profit.[40]

37 Lu Qiyuan, Xiamen, September 2011.

38 Communication of the Joint Meeting of Chinese Overseas (African) ETCZs and China–Africa Development Fund, Issue 2, July 2010.

39 Ibid.

40 Zambia Development Agency, Investor Guide, April 2016. Report on the Development of Zambia's China Economic and Trade Cooperation Zone

Apart from policies, both sides often encounter divergence regarding the model and strategy of zone development too. The Mauritian government held high expectations regarding the cooperation zone, providing limited state-owned land for the zone. In the original proposal for the zone, the Chinese developer Tianli Group sought to construct the zone as a regional managerial headquarters for Chinese companies in Africa. However, the 2008 financial crisis hit Tianli severely. The ownership of the zone has been altered several times since then and correspondingly the strategic goal of the zone has to be modified. New developers were not interested in building regional headquarters and changed the plan. The Mauritian government was very dissatisfied to see the purpose of the zone altered and the construction delayed.

Different understanding of the zone model also affects the progress of zone development in Egypt. Since 2009, TEDA had painstakingly negotiated with its Egyptian counterpart for a sustainable business model for the extension project of the zone. The Egyptian government initially considered the Chinese developer merely a contractor hired to construct an industrial park with complete infrastructure under the build–operate–transfer (BOT) model. They expected that ownership of the park would be transferred to the Egyptian government in fifty years, when the BOT contract expired. Accordingly, the zone developer's operations and authority were greatly restricted. TEDA disagreed with this presumption. According to their experience in China, they needed to spend heavily on the infrastructure construction and attract the investors with low land prices. Only after the business environment of the zone was comprehensively improved could the developer get returns from rising property value.[41] TEDA therefore asked for more land-use rights so that they would have more flexibility in attracting investors and could recover their investment from growth in land value.[42] After a "nearly 500-hour negotiation," both parties reached a consensus recognizing that the cooperation zone was not a BOT project but a comprehensive industrial development project.[43]

(*Guanyu zanbiya zhongguo jingji maoyi hezuoqu fazhanqingkuang de huibao*关于赞比亚中国经济贸易合作区发展情况的汇报), CNMC, May 30, 2014.

41 Li Zhiqun, Liu Yajun, and Liu Peiqiang, *Development Zone Deems Promising* (*Kaifaqu dayou xiwang*开发区大有希望) (Beijing: China Financial and Economic Publishing House, 2011), p. 287.

42 Internal communication of Suez ETCZ, Egypt, October 22, 2010.

43 Ibid.

In summary, China-Africa cooperation zones have hardly built functioning synergisms between the zones and the local societies in all the aforementioned dimensions. Apart from general problems of infrastructure and industrial support, the unique stakeholder structure of cooperation zones proves to be a major obstacle for replicating Chinese SEZ successes in Africa. Most of the zones in China, especially the early ones, are administered by a state-owned developer firm that is set up by the municipal government of its location. Under this arrangement, the developer could run the zone according to market mechanisms, while the government focused on providing public services. Since the zone developer company was owned by the municipal government, their interests aligned. The developer company was willing to invest large amounts of capital in infrastructure construction up front, even when it did not benefit the company's short-term profitability. Conversely, the municipal government offered preferential policies and other kinds of support to help attract investors to settle in the zone.[44] By comparison, China-Africa cooperation zones have three major stakeholders: Chinese government, Chinese zone developers, and African authorities, each of whose interests diverge from the others. The coordination in infrastructure, administration, policy, and other issues is therefore more challenging. In addition, different cultures, management styles, and industrial capacities between Chinese and Africans cause numerous unexpected incidents or incompatibilities. Consequently, the progress of the cooperation zones is slow. They have not yet generated significant impacts on the broad transformation in the host countries.

6.5 Approaches Toward Improved Synergism

Addressing the challenges encountered in the development practice of cooperation zones, both Chinese and African partners have taken measures for improvement. As diverging views and miscommunication are the main causes of delays and ineffectiveness of zone development, the stakeholders lay particular emphasis on enhancing exchange of ideas and strengthening linkage between the zones and local societies.

[44] Li Zhiqun, Liu Yajun, and Liu Peiqiang, Development Zone Deems Promising, pp. 43–59.

6.5.1 Chinese Initiatives

Chinese government and developers have realized that China's SEZ model cannot be simply replicated on the ETCZs. To find models which are fitting for zones in Africa, they have to rely on policymaking and regulation of African officials. Consequently, the Chinese pay much attention to exchanging ideas with African stakeholders and explaining concepts of economic zones to them in multiple manners, including training, workshops, site visits to China, and high-level dialogues.

China's MOFCOM has organized since 2005 a series of policy study workshops on the topic of zone development for officials from various African countries. African administrators in customs, tax, finance, port authority, and inspection departments were invited to attend seminars on operating SEZs and attracting FDI. They conducted field investigations of various zones in Shenzhen, Tianjin, Suzhou, and other Chinese cities in order to understand the policies, experiences, and management models China had cultivated at the development zones.[45] Some ETCZ developers organize their own programs for African partners. CNMC invited Zambian officials and parliament members to visit SEZs in Shenzhen and Shanghai for three weeks in 2009. The CEO of the Zambia zone Zan Baosen himself took part in designing the policy seminar. He was quite satisfied with the results of this tour. The participants brought their own questions to discussion in the seminar and wrote reports. Although Zambia does not have the same political system as China, the visitors understood Zan Baosen's main point, namely that a cooperation zone is not only a foreign investment but can also boost the Zambian economy. However, only about 20 out of 158 Zambian parliament members got the chance to take part in the

[45] Enrollment notification for African National Development Zone Construction Seminar (*Guanyu feizhou guojia kaifaqu jianshe yanxiuban de zhaosheng tongzhi*关于非洲国家开发区建设研修班的招生通知), Ministry of Commerce, July 15, 2005. www.mofcom.gov.cn/aarticle/h/jinckxx/200507/20050700168725.html (accessed July 16, 2020). 2016 Training Group of Developing Countries Inland Construction and Management Successfully Completed (*2016 nian fazhanzhong guojia neiludiqu kaifaqu jianshe yu guanli yanxiuban yuanman jieye* 2016年发展中国家内陆地区开发区建设与管理研修班圆满结业), Jiangxi College of Foreign Studies, July 19, 2016. www.jxcfs.com/html/2016/6-19/n06064899.html (accessed April 10, 2019).

tour. Zan found that there was still a long way to go in reaching mutual understanding with the Zambian politicians.[46]

Lu Qiyuan also invited Ethiopian ministers, mayors, and administrators to China many times. He described how after the Ethiopians saw Shanghai, Suzhou, and his hometown Zhangjiagang city, "they were astonished by the sights of things which were supposed to be seen solely in the West." In particular, he related how a field visit had changed the perception of the CEO of Ethiopian Industrial Parks Development Corporation (IPDC) Sisay Gemechu. "Sisay led people to visit Suzhou and Kunshan. He was already in the Suzhou industrial zone, but he still asked passersby in the street where the zone was located. After he realized that he was inside the zone, he understood that a zone is not merely made up of several roads or factories, but included finance, trade, commerce, housing, hospitals, schools (and many other things)."[47] This concrete experience helped the Ethiopian senior official understand the Chinese model of linking industrial zone development to urbanization.

Senior-level meetings also became the occasion for exchanging ideas in addition to diplomatic procedures. For example, when MOFCOM minister Chen Deming met the Ethiopian prime minister, he started every discussion by mentioning Eastern Industrial Zone, emphasizing the important role of development zones for attracting FDI and the need for preferential policies for zones to play such a role. The late prime minister Meles Zenawi agreed that the Eastern Zone was a good platform to share China's experience of zone management and market reform. He also instructed the Ministry of Finance and Ministry of Industry to design appropriate policies for the zone project.[48]

6.5.2 *African Initiatives*

The efforts of the Chinese stakeholders achieved various effects among the African partners. Most of the African officials who visited SEZs in

[46] Zan Baosen, CEO ZCCZ, Lusaka, July 29, 2013.

[47] Lu Qiyuan, Addis Ababa, January 2015.

[48] Minister Chen Deming's visit to Egypt (Chen Deming buzhang fangai qingkuang陈德铭部长访埃情况), Ethiopia Eastern Industrial Park, January 28, 2010. www.zjginvest.gov.cn/zjginvestnew/InfoDetail/?InfoID=01358ef0-5aa8-4afd-b202-353d411db6db&CategoryNum=012010004 (accessed August 18, 2011).

China acknowledge that the experiences were eye-opening and the discussions provided them with more insights into the zone development process. However, many of them also confess that the experiences learned can rarely be put into Africa's contexts because of various constraints. A Zambian official admired that Chinese government, from leadership to operating officials, attach so much importance to the special economic zones, whereas Zambian government put the MFEZ authority under the Ministry of Commerce for a while and then move it to Ministry of Finance. "Nobody takes it (MFEZ program) seriously."[49] Although CNMC put great efforts to promote the idea of zone development to high-rank politicians and officials, the effects are quite limited.[50] In Nigeria, the reform of the Nigeria Export Processing Zones Authority (NEPZA) has been delayed again and again. In Egypt, the political turbulence after the Arab Spring significantly slowed down the negotiation and development of the zone extension, as the Egyptian officials in charge were changed frequently.

While the lack of high-level initiatives in these African countries prevents the cooperation zones from building effective synergism, a remarkable example from Ethiopia showed that the cooperation zones may make a significant contribution once African policymakers take leading roles in the zone development. With the establishment of the Eastern Industrial Zone, the Ethiopian government gradually realized the importance of zonal development in building industrial capacity, creating employment, and attracting FDI.[51] To stimulate zone development in Ethiopia, the Ethiopian government hired Chinese consultants and actively selected the knowledge they wanted in the planning, implementation, and operation processes of the zone development. In 2013, the Ethiopian Ministry of Industry signed a consulting service agreement with China's Association of Development Zones.[52] Thirteen Chinese experts came to Ethiopia to

49 Interview with Zambian official, August 2016.

50 Zan Baosen, CEO ZCCZ, Lusaka, July 29, 2013.

51 Arkebe Oqubay, Made in Africa, pp. 3, 88.

52 China Development Zone Association and Ethiopian Government Signed "Ethiopia Special Economic Zone Advisory Service Agreement" (*Zhongguo kaifaqu xiehui yu aisaiebiya zhengfu qianshu "asaiebiya teshu jingjiqu zixun fuwu xieyi"* 中国开发区协会与埃塞俄比亚政府签署"埃塞俄比亚特殊经济区咨询服务协议"), China Association of Development Zones, September 2, 2013. http://yq.rednet.cn/c/2013/09/02/3131455.htm (accessed July 16, 2020).

draft a plan for the country's industrial zone program. Special Advisor to the Prime Minister Dr. Arkebe Oqubay read their report. Yet, it was said that Dr. Arkebe did not totally agree with the ideas proposed in the report because they seemed inappropriate for the Ethiopian context. To observe the real details of Chinese zones without diplomatic embellishments, he visited China on an ordinary passport. This "authentic" experience helped him devise the restructuring of the industrial zone program in Ethiopia.[53] Additionally, Ethiopian policymakers draw many lessons from the existing cooperation zones. For instance, Dr. Arkebe visited the Lekki Zone in Nigeria and witnessed its slow progress. In his view, the delay was caused by the fact that the host government was not the major owner of the initiative. Consequently, the Ethiopian government actively took part in the design and implementation of the new zone programs.

A dedicated state-owned enterprise, Ethiopian Industrial Parks Development Corporation (IPDC) was created in 2014 to develop and administer industrial parks according to international standards. From 2014 to 2019, IPDC plans to construct eleven industrial parks in various cities of Ethiopia. This structure is similar to that of SEZ in China; namely, state-owned zone developers take the initiative in construction and operations. Under this initiative, Chinese firms got contracted solely by IPDC to build and temporarily operate some of these zones. Ethiopian managers from IPDC will operate the zones in the long run. The new zones also serve the Ethiopian government's industrial policy more directly, allowing only those tenants that work in the export processing sectors, whereas the Eastern Zone does not select tenants according to sectors.

The Chinese side is indeed happy to see African partners taking initiative in the development of industrial zones, because these zones can better coordinate the comprehensive political-economic issues related. A few Chinese investors quickly moved into the government-owned industrial zones instead of the Eastern Industrial Zone. Chinese government and state-owned enterprises offered consultancy and management cooperation to help IPDC develop the zones. Furthermore, when China began collaboration with Congo Brazzaville to build a special economic zone at Pointe Noire in 2016, Chinese partners were very careful to serve in a supporting rather than a leadership

[53] Dr. Arkebe Oqubay, November 2018.

role. A senior Chinese official explained the structure of collaboration: "We insisted that the president (of Congo Brazzaville) should be the head of the Pointe Noir zone. They (Congolese partners) should lead the project; we should only be participating."[54] This position was appreciated and echoed by the Congolese partners. "It (the zone) is a cross-cutting project that engages the entire government. If our Chinese partners are mobilized for this project; We, Congolese, must be more so because we are the main beneficiaries," said Alain Atipault, Minister of Special Economic Zones.[55]

To conclude, the history of the cooperation zones is a good reflection of the pragmatism of Chinese engagements in Africa. First, the Chinese government and enterprises do not have a definite "China Model" of zone development for Africa. At the beginning, they were indeed troubled by different African political-economic contexts and experienced severe setbacks. The designed plans and strategies could not work effectively. Over a decade of experiments, the Chinese government and firms continuously modified and diversified their approaches to seek suitable modes of zone development in Africa. Second, relentless experimentation with cooperation zones has been driven primarily by the growing economic interests of China in Africa, as Chinese industrial investors require zones with good infrastructure. Meanwhile, Chinese partners strongly believe in the zones' potential to facilitate African industrialization and urbanization, especially due to their successful experience at home. China's need for further economic growth merges with Africa's demand for development in this regard. As Congolese Minister Alain Atipault pointed out, "China should reindustrialize itself and know that Africa needs to industrialize ... This (Pointe Noire SEZ) is neither a gift nor a loan, but deals with a direct investment that is open to other countries of the world."[56] Third, small pilot zone projects have gradually increased their policy impacts on Africa's structural transformation, in spite of

[54] Internal Speech, Official of China Ministry of Foreign Affairs, March 2017.

[55] Hervé Brice Mampouya, Pointe-Noire: La Réalisation de la Zone Économique Spéciale se Concrétise, l'Agence d'information d'Afrique centrale, January 25, 2017. www.adiac-congo.com/content/pointe-noire-la-realisation-de-la-zone-economique-speciale-se-concretise-60530 (accessed July 16, 2020).

[56] Loïcia Martial, Congo-Brazzaville: la Chine finance une zone économique spéciale, *RFI*, January 19, 2017. www.rfi.fr/fr/emission/20170119-congo-brazzaville-chine-finance-une-zone-economique-speciale (accessed July 16, 2020).

their seemingly mediocre performance. For instance, the Eastern Industrial Zone in Ethiopia served as a catalyst for the country's latest policies on industrialization and industrial zones. Lu Qiyuan, Chairman of the Eastern Zone, liked to call the zone as "the first person to eat crabs" in Ethiopia – that is, a pioneer who experiments with an unknown venture to open new possibilities. From negotiating preferential policies to providing sub-lease land certificates, the developer had to tackle numerous problems to make the first industrial zone a reality in Ethiopia. Therefore, progress was slow and costs were high.[57] However, one can make the case that the Eastern Zone project helped Ethiopian officials observe the zone development model closely and spurred the launch of the government's comprehensive zone program several years later.[58] Other zone projects have similarly become platforms for communication and experience sharing between Chinese and Africans, although their impacts vary. Chinese pragmatism influences Africa's structural transformation through interactive practices on the ground, rather than through grand strategies or fixed models.

[57] Lu Qiyuan, November 2011, Addis Ababa.
[58] Arkebe, Made in Africa, pp. 3, 88.

7 Employment and Training

7.1 Proletariat Friendship or Capitalist Exploitation?

Urafiki Textile Mill is a landmark enterprise in Dar es Salaam. "Urafiki" means friendship in Swahili. The name reminds people of the historic origin of the enterprise. It was an aid project established in 1968. In the late 1990s, with the direction of former premier Zhu Rongji, the malfunctioning aid project was converted into a market-oriented joint venture. To commemorate the remarkable background of the factory, a huge panel painted with "Long Live Tanzania-China Friendship" stands in a central position of the factory entrance. However, this symbolic project of international proletariat friendship was taken to court in 2008 by the Tanzanian labor unions.

The cause for the prosecution was the elevation of the minimal monthly wage standard for the entire textile sector from 57,000 Tsh (US$45) to 150,000 Tsh basic salary plus 65,000 Tsh welfare by Tanzania's Ministry of Labor in October 2007. The minimal wage of over 210,000 Tsh (US$266) was too much for the textile industry. All fourteen textile mills in the country protested and criticized that this regulation was based on an imprecise labor report. After several months of negotiation, the Minister of Labor agreed to lower the standard to 80,000 Tsh for the textile industry. However, the national worker union and its branch in the Urafiki mill did not accept the revision. They prosecuted the Urafiki mill together with the Ministry of Labor for violation of the constitution and demanded wage payments meet the 210,000 Tsh standard. The court finally ruled in favor of the unions and ordered Urafiki to compensate the workers according to the 2007 regulation.

This case was just a part of the complex labor challenges that impeded Urafiki's development over the past twenty years. The reputation and sale of Urafiki's products is actually quite good. The market demand surpasses the production capacity. Yet, the problems of labor relations have plagued the joint venture since its establishment in 1997. The arriving Chinese managers wanted to streamline the labor force to improve efficiency. They kept only 1,900 out the nearly 4,000 workers previously employed at the mill. However, most of the remaining staff were permanent workers and could not be laid off. A Chinese manager complained that these old workers "had obsolete ideas and low productivity." The rate of qualified products was only 40 percent in comparison with 90 percent in China. When workers took sick leave, managers could not verify whether they were truly sick or not. One day, the general manager expressed anger over the suspension of production: six of the ten workers assigned to move a stock of materials had gone on sick leave, causing chaos. Despite the good sales, the joint venture had been running at a loss for almost every year since its opening because of low productivity and apparent high labor costs.

Despite this, the worker union still demanded a salary increase and more welfare benefits. Chinese managers felt that the worker union did not care about the economic efficiency of the company, for they assumed that Chinese would not let this "child of Mao and Nyerere" fail. The political significance overweighed economic consideration.[1] By comparison, private enterprises in Tanzania can more effectively deal with worker unions through flexible approaches. As for the court case concerning minimum wage, all the other mills were able to negotiate with the unions privately to settle the dispute, but Urafiki, as a joint venture with government's participation, was not able to settle it through negotiation.

Researcher C. K. Lee pointed out that low wages formed the major grievance of Tanzanian workers at Urafiki. The workers' wages were hardly sufficient to cover the basic needs of a family.[2] She viewed it as a result of casualization of employment in Africa: previously socialist employment systems with high welfare provisions conceded to exploitative capitalist business logic.[3] Urafiki's Chinese and Tanzanian managers are aware that the wage paid to the local workers is meager. Yet,

1 Interview with Huang Lilan, general manager of Urafiki Textile, Dar es Salaam, July 2009.

2 Ching Kwan Lee, Raw Encounters: Chinese Managers, African Workers and the Politics of Casualization in Africa's Chinese Enclaves, *China Quarterly* (September 2009) 199, 111–112.

3 Ibid., pp. 100–103.

they have a different opinion on the cause. It is the low productivity and a stubborn labor system that make an increase of salary impossible. The overprotection of labor failed the enterprise and consequently affected the workers' salaries as well.

The Urafiki case exemplifies the complex controversies surrounding employment issues in the intensifying China-Africa economic ties. Public opinion and mass media have paid special attention to the employment practices of Chinese companies in Africa. Employment is an important aspect of socioeconomic structural transformation. The costs and skills of labor are essential factors that influence the progress of industrialization. The growing number of industrial workers also alters the sociopolitical structure of countries where rural peasants are still dominant in the population.

A critical tone underlies much of the public debate around Chinese employment practices. Some observers express concerns that Chinese companies bring large numbers of Chinese workers to Africa and are unwilling to hire local workers.[4] Ben Schiller reported that tens of thousands of Chinese laborers and engineers were imported to build infrastructure projects in Ethiopia, Sudan, and other African countries, thus worsening an already acute unemployment problem in Africa.[5] Others complain about low wages. The International Trade Union Movement's Hong Kong liaison office (IHLO) suggested that wages at Chinese companies are among the lowest in many African countries and they usually pay less than other foreign investors.[6] Doubts have also been raised about Chinese companies' contribution to the development of the continent's human capital. A World Bank research paper reported: "Chinese firms tend to rely on their own low-cost labor and do not invest heavily in the training and education of African

4 Antoinette Slabbert, Chinese Dump Local Labour for Imported Workers, *City Press*, September 1, 2012. http://m.news24.com/citypress/Business/News/Chinese-dump-local-labour-for-imported-workers-20120901 (accessed July 17, 2020); Southern Africa Resource Watch, Beware of Easterners Bearing Gifts? The Development Impact of China's Role in the Region, in Garth Shelton and Claude Kabemba, eds., *Winwin Partnership? China, Southern Africa and the Extractive Industries* (Johannesburg: Southern Africa Resource Watch, 2012), p. 128.

5 Ben Schiller, The China Model, December 20, 2005. www.opendemocracy.net/democracy-china/china_development_3136.jsp (accessed March 15, 2012).

6 IHLO, China's Exportation of Labor Practices to Africa, 2006. www.ihlo.org/CINTW/ArticleLabourPracticeExport.html (accessed March 15, 2012).

workers."[7] Southern Africa Resource Watch also stated that "technology transfer to local people is not a feature of most Chinese investment."[8]

Some of these observations are based on individual impressions alone, without any solid investigation on the ground. Others are based on scattered case studies. Systematic research in this area has been scarce. In this chapter, I aim to map out a more precise picture of Chinese employment patterns and their influence on Africa's development of human resources in the context of structural transformation. The following discussion will begin by outlining the major patterns of Chinese companies' employment practices in Africa. The practices reveal a dilemma of mutual causation between employment and skill. We will see that the solutions to this dilemma in China-Africa engagements are largely consistent with interactive pragmatism and the gradual altering of production and living styles in various African societies.

7.2 Truth of Employment Practices

It is widely believed that Chinese companies in Africa tend to bring workers from China instead of hiring local people, but this claim is not supported by the available data. Though it is not easy to obtain the exact numbers of African workers employed in Chinese companies, due to lack of official statistics, a number of fact-based reports and surveys still indicate a general trend. In 2007, the Angolan Ministry of Finance published a report listing the composition of employees at thirty infrastructure projects executed by Chinese companies. Out of a total of 3,136 employees, 1,872 were Angolans, making up 59.7 percent of the entire work force. In this case, the proportion of Chinese workers was still relatively high, more than 40 percent. However, this was because of the project's pressing deadline for completion and the lack of skilled labor in postwar Angola.[9] A survey conducted by the SACE foundation in Kenya in 2014 found that 78 percent of full-time employees in seventy-five

[7] Zafar, Ali, The Growing Relationship Between China and Sub-Saharan Africa: Macroeconomic, Trade, Investment and Aid Links, *The World Bank Research Observer* (2007) 22.1, 124.

[8] Southern Africa Resource Watch, Beware of Easterners, p. 149.

[9] Angola Ministry of Finance, Anexos Linha China II Semestre 2007. www.minfin.gv.ao/docs/dspProjGov.htm (accessed January 27, 2010).

Chinese companies are Kenyans.[10] Employment statistics from five active Chinese economic zones (Table 6.1) revealed that 33,973 African workers were employed in total, which accounted for more than 85 percent of the total workforce in those zones. McKinsey & Company, based on surveys of more than 1,000 Chinese companies in eight African countries, reported that 89 percent of employees in these firms were Africans, totaling up to more than 300,000 jobs.[11] The proportion of local employees is especially high in the Chinese manufacturing factories. A survey conducted by SAIS-CARI research center on a total of eighty-seven Chinese manufacturing firms across Ethiopia, Ghana, Tanzania, and Nigeria, from 2012 to 2014, reported the recruitment of 15,052 African workers and 688 Chinese workers. Through systematic surveys of 74 firms and 1,500 workers in Ethiopia and Angola 2016–2018, researchers from the School of Oriental and African Studies (SOAS), University of London found that the average proportion of local workers in Chinese companies was 74 percent in Angola, and above 90 percent in Ethiopia, similar to that of non-Chinese firms in these two countries.[12]

Such data not only suggests that Chinese companies employ a large number of African workers, but also indicates that the percentage of local workers varies by sector. According to another survey of 78 Chinese manufacturing and construction projects in Ethiopia for 2017–2018, the companies collectively employed 37,457 Ethiopians in total. There were also 3,153 expatriates in these factories. Most of them were Chinese but dozens were from Kenya, Mauritius, Sri Lanka, Myanmar, Vietnam, India, South Korea, and other countries. The garment making sector has the lowest expatriate ratio. In none of the eleven garment makers surveyed do expatriates make up more than 5 percent of the entire work force; the expatriate ratio is as low as 2.5 percent when accounting for all the 4,505 employees. Table 7.1 compares the employment structure in six major sectors. The factories in plastics, textile, and cement sectors use more expatriates, perhaps because their production depends on the operation and monitoring of

10 Business Perception Index Kenya 2014, SACE (Sino Africa Centre of Excellence) Foundation.

11 Dance of the Lions and Dragons, McKinsey & Company, June 2017, p. 40.

12 Carlos Oya and Florian Schaefer, Chinese Firms and Employment Dynamics in Africa: A Comparative Analysis, Synthesis Report, 2019.

Table 7.1 *Composition of employees in Chinese companies in Ethiopia by sector*

	Garment	Leather Products	Plastic Products	Textile	Cement and Gypsum	Construction
Ethiopians	4395	11830	3061	1840	2592	9767
Expatriates	110	440	150	152	291	1719
Ratio of local employment	97.56%	96.41%	95.33%	92.37%	89.91%	85.03%

Source: Author's survey

large sophisticated equipment, which require foreign technicians. The construction companies use a large amount of uncontracted day labor from neighboring areas; therefore the percentage of permanent staff is relatively lower.

Employment of local workers is both encouraged by governments and motivated by economic calculation. To combat high domestic unemployment, many African countries strictly regulate the employment of foreign workers and the issuance of work permits. For example, Egyptian law allows for one foreign employee for every nine Egyptians employed.[13] Angola has a similar policy, requiring that 70 percent of a company's staff be Angolans, though exceptions may be made for certain urgent public projects.[14] Even without government constraints, some Chinese companies prefer to hire more local employees in certain situations, because this allows them to greatly reduce labor costs. As Hai Yu, CEO of Huajian shoe factory in Ethiopia, told me in 2012, when the factory had just opened, "We have 200 Chinese expatriates now. It cuts into our profits. We have to double the wages of Chinese workers to attract them to work in Africa. We hope to reduce the number of Chinese workers as soon as possible."[15] Apart from higher salaries, Chinese employees require additional expenses, including food, accommodation, one or two trips to China per year, work permit applications

[13] Personal interview with an official in General Authority for Investment, Cairo, Egypt, June 2009. Transcripts in the author's possession.

[14] Angola's Basic Private Investment Law, Art. 54/1; personal interview with an official in National Agency for Private Investment, Luanda, Angola, July 2007. Transcripts in the author's possession.

[15] Hai Yu, CEO of Huajian Ethiopia, Dukem, Ethiopia, July 2012. Transcripts in the author's possession.

and extensions, and so on. Thus, a Chinese employee could cost up to three to four times more than a local employee in the same position.[16]

Still, most Chinese companies find that they have to bring a number of Chinese workers to Africa, at least at the beginning. In the first place, Chinese workers are familiar with the companies' organization and processes. They can get operations running quickly, especially in the case of urgent projects. Second, Chinese technicians are needed to install and test machinery, as most equipment is imported from China. Once local workers become familiar with machine operations, most Chinese technicians will leave Africa; only a small number stay, usually to conduct maintenance and repairs. Third, experienced Chinese workers can teach their local colleagues on the job. Over a period of time, Chinese employees can demonstrate and transfer their work skills to their African colleagues.

In several cases, a steadily decreasing number of Chinese staff has been evident. My survey in the Democratic Republic of Congo (DRC) found that companies that had been in the country for five years or less employed Chinese in almost one-third of their positions, whereas companies with a history of more than five years had reduced the proportion of Chinese staff to 16.8 percent.[17] At Zambia's Zambia-China Economic and Trade Cooperation Zone (ZCCZ), around four hundred Chinese and five hundred Zambians were employed in the early phase of construction, machinery installation, and training, but the percentage of Chinese workers went down to less than 20 percent once the production process became stabilized.[18] In Ethiopia, China-Africa Overseas Tannery reduced the number of Chinese technicians from thirty-three to twenty-three within one year, as local engineers were promoted to supervisory positions.[19] Huajian shoe factory moved even faster. It started operations in January 2012 with over three

[16] Tang, Xiaoyang, Bulldozer or Locomotive? The Impact of Chinese Enterprises on the Local Employment in Angola and the DRC, *Journal of Asian and African Studies* (2010) 45.3, 354.

[17] Ibid., p. 362.

[18] Email communication with Haglund, Dan, University of Bath, December 10, 2009. Quoted from Deborah Brautigam and Xiaoyang Tang, China's Investment in Special Economic Zones in Africa, in Thomas Farole and Gokhan Akinci, eds., *Special Economic Zones* (Washington, DC: World Bank, 2011), p. 90.

[19] Personal interview with Ethiopian Human Resource Manager, China-Africa Overseas tannery, Sululta, Ethiopia, July 16, 2012. Transcripts in the author's possession.

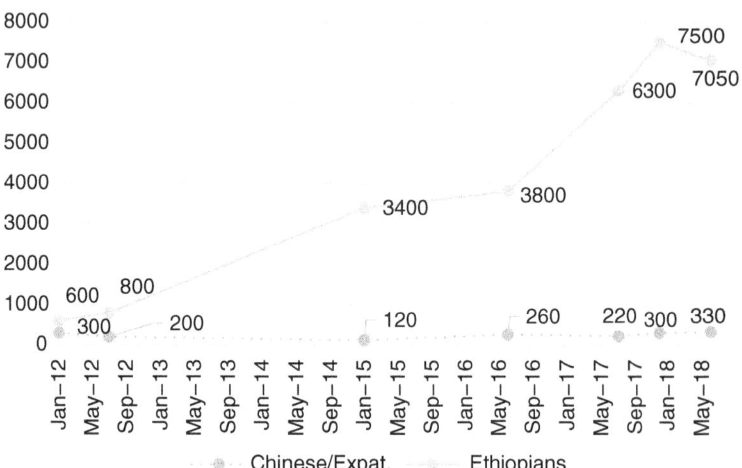

Figure 7.1 Composition change of employees at Huajian factory in Ethiopia, 2012–2018.
Source: Author's survey

hundred Chinese. By July 2012, approximately 100 Chinese expatriates had already been replaced by local workers.[20] The trajectory of the composition of employees at Huajian can be seen in Figure 7.1. Apart from small fluctuations due to new trainings, the company has significantly raised the portion of Ethiopian workers over six years.

As for the perception that wages at Chinese enterprises are low, the findings of various studies have not provided a unanimous answer to this question. C. K. Lee reported that a Chinese-owned major company, NFC Africa Mining Plc (NFCA), was known to pay the lowest wages among all major mining companies in Zambia.[21] Her study on Urafiki Textile and Andrew Brook's study on Mulungushi Textile showed that low wages was a major source of labor conflicts in both projects.[22] However, a World Bank survey in Ethiopia 2011 concluded that the average monthly salary for local employees at Chinese enterprises was US$85, about 13 percent above the estimated national

[20] Personal interview with Chinese supervisor, Huajian shoe factory, Dukem, Ethiopia, July 10, 2012. Transcripts in the author's possession.
[21] Lee, Raw Encounters, p. 111f.
[22] Andrew Brooks, Spinning and Weaving Discontent: Labour Relations and the Production of Meaning at Zambia-China Mulungushi Textiles, *Journal of Southern African Studies* (2010) 36.1, 121.

average salary.[23] In my own interviews in Ethiopia, I found wide diversity among Chinese investors. Some were paying as low as US$35–40 per month to workers on assembly lines, whereas others paid US$100 a month to technicians or US$600 per month to managers, in order to attract them from other competitors. [24] It is necessary to take a closer look at the reasons behind these differences.

Apart from several joint ventures struggling with the historical burdens, the newly arriving Chinese enterprises set their wage schemes according to the business needs. The reasons for these divergent salary levels can be found in the concrete market conditions of various projects. Li Pengtao compared NFCA with other mines in Zambia to assess its labor standards. When NFCA bought Chambishi mine in 1998, it had been closed for thirteen years. The reconstruction of the mine cost the company US$160 million, and all employees were newly recruited. In contrast, Swiss-owned Mopani and Indian-owned KCM bought mines that were already in operation with established salaries in place. To recover the huge investment that they made in infrastructure and training, NFCA initially paid considerably lower salaries than other mines, although an annual increase was granted.[25]

Similar business logic can also be found at Huajian. The shoe company invested heavily to set up a highly mechanized factory, but they paid their workers merely 600 birr (US$35) per month at the beginning of the operation, far below the national average. Many Ethiopians could not accept this kind of argument and the turnover rate was very high initially. More than seventy of the eighty-six workers who were trained in China left the company within six months. Low wages were quoted as the main reason for their departure.[26] CEO Hai Yu

23 Michael Geiger and Chorching Goh. Chinese FDI in Ethiopia: A World Bank Survey (Washington, DC: World Bank Group), November 2012, p. 12.

24 Tang Xiaoyang, Does Chinese Employment Benefit Africans? Investigating Chinese Enterprises and Their Operations in Africa, *African Studies Quarterly* (2016) 16.3–4, 107–128.

25 Pengtao Li, The Myth and Reality of Chinese Investors: A Case Study of Chinese Investment in Zambia's Copper Industry, Occasional Paper no. 62, South African Institute of International Affairs, 2010, p. 9. But he mistook Chambishi for Luanshya; see Caixin Online, Zambian Workers Return to Jobs at Chinese-Owned copper mine, October 23, 2011. www.caixinglobal.com/2011-10-23/zambian-workers-return-to-jobs-at-chinese-owned-copper-mine-101016408.html (accessed July 17, 2020).

26 Personal interview with former Huajian workers, Debre Zeit and Addis Ababa, Ethiopia, July 2012. Transcripts in the author's possession.

tried hard to persuade the workers to stay with China's development experience, "China used to be poor too 30 years ago . . . . . . It took time and hard work to become successful. People need to be patient and have foresight for the future."[27] Although such words were not effective in general, a few Ethiopians agreed with her. Two young Ethiopians on the assembly line at Huajian told me that they quit a company in Addis Ababa to work at this factory, even though they had received higher salaries at the previous company. They pointed to the roaring machines around them and to their new uniforms with Huajian's logo, "We can learn many things here: making shoes, using machines and also speaking Chinese. We feel security for the future." As the remaining workers gradually improve their skills and productivity, their income rose correspondingly. After three years, experienced sewing machine operators of at Huajian can earn 1200 birr on average and after six years, more than 2,000 birr.[28]

Both the Huajian and NFCA cases suggest that low wages at the beginning of the new projects are designed by the Chinese investors for the following reasons. First, investors expend considerable initial capital on machinery and try to cut costs on other parts until the projects become profitable. Second, the low initial salary can provide enough room for a wage increase later. Third, the salary raise should be linked to productivity improvement. Since newly recruited workers often lack sufficient skills, their salaries are low. These are indeed common calculations for businesses everywhere. Korean, Indian, and European investors adopt similar wage schemes when they set up new projects from scratch. A large number of Chinese investors arrived in Africa just recently to open their businesses, especially in the labor-intensive manufacturing and construction sectors, and hired tens of thousands of unskilled and semiskilled laborers. This may contribute to the impression that Chinese firms provide lower wages, but in fact it reflects a common phenomenon in the early stage of industrialization, which many African countries are entering now.

A systematic survey done by Carlos Oya and Florian Schaefer of 1,500 Ethiopian and Angolan workers in different enterprises confirmed that the workers' wages were more closely related to the skill

[27] Mulu, Dani, Felke, Surafei, Sebdesse, former Ethiopian employees at Huajian shoe factory, Debre Zeit, July 2012.

[28] Interview with Huajian managers and workers, 2012–2018.

level, working sector, and regional income level rather than to the origin of the investors.[29] Consequently, skill and productivity improvement become the key to expanding the employment of African workers as well as increasing their income. Most of the local workers come to the factories from rural areas. They had never worked in factories and operated on machines previously. How effective are the training processes in the Chinese factories? These questions do not merely concern the benefits of the workers, but also affect the speed of industrialization in Africa. In the following sector, I will concentrate on the training of industrial work ethics to illustrate the mutual influences between Chinese employers and African employees.

7.3 Dilemma Between Work Ethics and Industrial Practices

For a large part of the factory managers, the primary problem that affects African workers' productivity is their work ethics. In my survey of 87 Chinese manufacturing firms across Ethiopia, Ghana, Tanzania, and Nigeria, from 2012 to 2014, 56 percent of the managers held negative views toward African workers for being "slow," "inefficient," "lazy," or "lacking discipline." For example, one Chinese manager at a glove-making factory in Addis Ababa accused his Ethiopian trainees of tardiness: "The workers should start working at 7:30 a.m., but … … after they [arrive in the factory,] greet each other and get prepared for work, half an hour is lost. The company pays the workers for every minute, but they don't work every minute."[30] Such perceptions of the inefficiency of local workers make Chinese employers unwilling to hire and promote more Africans.

A common explanation for this is that the diverging work ethics are caused by cultural differences. Mulu Gebre was one of the first Ethiopian employees in Huajian shoe factory, but she quit six months later, citing cultural differences: "All [Chinese] supervisors like to shout. The Chinese are doing everything fast, but Ethiopian culture teaches people to act slowly."[31] Karsten Giese recorded what a Ghanaian at a Chinese-owned hotel outside Accra told him: "There are big cultural differences that make working for the Chinese difficult.

29 Carlos Oya and Florian Schaefer, Chinese Firms and Employment Dynamics in Africa: A Comparative Analysis, Synthesis Report, 2019.

30 Billy Yang, manager of Pittards Glove Factory, Addis Ababa, July 2012.

31 Mulu Gebre, former employee of Huajian shoe factory, Debre-zeit, July 2012.

The Chinese themselves are working around the clock. They are very hard-working and it seems they never sleep."[32] In another study, Chinese traders thought "too much culture" in the Ghanaian community distracted local workers who missed work to attend funerals or clan events.[33]

Various scholars support a culturalist explanation of Chinese work ethics. Melissa Wright argues that draconian disciplinary measures for controlling labor in China are influenced by Confucian cultural expectations.[34] Tai Hung-Chao stresses that millennium-long Chinese cultural traditions have shaped the "Oriental model" of diligent and frugal Asian workers.[35] Geert Hofstede and Michael Bond attribute East Asia's economic growth to regional cultural roots that emphasize hard work as a Confucian virtue.[36] Herman Kahn identifies two aspects of Confucian ethics as important to modern development: "the creation of dedicated, motivated, responsible, and educated individuals" and "the enhanced sense of commitment, organizational identity, and loyalty to various institutions."[37] These studies argue that collectivist Confucian values emphasizing diligence, loyalty, and education are largely responsible for creating a sense of discipline and industriousness that has supported China's economic take-off since the 1980s.[38]

However, as Susan Greenhalgh critiques, such scholarship simplistically "uses Orientalist cultural categories to understand Oriental economic outcomes."[39] Before China entered its period of rapid

32 Karsten Giese. Same-Same but Different: Chinese Traders' Perspectives on African Labor, *The China Journal* (2013) 69, 134–153.

33 Marcus Power, Giles Mohan, and May Tan-Mullins, *China's Resource Diplomacy in Africa: Powering Development?* (Basingstoke: Palgrave Macmillan, 2012), p. 174.

34 M. W. Wright, Factory Daughters and Chinese Modernity: A Case from Dongguan, *Geoforum* (2003) 34, 291–301.

35 Hung-Chao Tai, ed. *Confucianism and Economic Development: An Oriental Alternative?* (Washington, DC: Washington Institute Press, 1989).

36 Geert Hofstede and Michael Bond, The Confucius Connection: From Cultural Roots to Economic Growth, *Organizational Dynamics* (1988) 16(4), 5–21.

37 Herman Kahn, *World Economic Development: 1979 and Beyond* (Boulder, CO: Westview Press, 1979), p. 122.

38 Huang Kuang-Kuo also explored the connection between Confucian ideas and East Asian modernization. See Kuang-kuo Huang, *Rujia sixiang yu dongya xiandaihua* (*Confucianism and East Asian Modernization*) (Taipei: Zhulin chubanshe, 1988).

39 Susan Greenhalgh, De-Orientalizing the Chinese Family Firm, *American Ethnologist* (1994) 21(4), 746–775.

growth in the 1980s, Chinese cultural traditions were often considered backward and disadvantageous for modernization. Chen Xi describes Chinese workers as being "lazy" during the early period of economic reform and attributes this characteristic to traditional perceptions of time in rural Chinese society, which contrasted sharply with modern perceptions of time in Western industrial society:

Even if [the Chinese] have working plans, they are easily distracted and interrupted by other things. This is demonstrated by the fact that people seldom make appointments in advance for social activities, do not keep strict time ... and are tolerant even when people do not keep appointments. In some offices, people may chat and work at the same time. When one thing is not finished, they can leave it for tomorrow. Although ancient people have mottos like "life is short" and "time is precious," these have never become part of common awareness.[40]

Likewise, in her study on Chinese female workers, Pun Ngai records the thoughts of Hong Kong managers who considered mainland Chinese workers to be too socialist and too rural for capitalist production: they were "uncivilized," undisciplined, and left their work at will.[41] Today, such comments sound similar to how Chinese managers describe African workers. Hence, the validity of a purely culturalist explanation of work ethics is questioned. Furthermore, these historical narratives of Chinese "laziness" raise questions about why Chinese work ethics have changed so much in the process of industrial development.

The preceding discussion suggests that the work ethics in the factories have a close relationship with the perceptions of time, as the ethics divergence deals primarily with notions such as punctuality, quickness, efficiency, willingness to do overtime, as well as slowness and delay. Different time perceptions, which reflect different manners of social production and organization, may lead to departing views on work ethics. While Chinese workers from rural areas were considered undisciplined and uncompetitive by Western and Hong Kong standards of efficiency in the modern workplace, they were still described as working from dawn to dusk without rest and painstakingly taking care of

[40] Xi Chen, Zhong-Xi chuantong shijian guan bijiao (A Comparison of Chinese and Western Traditional Concepts of Time), *Shidai jiaoyu* (2007) 9, 54–55, translated by the author.

[41] Ngai Pun, *Made in China: Women Factory Workers in a Global Workplace* (Durham, NC: Duke University Press, 2005), pp. 79–81.

crops.[42] Similarly, observers have described tireless African bus drivers and street vendors who work around the clock in cities across the African continent. Former Chinese ambassador Cheng Tao writes, "In fact, Africans are very capable. African women are especially diligent and capable. They work in the field and take care of the household. We often see them lift heavy stuff on their head, a large bag of crops or a large bunch of wood, even a large container of water."[43] Hence, the same group of people can be viewed as hard-working or lazy under different standards. However, heavy domestic work or laboring with antiquated farming methods do not necessarily count as desirable work ethics in the factory workplace of modern industrial capitalism.

Labor historians have argued that industrial capitalism requires a particular set of work ethics, characterized by a close relationship between time and monetary value. As Benjamin Franklin wrote in 1978 in *Advice to a Young Tradesman*, "Time is money."[44] E. P. Thompson distinguished between leisurely task time where a sense of time depended on simply finishing a task as needed, "so effort varied seasonally ... [and] work rhythms were integrated into patterns of social life," and rigid clock time, where the rise of wage labor and strict discipline in the factory leads to the capitalist wanting to "get his precise due" by buying his laborer's time.[45] Task time corresponded to preindustrial Europe; clock time arrived only after the rise of industrial capitalism. Workers in the West used to follow a flexible working schedule without connecting hours worked with money earned.[46] However, a new time discipline was gradually imposed on European workers in the eighteenth and nineteenth centuries through "the division of labor; the supervision of labor; fines; bells and clocks; money

42 Arthur Smith, *Chinese Characteristics* (New York: Fleming Revell Company, 1894), pp. 30–31.

43 Tao Cheng, Feizhou de di, shi he ren – huijilu (Africa's land, objects and people – a memoir). Guojiwang, December 29, 2012. memo.cfisnet.com/2012/1229/1293993.html (accessed July 17, 2020).

44 Benjamin Franklin, Advice to a Young Tradesman, 1748. http://founders.archives.gov/documents/Franklin/01-03-02-0130 (accessed July 17, 2020).

45 Frederick Cooper, Colonizing Time: Work Rhythms and Labor Conflict in Colonial Mombasa, in Nicholas Dirks, ed., *Colonialism and Culture* (Ann Arbor, MI: University of Michigan Press, 1992), pp. 209–246.

46 E. P. Thompson, *The Making of the English Working Class* (London: Penguin Books, 1963), p. 357.

incentives; preachings and schoolings; the suppression of fairs and sports."[47] Thompson wrote that for those "accustomed to labor timed by the clock," the traditional task-based ethic to labor appears "wasteful and lacking in urgency."[48]

Similarly, Moishe Postone traced the origins of working hours to the cloth-making industry in western Europe in the fourteenth century. Unlike most medieval "industries" of boutique workshops producing for the local market, the cloth-making industry was the first to engage in large-scale production for export. Hiring thousands of wage laborers, the merchants could no longer rely on "natural time" marked by sunrise or sunset. Towns began using work bells to announce the beginning and end of the workday and meal intervals. Disciplining and coordinating workers through standardized hours were considered effective measures to improve productivity. The merchants, whose profits came from the difference between the value of the cloth produced and the wages paid, were keen to increase the productivity of workers in a given time.[49] In contrast, the notion of productivity was apparently unknown in ancient China, where production was not monetized on a large scale and the number of wage earners was limited.[50]

In fact, until half a century ago, Chinese rural society maintained a traditional notion of time perception. In the late nineteenth century, Arthur Smith described how the Chinese worked long hours but disregarded efficiency: "They are perpetually stopping to drink tea. They make long journeys to a distant lime-pit carrying a few quarts of liquid mud in a cloth bag, when by using a wheelbarrow one man could do the work of three; but this result is by no means the one aimed at. If there is a slight rain all work is suspended. There is generally abundant motion with but little progress, so that it is often difficult to perceive what it is which represents the day's 'labour' of a gang of men."[51] In 1955, Yang Lien-Sheng wrote, "Modern Westerners sometimes criticize the Chinese for their lack of a sense of time in their daily affairs. One must remember that China was an agricultural state in a pre-machine

47 E. P. Thompson, Time, Work and Industrial Capitalism, *Past and Present* (1967) 38, 56–97.

48 Ibid., p. 60.

49 Moishe Postone, *Time, Labor, and Social Domination* (Cambridge: Cambridge University Press, 1996), pp. 209–210.

50 David S. Landes, *Revolution in Time: Clocks and the Making of the Modern World* (Cambridge, MA: Harvard University Press, 1983), p. 25.

51 Smith, *Chinese Characteristics*, p. 44.

age where there was little need to be particular with time to the minute or second."[52]

The Chinese notion of work ethics started to change as capitalism impacted the country. Yeh Wen-hsin noted how the landmark Custom House clock in Shanghai introduced modern, urban time discipline to dominate the practices of the emerging urban capitalists, merchants, and white collar and industrial workers. As a pioneer, Bank of China used a stringent schedule of work, vocational study, and communal life to train its employees, in a largely self-contained environment, not only to get accustomed to the concept of uniform time, but also to develop a work ethics closely related to time discipline.[53] This model evolved to become the work unit (*danwei*, 单位) in the socialist era, which continued training workers by regulating their work and life according to standardized clock-time. However, the Chinese Communist Party despised the maxim "Time is money" as representing capitalist values and cut off the links between time and monetary value.[54] Consequently the concept of industrial work ethics became distorted. Political campaigns occasionally promoted time discipline and production efficiency to boost industrialization. Yet, as an increase in profit was no longer the goal of production, the efforts to improve punctuality and efficiency depended on political instructions and were thus sporadic and inconsistent. Efficiency-oriented production was just *one of* the work manners that could coexist side-by-side with traditional lifestyles and egalitarian (*daguofan*, 大锅饭) communism.

By comparison, efficiency-oriented production is *the* one work manner of industrial capitalism, for profit-seeking enterprises target nothing but productivity growth. To achieve more profit and survive in a competitive landscape, every producer under capitalism has to constantly improve efficiency and keep up with a stringent time schedule. Therefore, it was not until the beginning of market reforms that the industrial notion of time perception became significant and rapidly spread throughout the entire society. When China set up its first special

52 Lien-sheng Yang, Schedules of Work and Rest in Imperial China, *Harvard Journal of Asiatic Studies* (1955) 18(3/4), 301–325. DOI: 10.2307/2718436.

53 Wen-hsin Yeh, *Shanghai Splendor: Economic Sentiments and the Making of Modern China, 1843–1949* (Berkeley: University of California Press, 2007), pp. 79–100.

54 Gao Chenglin, Analysis of "Time Is Money" (*"Shijian jiushi jinqian" xiyi* "时间就是金钱"析义), *Finance & Economics* (1985) 6, 79–80.

economic zone in Shenzhen in 1980 to experiment with a market economy, a large billboard was erected in front of the zone with the slogan, "Time is money, efficiency is life." This served as a symbolic event in bringing back a capitalist drive. A national debate unfolded. The slogan attracted criticisms of "restoring capitalism." Only after leaders such as Deng Xiaoping showed their approval of the slogan did Chinese society come to widely accept the connections between time, money, and efficiency.[55]

The changed perceptions about time and economic value were experienced concretely by numerous Chinese factory managers and laborers. In a study of Liton (China) Electronics Limited in Shenzhen in the early 1990s, Ching Kwan Lee describes a new class of workers (*dagongzai*, 打工仔) as "workers laboring for the bosses" in a system of both "modernity and prosperity" and "ruthless exploitation."[56] One worker recounted, "We Chaozhou girls have a tradition of doing embroidery work at home ... ten to fifteen girls sitting together, joking while working ... when you work you can arrange your time freely, but when you *dagong*, there are rules from your boss."[57] Another woman felt she was "kicked around like a football," moved from one position to another for greater efficiency.[58] Likewise, in Pun Ngai's study, Hong Kong managers positioned Chinese workers in the assembly line to impose discipline and encourage efficiency, making the "socialist and rural" bodies work for capitalist production.[59]

Most opinions of different work ethics between Chinese and Africans also refer to "hard work" in terms of efficiency, speed, and long hours. A local employee at Tooku Inc., a Chinese-owned garment factory in Dar es Salaam, described the Chinese preference for working fast: "The Chinese really work hard, and they expect us to work hard as well. At times, they really push you. They say Tanzanians are slow, especially when we receive big orders and the workload is high."[60] Meanwhile, Adeyemo Thompson, Nigerian deputy managing director

55 Yan Jun, Time Is Money, Efficiency Is Life – Out of the Imprisoned Mindset (*Shijian jiushi jinqian, xiaolv jiushi shengming – chongpo sixiang jingu de diyisheng nahan*时间就是金钱, 效率就是生命 – 冲破思想禁锢的第一声呐喊), *Inheritance and Innovation* (February 2008) 1–3.

56 Ching Kwan Lee, *Gender and the South China Miracle: Two Worlds of Factory Women* (Berkeley, CA: University of California Press, 1998), pp. 110–115.

57 Ibid., pp. 114–115. 58 Ibid., p. 115. 59 Pun, *Made in China*, pp. 79–81.

60 Interview with Tanzanian worker in quality control department, Kiswahili, March 2015.

of the Lekki Free Trade Zone (LFTZ), considered working overtime an example of Chinese-style hard work: "Nigerians are learning to work harder by following their Chinese colleagues and staying in the office every weekend."[61] Furthermore, "discipline" is related to punctuality. Workers at East Star shoe factory in Dar es Salaam described: "The Chinese are very much on time, and they even arrive a bit earlier to start work."[62]

Hence, judgment of work performance in modern industries, no matter in Europe, China, or Africa, universally highlights the importance of rigid discipline with respect to time. Modern perceptions of uniformly divided hours, punctuality, time value, and productivity were developed out of capitalist economies and large-scale industries. As industrial capitalism spread, both Western and Chinese societies gradually adopted a corresponding view that "time is money." Although teachings of "hard work" and "discipline" existed in ancient China, they held significantly different meanings from their association with Chinese work ethics today under industrial capitalism. Working overtime in the evenings or on weekends, emphasizing efficiency and productivity of time, and adhering to punctuality are behaviors based on Chinese society's evolved notions of time rather than on any static, culturally rooted devotion to work that characterizes Chinese workers.

African societies have also experienced changes in working styles with modern shifts in time perception. Keletso Atkins describes the influence of churches, municipalities, and factories in urban South Africa in detaching African workers from old traditions and integrating them into new rhythms of the industrial workplace.[63] Frederick Cooper argues a British colonial administration that decasualized labor transformed the meaning of time for local dock workers by promoting adaptation to "the work rhythms of industrial capitalism: to the idea that work should be steady and regular and carefully controlled."[64] Bill Freund noticed that work patterns in different African urban areas diverged depending on their adaptation to modern industrial society; for example, miners in the Zambian copper belt

61 Adeyemo Thompson, deputy managing director, Lekki.

62 Interviews with workers at Eaststar shoe factory, Dar es Salaam, March 2015.

63 Keletso Atkins, "Kafir time": Preindustrial Temporal Concepts and Labour Discipline in Nineteenth-Century Colonial Natal, *The Journal of African History* (1988) 29(2), 229–244.

64 Cooper 1992, p. 209.

became much more disciplined and professionalized than dwellers in Addis Ababa because of booming mineral development.[65] Post-independence industrialization efforts have further led to a relatively strong working class in some countries, but the continent is still vastly a rural-based economy.[66] Employment in industry made up 46.9 percent of total employment in China in 2011, but only 14.4 percent in Ghana, 9.5 percent in Zambia, 8.5 percent in Nigeria, 7.4 percent in Ethiopia, and 6.4 percent in Tanzania around the same time.[67] Most African countries lag behind China in industrial development and are not fully adapted to the time perception of industrial capitalism.[68] Therefore, diverging judgments on time perception between Chinese and Africans lead to conflicts regarding work rhythms in daily operations.

Increasingly, Chinese firms in Africa are trying to solve the problem of diverging work ethics and transform local workers' time perception to match the requirements of industrial capitalism. As work ethics are shaped by broad social practices, the Chinese firms face challenges different from those of other foreign powers in Africa and those in China's own reform. On the one hand, individual Chinese investors have neither a government's administrative capacity nor the help of churches or other social institutions; instead, they must rely on the

65 Bill Freund, *The African City: A History* (Cambridge: Cambridge University Press, 2007), pp. 82–92.

66 Kevin R. Cox (with David Hemson and Alison Todes), Urbanization in South Africa and the Changing Character of Migrant Labor, *South African Geographical Journal* (2004) 86.1, 7–16; Frederick Cooper, Urban Space, Industrial Time, and Wage Labor in Africa, in Frederick Cooper, ed., *Struggle for the City: Migrant Labor, Capital, and the State in Urban Africa* (Beverly Hills, CA: SAGE, 1983), pp. 7–50.

67 Employment in Industry (% of Total Employment), World Bank. data.worldbank.org/indicator/SL.IND.EMPL.ZS. The industry sector consists of "mining and quarrying, manufacturing, construction, and public utilities." The statistics for each country vary by year: Ghana (2013), Zambia (2012), Nigeria (2007), Ethiopia (2013), and Tanzania (2014). The percentage of employment in industry in southern Africa is higher than in other parts of sub-Saharan Africa: 23.5 percent for South Africa in 2014 and 17.5 percent for Botswana in 2010.

68 Notably, African migrants in Europe were considered to work harder and more efficiently than Africans at home. [See Hein de Haas, The Myth of Invasion: The Inconvenient Realities of African Migration to Europe, *Third World Quarterly* (2008) 29.7, 1305–1322]. This supports the notion that the societal context of developed industrial countries was a factor in inducing Africans to work according to the requirements of modern industries. It is not African culture but the lack of industry that has hindered Africans to work efficiently.

power of factory management. On the other hand, even though the time discipline of industrial capitalism applies a universal clock time, manners of adaptation vary across different social and cultural contexts. The interaction between Chinese managers and African workers must involve cross-cultural communication and convergence. While culturalist views cannot fully explain the transformation of work ethics, it is shortsighted to exclude culture completely. Fredrick Cooper once criticized labor historians for merely emphasizing "what the workplace brought to African workers rather than the other way around."[69] In other words, local workers have agency. Chinese and Africans have to work together to overcome the divergence of work ethics and create a modern work force in Africa.

7.4 Pragmatic Approaches Toward Convergence

In this section, I will use two case studies to illustrate how Chinese managers are trying to change African work ethics and time perception. Both cases are of Chinese investments in manufacturing, a sector that emphasizes disciplining labor to clock-time. As Thompson explains, while in other industries, precapitalist and capitalist work ethics coexisted side by side, manufacturing factories such as textile mills were the first to adopt a strict working time schedule.[70] Out of the manufacturing projects visited in African countries, I select Urafiki and Huajian again for several reasons. First, both firms employ a considerable number of workers. Fewer than ten Chinese manufacturers in Africa reported more than 800 local workers. I believe that the effects of time discipline and coordination can be seen more clearly in factories with a critical mass of employees. Second, they represent two different trajectories. One factory is a Chinese aid project from the socialist era that was turned into a market-oriented joint venture in Tanzania, while the other factory is a new private investment in Ethiopia. Different countries and backgrounds illustrate different patterns of interactions between traditional environments and industrial capitalism, but they are comparable due to their common pursuit of time value and discipline. Third, both projects are considered "flagship" cases in the China-

[69] Frederick Cooper, Work, Class and Empire: An African Historian's Retrospective on E. P. Thompson, *Social History* (1995) 20(s), 235–241.

[70] Thompson, *The Making of the English Working Class*, pp. 337–380.

Africa relationship by government, media, and researchers, with studies already conducted at both factories.[71] Analysis of these projects' labor management provides lessons for tackling the challenges, and understanding the impacts of, a new trend of African industrialization for a broad range of readers. I chose Tanzania and Ethiopia also because their current industrialization levels, like those of most sub-Saharan African countries, are relatively low and the transformation process is identified more clearly. I visited both factories several times since 2009. In each factory, three or four separate day-long, on-site observations were conducted. Both Chinese and African managers and employees were interviewed. Except from top management interviewees, I selected Chinese and African workers randomly in the workshop for conversation.

The case studies are based on phenomenological interpretations of dynamic daily practices in two factories. Real-life experiences and interactions in the workplace never follow fixed rules, especially in a diverse intercultural context, even when modern factories strive to standardize them. Therefore, I chose not to measure the transition of work ethics with a standardized dataset or quantitative models; instead, I depict changes in individual mindsets by presenting cases from the field research. These cases cover various aspects of temporal perceptions in different places. Weaving them together, I do not aim to demonstrate *how much* Chinese employers have effectively changed African work ethics, as it is extremely difficult, if not impossible, to measure such changes. Instead, I have a more modest goal: to show that Chinese investments *have indeed* been changing the time perception of local workers and converging previously divergent work ethics.

7.4.1 Urafiki Textile Mill

As noted in Section 7.1, the old workers in the Urafiki mill had developed a certain sense of industrial clock time from the socialist era, for they were clearly aware of their work schedule. Yet, they did not link

71 See Lee, Raw Encounters; Deborah Brautigam, *Dragon's Gift: The Real Story of China in Africa* (Oxford: Oxford University Press, 2009), pp. 197–201; Justin Yifu Lin and Yan Wang, *Going Beyond Aid: Development Cooperation for Structural Transformation* (Cambridge: Cambridge University Press, 2017), pp. 131–149.

time discipline with economic efficiency, and this therefore sparked conflict with the newly arriving Chinese managers.

In 2013, to improve worker productivity and respond to demands for a salary raise by the worker union, the general manager Wu Bin introduced a new incentive system based on "a combination of the 'overall' and the 'individual'."[72] On the one hand, he gave salary bonuses and extra food to all employees during local holidays and festivals; such egalitarian methods were commonplace in China's socialist past. This is what Wu meant by the "overall." On the other hand, he attached more importance to giving bonuses and overtime pay to the "best workers," that is, those who produced the most in a given period of time. Workers in the weaving department could receive a bonus of 30,000 Tanzanian shillings (US$20) if they reached a preset monthly target. For every additional meter of cloth weaved, another 20 shillings was offered. Overtime was paid as well, rewarding those who worked long hours. The most productive workers could earn as much as 250,000 shillings per month, whereas the fixed income for a worker without any bonus was usually about 100,000 shillings.[73] This is what Wu meant by the "individual."

Many other Chinese firms introduced similar measures to reward productivity, but the results were not always satisfactory. Some enterprises reported that local workers were not willing to adopt the piece-rate system, the practice of paying according to output, because they were not skilled enough to produce large quantities and afraid they would make less income than on the default system.[74] A Chinese manager in the Tooku Garment Factory located near the Urafiki Textile Mill reported that local workers used to return their bonuses because they felt uncomfortable being singled out among peers.[75] Worker unions in Tanzania also tend to resist a piece-rate wage system, viewing it as threatening to the workers' guarantee of income.

However, the bonus system in the Urafiki Textile Mill worked owing to three conditions. First, Wu noticed that the workers' fixed salary of 100,000 shillings per month, slightly above the minimum wage, was barely sufficient to support local workers and their families in Dar es Salaam. Therefore, workers were eager to earn additional income. In

[72] Wu Bin, August 2014. [73] Ibid.
[74] Sun Linhua, director, Best Hubo Garment Company, Rangoon, January 2016. The factory is located in Yangon, Myanmar.
[75] Hu Xianjun, manager, Tooku Garment Factory, Dar es Salaam, August 2014.

Wu's words, "The marginal effect of the 10,000 shilling bonus and overtime pay on top of the 100,000 shilling fixed salary is significant."[76] Second, he calculated the bonuses not just according to the output of the individual worker, but rather to the output of a group of workers. Workers were divided into teams under local supervisors; supervisors' bonuses were calculated on the basis of the average bonuses of their team members. Supervisors were therefore motivated to encourage the entire team to work more efficiently for longer hours. As a group, workers were more likely to be productive. Third, Wu ensured that all workers understood the firm's target by breaking it down into concrete parts. Urafiki needed to produce at least 8 million meters of fabric per year to break even, but the factory usually could only produce 5–6 million meters. To make this target less daunting, Wu divided the quota into smaller targets for each group. In the last month, supervisors monitored their group's target each day, checking whether members had finished their daily targets before going home; if they had not, the whole group voluntarily worked overtime. As a result, the mill ended up producing 8.08 million meters of fabric that year.[77] Wu had created a factory culture in which raising productivity was a collective experience, and where workers were experiencing a direct connection between the hours they worked and the money they and the firm earned.

Soon, Wu noticed changes in the perceptions of the Tanzania Union of Industrial and Commercial Workers (TUICO). In the past, the Union directly requested an increase in wages without any connection to the workers' production. But, in its 2014 May Day speech, the Union requested the factories' management "to increase the workload so that the pay increases." On behalf of the workers, the Union also stated: "We need to increase production this year. We are ready to work … Planned production targets must be known to workers and the TUICO branch should be informed about these targets so that it can cooperate fully in the reaching of the targets."[78] Wu was delighted with these requests: "They [the Tanzanian workers] have realized that they should make money through more work, and not simply demand a raise."[79] The Union appeared to have revised its view of the relationship between time

76 Wu Bin, August 2014. 77 Ibid.

78 May-Day speech given by workers' representatives, Tanzania-China Friendship Textile Company, Dar es Salaam, June 24, 2014 (written version).

79 Wu Bin, July 2014.

and money. Now, workers who wanted to earn more income thought of improving production efficiency and increasing their overtime.

A Tanzanian supervisor who has worked at Urafiki since 1968 described his impression of the changing management style of the Chinese: "Previously, the Chinese mainly paid attention to production itself, but currently they think more about business. They focus their attention on how to save time and how to reduce loss. Previously, they would teach Tanzanians again and again if Tanzanians could not grasp the skill within a short time. But now they would give a worker one week to learn a skill, and if he cannot get it, it's over."[80] His observation revealed that he understood the essential characteristic of the new Chinese work ethics as not simply focusing on industrial production but on a close link between time and value.

7.4.2 Huajian Shoe Factory

I choose Huajian Shoe Factory as the second case to demonstrate how a Chinese private enterprise trains its workers (see Figure 7.2). In comparison with Urafiki, the requirements of discipline and efficiency are stricter in the Huajian Factory. First, the factory prioritizes punctuality. Inside the workshop is a large banner in Amharic, English, and Chinese that reads: "Late arrival is delay, early arrival is waste, punctuality is integrity." Managers encourage punctuality with rewards and discourage tardiness with punishments. Workers who arrive on time every day for a month receive a bonus on top of their regular salary. If they are late once, they lose their entire bonus for the month. The factory also provides shuttle buses for the workers to commute between two nearby towns and the factory. This is not merely beneficial for the workers but also important for the factory. A factory manager described how the shuttle buses helped workers to arrive on time: "Otherwise, they would arrive scattered, some may come at 10 o'clock [in the morning]."[81] I observed that the workers all assumed their proper places when the clock approached 8 a.m. A supervisor stood in front of every production line, making final inspections before work

80 Interview with Tanzanian workshop supervisor, Urafiki Textile Mill, Dar es Salaam, March 2015.

81 Chen Jixiang, factory production manager, Huajian shoe factory, Addis Ababa, July 2017.

Figure 7.2 Huajian production line in Addis Ababa, Ethiopia, 2017.

began. With the shrill blow of a whistle, the entire factory floor erupted simultaneously into operation.

The firm employs military-like drills for newly recruited workers, who undergo a week of physical training before starting work on the factory floor. One "formation drill" that workers participate in everyday consists of standing for long hours in the sun and going through coordinated exercises as a group, "turning left," "turning right," and "lining up in good order." The exercises, which simulate synchronized movements in the factory, are meant to impose discipline. New recruits who are not able to finish the training have to leave. CEO Hai Yu appeared satisfied with these methods of changing workers' attitudes: "Through militaristic training … their [the local employees'] morals and appearances become very different from those of the people who are still waiting for jobs outside the factory gate. It [the training] is harsh, but it's good for them."[82]

To improve efficiency, Huajian uses a bonus scheme, and like at Urafiki, the bonus is calculated based on group performance. But at

[82] Helen Hai, Huajian shoe factory, Addis Ababa, July 2012.

Huajian, not only do teams that achieve their targets get bonuses, but teams that produce the most output get additional rewards. Each team is made up of twenty to thirty Ethiopian workers led by a Chinese supervisor and competes to produce the most output as recorded by factory management. Each week, a winning team is selected. On a field visit, I observed this in action. Workers were set up into parallel teams that made the same items. A blackboard recorded each team's output every hour. After a week, the factory manager announced the winner of this competition with a reward of a bonus and workplace honors. In total, three teams were selected as winners every week. The first team received 1,000 birr (approximately US$50), with each individual on the team receiving about 50 birr. The second and third placed teams received less. Factory managers hung red banners over the assembly lines of winning teams to signify their success.

One morning, a team supervisor, Zhou Fei, checked the tables of hourly outputs of all the teams. When he found his team was slowing down, he urged each worker to speed up. Before lunch, he summoned his team for a briefing on their performance. His team had won the competition the week before and Zhou praised them for making good shoes and earning money. In the afternoon, he continued urging his team on, giving shoulder massages to several members to encourage them to work harder. Meanwhile, a supervisor of another team complained that his team could not win because the local workers were not interested in the competition.[83] In general, however, a competitive environment turned out to be an effective approach to increasing production efficiency. The emphasis on speed has reached the point where the factory's boss, Zhang Huarong, has encouraged local workers to do more, even if they make mistakes, because he does "not like workers who make fewer mistakes by doing less."[84] He argued that efficient workers are those who finish their tasks on time.

These two cases show the gradual and interactive influence of Chinese manufacturing investments on local employees' professionalism and work ethics. As industrialization spreads, corresponding production activities and time perception become dominant, replacing traditional work practices and modes of social life. However, the

[83] Zhou Fei and Wu Runlu, Huajian shoe factory, Addis Ababa, July 2012.

[84] Diro, Fasel, Esrael, Ethiopian workshop supervisors, Huajian shoe factory, July 2017.

transition from traditional customs to modern capitalism is never the same. As Thompson writes, "There is no such thing as economic growth which is not, at the same time, growth or change of a culture; and the growth of social consciousness, like the growth of a poet's mind, can never ... be planned."[85] The adaptation of standardized production into a society is an interactive process between incoming industrialization and existing traditions in the country. Although modern factories appear uniform and standardized, they reflect local history and culture. Modern European, American, and East Asian societies agree on the merits of punctuality, efficiency, and accumulation, but still differ from each other in terms of degree of discipline, lifestyle, and visions of the future.[86]

The divergence and convergence of work ethics between Chinese and Africans today can be viewed as a new episode of the clash between "modern" and "traditional" societies. This latest tension is similar to previous ones with the more industrialized society, which attaches normative values to perceptions and behaviors related to rigid clock time, viewing the culture of the less industrialized society as backward.[87] Yet, this new episode is also unique. Since most Chinese adopted modern work ethics only in recent decades, it is possible that they have not yet developed a deep-rooted sense of superiority or established clearly systematic practices of discrimination. Chinese views of Africans, like African views of Chinese, are based on scattered observations mixed with prejudice.[88] The interaction between Chinese and Africans in the workplace may help reduce prejudices on both sides, as time perceptions and work ethics gradually converge through cooperation and mutual adaptation. I do not intend to generalize and speak for all "Chinese" and "Africans," and I emphasize my observations are based on specific cases which vary across time and space.

Furthermore, the case studies demonstrate that dynamic changes to work ethics are taking place in Chinese factories in Africa in a mutually interactive manner. Chinese managers often borrow their experiences of training workers back home (e.g., military-like physical training or

85 Thompson, Time, Work and Industrial Capitalism, p. 97.

86 Edward T. Hall, *The Silent Language* (New York: Doubleday, 1959), pp. 25–35.

87 Thompson, Time, Work and Industrial Capitalism, p. 94.

88 Marte Kjaer Galtung and Stig Stenslie, *49 Myths About China* (London: Rowman and Littlefield, 2015).

team competitions) to influence their African workers' behaviors. But there are also signs that the modifications are being managed to fit the local cultural context (e.g., promoting piece-rate wages by group). African workers do not simply resist or accept Chinese management; rather, they respond to new production practices. Without state administrative power, Chinese managers can only influence local workers incrementally through daily operations. This is not necessarily a negative development, as it facilitates more communication and reduces the risk of simply imposing industrial discipline on local traditions. I believe such concrete changes are helping to develop a qualified African work force in the manufacturing sector and can eliminate the perception of "lazy" Africans in the Chinese context. New forms of work ethics will gradually emerge in workshops in Africa through joint efforts between foreign investors and local workers. [89]

Even as Chinese managers deliberately explore optimal methods for working with Africans, the standalone arrival of numerous Chinese firms and their employment of tens of thousands of Africans seem to have already facilitated the emergence of modern work ethics. Even when local workers are not yet fully integrated into factory operations, they become increasingly familiar with the concrete requirements of a new factory in the context of modern industry. As a Tanzanian worker described:

> The most important reason [for the lack of discipline] is that Tanzanians do not have relevant knowledge. We know which rules and procedures to follow at work only after we see the factory and machines. This knowledge was not given to us when we were born, but can only be learned later. For example, after I see the machines and the professional work done by Chinese in the shoe factory, I hope to be able to work like the Chinese. But without the factory and the machines, how can I know which rules I should follow? We cannot understand these things until we get jobs, such as I should go to work at what time in the morning, I should work how long every day and how much I can earn monthly. These are rules at work. Therefore Tanzanians do not intentionally disobey work disciplines. They do not follow the rules because they do not have jobs.[90]

[89] Tang Xiaoyang and Janet Eom, Time Perception and Industrialization: Divergence and Convergence of Work Ethics in Chinese Enterprises in Africa, *China Quarterly* (2019) 238, 461–481.

[90] Simba, Tanzanian workers at T-better shoe factory, Dar es Salaam, March 2015.

Similarly, Sun Linhua, a Chinese manager who has worked in the garment sector in southern Africa for a decade, believes that skills improvement and discipline is a matter of time: "The workers will gradually learn the details of work after several years, as long as they are working in the factories. This is the case in China, Southeast Asia, and Africa."[91]

If this is true, the key to nurturing modern work ethics in Africa is the employment of large numbers of Africans in factories. This seems paradoxical: an existing lack of skills and work ethics hinders the employment of local workers in the first place, and so the local labor force has limited opportunities to improve these skills and work ethics, in the factory or elsewhere. Nonetheless, this solution reveals an important point: internalizing work ethics is a dialectic, not straightforward, process between individuals and their environment. Suitable circumstances can facilitate individual workers to change their habits, and these individuals in turn can contribute to the transformation of the societal context, whereas it is much more difficult to directly urge individuals to change their habits without any alterations to their environment. These trends are initiated by increasing investments from China in Africa, particularly in manufacturing. If these pioneer investments can effectively build a professional African work force, they will attract even more manufacturing and improve the African environment for industrialization. The convergence of work ethics is not merely beneficial to existing enterprises but may also accelerate a virtuous cycle of wider industrialization across Africa.

91 Sun Linhua, director, Best Hubo Garment, Rangoon, January 2016.

8 *Social and Environmental Responsibility*

8.1 Water, Wind, and Wild Animals

When somebody visited Kampala, capital of Uganda, between 2017 and 2019, he might be struck by the contrasting view of two sewage systems. On some sites, constructions of wastewater canals were half wrecked and piles of garbage accumulated in ditches. Sewage overflew on the road surface, diffusing stench all around. Yet, some other sewers not far away were lined with stones or concrete blocks. The ditches were almost clear of debris so that the water flew smoothly. During an interview in September 2019, Chen Huanbo, country manager of China Jiangxi International Economic and Technical Cooperation Co. (CJIC), explained that the upgrading of Kampala's sewage network was just halfway toward completion. His company, together with several other Chinese and Indian firms, was awarded by Kampala municipality with contracts to improve the sewer lines 2016. However, the municipality encountered a serious shortage of funding after the construction began. Consequently, several contractors halted work for months and did not resume until the funds arrived. By comparison, CJIC did not delay the project because of funding issues, but instead used its own money to pay for construction materials and labor in advance and completed its contracted work according to the original schedule. Thinking highly of such commitment, Kampala municipality rewarded CJIC with additional contracts later.

Chen Huanbo recalled that a speedy upgrading of sewage network was very needed for the city at that time. When the rainy season began, more garbage would be flushed by rain water to block the dysfunctional sewers. With the improved ditches, the municipality staff was able to clean the garbage with ease and keep the sewage system running. Yet, he admitted that the company was willing to advance funds for project completion also out of commercial consideration.[1] There were more than a dozen of firms, local and foreign, doing similar business in this small land-locked country. CJIC had to try its best to outcompete others for the market share.

The next day, I met a representative of another Chinese company working on environment-related projects. Yu Qianming from Zhongmei Engineering Group told me how they built water supply pipelines for two towns in the mountainous Rwebisengo region, 300 kilometers west of Kampala. For centuries, the inhabitants of this region had sourced their drinking water from Albert Lake, which has a high salinity level. The project plan included construction of a dam and reservoir on a stream. To avoid disrupting the drinking habits of wild animals, the project team constructed a bifurcated canal to dam only half of the stream. Additionally, the team designed a mechanism of using gravity to transport water so that no power supply is required and operational costs are reduced. Such arrangements addressing local conditions and demands were appreciated by the Ugandan environment authority.[2]

Apart from contracting business, China also funded a number of ecological projects around Africa, including solar energy, biogas, waste treatment, and so on. A symbolic example is Adama wind farm in Ethiopia. While relentlessly promoting industrialization in the country, Ethiopian policymakers highlight the importance of utilizing renewable energy to protect the environment.[3] China has been the leader for the world's wind power industry since 2009. Financed through two concessional export credit lines of more than US$450 million in total from China Exim Bank, a consortium of Hydro China and CGCOC installed 136 gigantic wind turbines with overall capacity of 204 megawatts in Adama region between 2011 and2017, making it the largest wind farm in sub-Saharan Africa to date. The geographic location of the wind farm is perfect. Perennial strong air flows passing the Great Rift Valley keep the turbines rotating at their full capacity most of the time. However, the cost per kilowatt-hour electricity generated by the

[1] Chen Huanbo, country manager, China Jiangxi International Economic and Technical Cooperation Co., Kampala, September 2019.

[2] Yu Qianming, country representative, Zhongmei Engineering Group, Kampala, Uganda, September 2019. Jamil Wesigomwe, chief engineer, Ministry of Environment and Water, Uganda, October 2019.

[3] National Planning Commission, Growth and Transformation Plan II (GTP II), May, 2016, Addis Ababa.

wind farm, which is owned and operated by Ethiopian Electric Power Corporation, is still higher than the market price for electricity in Ethiopia, which relies on cheap hydropower. Correspondingly, the Ethiopian government offers subsidies to compensate the excessive costs of wind energy. An engineer from Hydro China had the impression that Ethiopians are truly enthusiastic about the concept of green energy and not much concerned about economic calculation.[4] In 2017 China Exim Bank signed another agreement of US$257 million to finance phase I of Ayisha wind farm in eastern Ethiopia.

However, China in the meantime invests heavily in conventional sources of energy in African countries, which attract many controversies. International Energy Agency (IEA) reported that 27 percent of coal-fired power plants and 58 percent of hydropower dams built in sub-Saharan Africa between 2010 and 2015 were constructed by Chinese enterprises, mostly with Chinese financing.[5] The mixture of these assumed "green" and "not-so-green" practices confuses some international observers, who criticize China for being inconsistent in promoting climate cooperation and environmental preservation.[6] Liu Shiyu, a director at China Electric Power Design Institute, pointed out that coal-fired power should not be simply equated with carbon pollution. In his view, electricity supply through advanced power plants can replace traditional manners of burning coal and wood in developing countries so that pollution actually decreases. Wind and solar power, being too dependent on weather conditions, cannot on its own guarantee stable large amounts of supply for industries and urban area. Especially in developing countries where demand growth is hard to predict and national grid lacks capacity of coordination and adjustment, coal power and hydropower are still the most reliable options and often the least costly ones as well. As long as the amount of carbon emission stays in line with national and international requirements, Liu believes that more coal power plants should be built and should not be demonized.[7]

4 Liu, Engineer, Hydro China, Adama, Ethiopia, May 2018.

5 International Energy Agency, *Boosting the Power Sector in Sub-Saharan Africa: China's Involvement* (Paris: International Energy Agency, 2016).

6 Lili Pike, "Are China's Energy Investments in Africa Green Enough?", *China Dialogue*, September 3, 2018. www.chinadialogue.net/en/energy/10799-are-china-s-energy-investments-in-africa-green-enough/ (accessed July 18, 2020).

7 "煤电'十四五'命途", 环保网, November 12, 2019. https://ecep.ofweek.com/2019–11/ART-93008–8110-30416874.html (accessed July 18, 2020).

Similar controversies can also be found about the environmental issues of China-African engagements in general. As the bilateral cooperation is dedicated to promote industrialization and economic development, policymakers, members of civil society, and ordinary citizens are wondering how it may impact the continent's environment. Africa is well known for its pristine forest and savanna, for the natural life still relatively untouched by industrialization, and for the unique but fragile ecosystems facing serious challenges from global climate change. When a large number of Chinese enterprises enter the continent to conduct construction, manufacturing and other operations on a grand scale, they are bound to greatly alter the landscape. Unfortunately, Chinese enterprises do not have a particularly good reputation for environmental practices in Africa. They are often accused of engaging in reckless commercial exploitation without sufficiently considering the social-environmental consequences. For instance, in 2006, the major Chinese state-owned oil conglomerate Sinopec was accused of illegally prospecting for oil in Gabon's Lonango National Park. It was said that the company carved roads through the forest, dynamited areas of the park, and caused mass pollution.[8] In June 2013, Ghanaian authorities arrested more than 100 foreign gold miners, most of whom were Chinese. These Chinese businessmen not only illegally invested in small-scale mining, but also polluted lakes and rivers with their poor operational practices.[9] In August 2013, the Chadian government suspended another Chinese oil giant China National Petroleum Corporation (CNPC)'s license for oil exploration in the country. In the firm's operational area, large quantities of oil spill were reportedly discovered.[10]

[8] Ian Taylor, China's Environmental Footprint in Africa, *China Dialogue*, February 7, 2007.

[9] 124 Chinese Citizens Arrested in Ghana, Police Urge Villagers to Ransack Chinese (*124 ming zhongguo gongmin jiana beibu, junjing songyong cunmin xijie huaren* 124名中国公民加纳被捕军警怂恿村民洗劫华人), *Tencent*, June 6, 2013. news.qq.com/a/20130606/000651.htm (accessed July 18, 2020); Ghana Deports Thousands in Crackdown on Illegal Chinese Goldminers, *The Guardian*, July 15, 2013. www.theguardian.com/world/2013/jul/15/ghana-deports-chinese-goldminers (accessed July 18, 2020).

[10] Chad Suspends China Petroleum Oil Exploration Activities, Claiming Violation to Environmental Regulations (*Zhade zanting zhongshiyou kaicaihuodong, chengqi weifan huanjing fagui*乍得暂停中石油开采活动 称其违反环境法规), *Global Times*, August 15, 2013. https://world.huanqiu.com/article/9CaKrnJBNSu (accessed July 18, 2020); Natasha Howitt, Chad Suspends CNPC's Oil

Research literature presents more comprehensive and multilayered pictures. Ian Taylor argued that China's environmental concerns at home had driven its firms to go to Africa for resources, likely leading to exploitation of Africa's environment.[11] Michelle Chan-Fishel, Marcel Kitissou and Tina Butler pointed out that China's mineral and timber operations in Africa did not have good environmental records, but they also argued that Chinese firms' track records were not markedly different from those of other nationalities.[12] Oliver Hensengerth studied the construction of Bui dam in Ghana by Sinohydro. He argued that even if their environmental practices were not stellar, the Chinese company appeared to abide by local laws.[13] At the policy level, Peter Bosshard claimed that strengthening the regulation of socioenvironmental impacts of overseas Chinese investments would serve China's own interest, but the regulatory framework was still too simple and weak.[14] Daniel Compagnon and Audrey Alejandro saw promising progress in China's externally oriented environmental policy, but noted that the real effects of these policy changes on outbound investments have not been sufficiently examined.[15]

This chapter aims to analyze the diverse practices of Chinese government and enterprises in Africa in regard to environmental and social

Operations After Oil Spill, August 22, 2013. www.chinadialogue.net/en/energy/6315-chad-suspends-cnpc-s-oil-operations-after-oil-spill/ (accessed July 18, 2020).

[11] Ian Taylor, China's Environmental Footprint in Africa, *China Dialogue*, February 7, 2007. https://chinadialogue.net/en/energy/741-china-s-environmental-footprint-in-africa/ (accessed July 18, 2020).

[12] Marcel Kitissou and Tina Butler, Growing Pains and Growing Alliances: China, Timber and Africa, in Marcel Kitissou, ed., *Africa in China's Global Strategy* (London: Adonis & Abbey, 2007); Michelle Chan-Fishel, Environmental Impact: More of the Same, in Firoze Manji and Stephen Marks, eds., *African Perspectives on China in Africa* (N.p.: Fahamu/Pambazuka News, 2007), pp. 139–152.

[13] Oliver Hensengerth, Interaction of Chinese Institutions with Host Governments in Dam Construction: The Bui Dam in Ghana, German Development Institute, March 2011. www.die-gdi.de/uploads/media/DP_3.2001.pdf (accessed July 18, 2020).

[14] Peter Bosshard, China's Environmental Footprint in Africa, SA Institute of International Affairs, China in Africa Policy Briefing, No. 3, April 2008. https://saiia.org.za/wp-content/uploads/2008/04/chap_brf_03_bosshard_200804.pdf (accessed July 18, 2020).

[15] Daniel Compagnon and Audrey Alejandro, China's External Environmental Policy: Understanding China's Environmental Impact in Africa and How It Is Addressed, *Environmental Practice* (2013) 15.3. 220–227.

preservation. Socio-environmental sustainability has increasingly become an essential part of sustainable development today, as economic growth without addressing environmental constraints and social challenges cannot sustain. Accordingly, my research tries to understand the socio-environmental issues in China-Africa cooperation in light of the general goal to promote sustainable productivity growth. I argue that the puzzling blend of various kinds of behaviors indeed are consistent with the spirit of coevolutionary pragmatism. Being convinced that industrialization inevitably alters original societal structure and natural environment, China does not insist on intact socioenvironmental preservation in developing countries but strive to balance economic growth and socioeconomic transformation under concrete circumstances in order to sustain development.

In the following, I will first investigate socioenvironmental practices of various types of Chinese enterprises in different sectors, followed by a review of related government policies and legal framework. I will then depict how Chinese business associations and banks provide pragmatic assistance to promote corporate social responsibility among Chinese investors overseas. Section 8.4 examines diverging viewpoints on the relationship between economic development and the environment, and sheds light on how Chinese evaluate socioenvironmental impacts of industrial projects in Africa.

8.2 Chinese Enterprises' Environmental Footprint in Africa

As thousands of Chinese enterprises operate in diverse ways across the African continent, environmental practices may vary greatly according to different countries' regulations, the size of investments, ownership, and industrial sectors. Each of Africa's fifty-four countries and multiple regional groupings has its own environmental regulations, which shape diverse entrepreneurial behaviors. To situate the discussion of environmental practices within a context of structural transformation, I will look at company characteristics by ownership and by sector, as the former is useful for understanding entrepreneurial decision-making, and the latter reflects the differences in business and regulatory forces of various industries.

Ownership and size of investment make a big difference when it comes to compliance with environmental standards and willingness to invest in proactive socioenvironmental preservation. Generally speaking, a divide can be seen between large state-owned enterprises (SOEs) and small private businesses. The larger companies (with capital of more than US$10 million), most of which are SOEs, pay more attention to socioenvironmental issues, whereas smaller private business often evade government control and sometimes unscrupulously pursue short-term profits at the cost of environmental and social goods. As an official in the Chinese Ministry of Environmental Protection (MEP) said,

> Large state-owned enterprises are doing fine with Corporate Social Responsibility (CSR). They have the capacity and awareness to do it. The small private companies are more problematic, especially the mining and timber traders. They cause damage to Africa's environment and are very difficult to manage.[16]

There are several reasons for this gap. First, large companies usually have long-term investment goals. Hence, they have a stake in creating a friendly investment environment in the host country. Private businesses, by contrast, maybe focused only on the short term. Many smaller companies are run by founder-owners, entrepreneurs who aim to eventually return to China to retire rather than building businesses in Africa in perpetuity. Hence, they are more likely to simply move to another country if business prospects sour due to environmental or social damage. Second, large companies are often scrutinized more closely by the authorities and by the public. Thus, quite a few of them have dedicated departments and more sophisticated attitudes, as well as resources to implement internal controls related to socioenvironmental issues. In contrast, smaller private companies are more inclined to solve problems that arise in an ad hoc manner, or "under the table." Last but not least, Chinese embassies and government commercial offices located in African countries regularly contact and visit larger companies, but they have no capacity to track smaller companies, except in crisis situations.

Nonetheless, large SOEs are better only in a relative sense. Negative reports of these firms' practices, such as the earlier mentioned stories about Sinopec, are not uncommon in African media. It is important to note that large SOEs make up 38 percent of the investments registered

[16] Interview with an official of the Chinese Ministry of Environmental Protection, Beijing, September 2014.

in the Chinese Ministry of Commerce (MOFCOM) database. Of these, roughly half are central government-owned enterprises, and half are provincial government-owned, which are on average smaller than the central SOEs. However, a number of Chinese overseas investments, particularly small private firms, do not register with MOFCOM, so the real proportion of purely private Chinese investment is likely to be much greater than 60 percent. Even so, the scale of SOEs' operations in Africa dwarf that of typical private investors; hence, their environmental impact may in fact be just as or even more consequential.

Another reason for the diversity of environmental impact is the industrial sector in which a firm operates. I have chosen four sectors – manufacturing, mining, construction, and agriculture – for in-depth analysis here. In the first place, Chinese investments are concentrated in these sectors. According to the MOFCOM database for outward FDI registration, as of January 2015, 46.5 percent of Chinese investments in Africa were reported to be in manufacturing, 44.5 percent in mining, 24.2 percent in construction, and 7.7 percent in agriculture.[17] Another reason is that these sectors are particularly significant for environmental concerns. Meanwhile, developments in the manufacturing and construction sectors are key drivers for structural transformation. Agriculture and mining are vital to many African countries' economies as well.

8.2.1 Manufacturing

As noted in Chapter 5, Chinese enterprises are active in a wide range of manufacturing sectors in Africa, processing raw materials, plastics, clothing, furniture, and food. Their environmental practices vary largely according to their products and business models. Some of these firms serve domestic African markets, especially in populous countries like Nigeria. Others set up factories in Africa to supply manufactured products such as clothing and footwear to European and American clients such as Levi's, Gucci, or Nike. This trend was accelerated in the wake of the African Growth and Opportunity Act (AGOA), which provides tariff-free access to the US market for certain African countries. Such firms must abide not only by the regulations of African countries, but also by the Corporate Social Responsibility (CSR) standards of their Western clients. During recent years,

[17] MOFCOM database for outward FDI registration, January 2015.

European and American firms have significantly raised the bar on environmental and social compliance for their business operations, as well as for those of their suppliers. In the face of increasing pressure from public opinion and civil society in Europe and the United States, suppliers must provide proof that they have not used chemicals or processes that are hazardous to the environment, while they are also subject to regular inspections. These additional CSR requirements supplement African governments' local administration to contain the environmental impact of industrialization within a limit that is socially acceptable.

In cases in which Chinese manufacturers are not subject to outside customer pressures and are monitored by African authorities alone, the situation is often more challenging. One problem is that African countries have different regulatory systems than those in China, and some Chinese firms are unaccustomed to such systems. For instance, a Chinese factory owner in Botswana complained that he had to hire a third-party consulting firm to complete a required environmental inspection report. He perceived this to be an additional cost burden for him because in China, the inspection would be done by the officials themselves.[18] Lack of applicable standards is another common problem. A Chinese sisal farm in Tanzania said that wastewater from sisal processing has a high concentration of organic materials. The discharge of wastewater was regulated in China and other countries, but Tanzania did not have any requirements for it yet. Consequently, sisal farms in Tanzania did not follow any common strict standard for treating waste water.[19] This is understandable from the perspective of an enterprise, as every competitor in Tanzania does what it can to lower costs, but unregulated practices may eventually harm waters in surrounding areas. As more Chinese firms enter Africa's underdeveloped manufacturing sectors, they often bring machines, technologies, and production processes that are new to African markets. Local authorities face serious capacity constraints in regulating these newcomers appropriately.

It is notable that quite a few newly arrived Chinese manufacturers work in sectors that tend to cause more pollution, such as small-scale steel production and leather processing. As Chinese social awareness of the need for environmental protection has risen steadily alongside the

[18] Interview with Chinese factory owner, Gaborone, August 2013.
[19] Interview with manager of Chinese Sisal Farm, Dar es Salaam, August 2014.

tightening of environmental regulations in China, factories that generate waste and hazardous materials need to spend increasing amounts of money on waste treatment. These factors push factory owners to relocate the polluting parts of their businesses to regions with lower production costs and less public resistance. Seeing that some African jurisdictions have relatively lower requirements for waste treatment, some Chinese factories have shifted their production bases to Africa. Among these are factories for the processing of raw animal hides, manufacturing of non-biodegradable plastic bags and steel production using relatively older, more polluting technology. Trading environment costs for production costs is a common practice in the history of development. China, Japan, the United States, and other countries all underwent periods of rapid industrialization alongside environmental deterioration.

Yet, Chinese investments in the polluting sectors have silver linings. Compared with indigenous firms, Chinese investors often have higher awareness of environmental protection due to their experience within China. For instance, a manager in Ethiopia's Eastern Industrial Zone recalled that local authorities did not care about wastewater discharge, telling the zone to simply "discharge the water outside." The zone developer, however, knew the importance of environment protection from China's lessons and built a wastewater treatment plant anyway. Local officials did not attach importance to the treatment of wastewater until seven or eight years later.[20] A study on the tanneries in Ethiopia proves that two Chinese tanneries had relatively better environmental practices vis-à-vis local tanneries and an Indian firm in Ethiopia, albeit their discharges exceed most of the limit values set by Ethiopian authorities too.[21]

8.2.2 Extractives

More than other industries, Chinese extractives make up a bifurcated bunch. On one end of the spectrum, large state-owned oil companies, such as Sinopec, have well-staffed, dedicated CSR departments and issue annual reports on sustainability. On the other end of the spectrum,

20 Jiao Yongshun, deputy director of Eastern Industrial Zone Management Committee, August 2017.

21 Birhanu Hayelom Abrha, Physico-Chemical Analysis of Effluents from Tannery Industry in Ethiopia, *International Journal of Scientific & Engineering Research* (January 2017) 8.1, 1101.

small, fly-by-night mining companies regularly flout local regulations and engage in environmentally and socially destructive practices.

Small-scale private Chinese mining companies have caused serious environmental damage in several countries. In Ghana, hundreds of illegal Chinese gold miners along with miners of other nationalities were arrested in June 2013. These small-scale miners were accused of water and soil pollution. A large number of small-scale Chinese miners have also operated in the Lubumbashi area of the DRC. The administration in this region is apparently weak, and environmental damage caused by mining activities is reportedly significant.[22] Larger-scale firms do have better environmental practices, but they are still involved in accidents and violations. Because of their larger size, these incidents may cause greater damage and attract more public attention.

Although almost half of Chinese investments registered with MOFCOM claimed that they were involved in the extractives business, the reality of mining investments looks quite different. Most Chinese investments in the extractives sector are only at the prospecting or exploration stages. As rights to most large proven oil and gas reserves were scooped by Western companies in the 1960s and 1970s, Chinese companies do not have control over many operative oil fields or mines in Africa. Using Tanzania as an example, MOFCOM data show that nineteen firms are registered for mining in the country. However, during field visits conducted in August 2014, I found that on the ground, none of these companies were really operating any mines. Only one firm was preparing to open a coal mine, and others were merely prospecting or trading minerals. There are exceptions: Chinese firms own large mines in Zambia and the DRC. Similarly, China imports large volumes of oil from Africa, but Chinese firms do not have shares or operatorships in many oil fields because of technological constraints and their late entry into the market. For example, although exports to China accounted for 47.99 percent of Angola's total oil production in 2014, Sinopec was the sole investor from mainland China in Angola's oil sector and held shares in merely four blocks out of thirty-four in total. Moreover, it did not have an operatorship of any of these blocks. The major foreign shareholders and operators in Angola's oil blocks are European and US giants such as BP, Chevron,

[22] Chinese Mining Operations in Katanga Democratic Republic of the Congo, RAID, September 2009.

and Total.[23] Therefore, with some exceptions, the impact of Chinese investments on Africa's environment in relation to extractive sectors is likely still limited.

8.2.3 *Construction*

Chinese construction companies in Africa generally follow local regulations and conduct social and environmental evaluations (SEAs) before beginning projects. Usually, a Chinese investor commissions an institute in China to design the project and draft the SEA, then submits it for approval to African authorities. Large investors generally follow this practice in African countries, but in several cases, Chinese institutes did not know the specifics of Africa's environment and simply copied the Chinese model in their project design. For example, the original designer of Zambia Lusaka Multi-facility Economic Zone and Angola Kilamba New City, both developed by Chinese companies, had never been to Africa when he conceived both projects. Had the developers not later revised their design in light of foreseen difficulties with implementation, these unrealistic plans would have generated significant unexpected environmental consequences.

The standard process described in the foregoing is also vulnerable to unlawful behavior on the African side. Local environmental officials are responsible for evaluation and approval, and some Chinese managers have the impression that these officials are more interested in asking for money than seriously evaluating the plan. My interviewees reported cases in which African government officials gave them the impression that environmental considerations are a mere formality as long as a sufficient bribe is provided. Consequently, some firms would rather pay bribes to get through the approval process instead of spending on real environmental assessment and protection.

8.2.4 *Agriculture*

We have seen in Chapter 4 that the number and size of Chinese agricultural investments in Africa are quite limited. Nonetheless,

[23] Tang Xiaoyang, Models of Chinese Engagement in Africa's Extractive Sectors and Their Implications, *Environment: Science and Policy for Sustainable Development* (March 2014) 56.2, 27.

Chinese farmers' views and behaviors reflect their understanding of the relationship between environment and development.

On the positive side, many Chinese farmers in Africa appreciate the continent's relatively unspoiled natural environment, and, drawing lessons from China's history of environmental deterioration, actively take measures to preserve the ecosystem. For example, Wanbao rice farm in Mozambique does not use machines to repel birds like local farmers do. In Wanbao's opinion, local farmers repel birds because they believe birds eat a large portion of their grains. However, Wanbao is able to achieve better yields through advanced technology and management. Consequently, the volume of crops that birds consume is relatively insignificant. Seventy percent of what birds eat are pests, so they actually benefit farming activity. Moreover, Wanbao does not use pesticides and instead uses herbicides and a small amount of urea as fertilizer. As the manager said, "In China, the use of pesticides created a vicious cycle. Pesticides killed both insects and the insects' predators, namely birds. The reduction of the bird population caused an increase in pests, making farmers more reliant on pesticides."[24] Learning from this lesson, Wanbao attaches great importance to maintaining the existing ecological system. Here, we can see how voluntary action by firms is driven by self-interest, as firms recognize that investment in environmental protection today will mitigate costs in the future.

On a more problematic note, illegal logging and timber smuggling by Chinese firms constitute a serious threat to Africa's ecosystem. In response to these concerns, in 2009, the Chinese State Forestry Administration (SFA) and the Chinese Ministry of Commerce jointly issued "Guidelines on Sustainable Overseas Forests Management and Utilization by Chinese Enterprises." Chinese officials mainly blame private businessmen for these unlawful activities. Their suspicions have been confirmed by a report from the Center for International Forest Research (CIFOR), which has tracked this issue in detail.[25]

Overall, we can see that the extent of Chinese firms' impact on the environment varies widely by ownership and by sector. At the firm level, decision-making with regards to the environment is driven by

24 Interview with manager of Wanbao rice farm, Xai-Xai, Mozambique, August 2014.

25 The Africa-China timber trade, CIFOR, Brief No. 28, March 2014. www.cifor.org/publications/pdf_files/infobrief/4518-brief.pdf?_ga=1.149960179.475458375.142022011 (accessed July 18, 2020).

several factors, including business logic (e.g., farms preserving the environment in order to save fertilizer costs), customer preferences (e.g., manufacturers fulfilling the CSR requirements of their buyers), managers' abilities and expectations (e.g., the ability to conduct required assessments in-house), and the microdynamics of interaction with local African government officials (e.g., construction firms encountering local officials asking for bribes).

8.3 Regulatory Efforts from the Chinese Side

Chinese enterprises in Africa are first and foremost subject to regulation by local authorities. From environmental impact assessment to regular environmental inspections, each African country's legislation and administration has set up regulatory frameworks that all investors, whether from China or elsewhere, must follow. Traditionally, China has been a strong advocate of the principle of judicial sovereignty, the notion that outsiders should not interfere in African authorities' regulation of enterprises within their own countries. In line with its famous foreign policy principle of "noninterference," the Chinese government has long stressed that Chinese investors overseas should fully abide by local regulations.

However, the rapid increase of Chinese investments in Africa and the accompanying controversies about Chinese enterprises' environmental practices have brought growing pressure on the Chinese government to regulate. Reported incidents such as illegal Chinese gold mining in Ghana or the oil spill in Chad tarnished China's international image. A survey by the Ethics Institute of South Africa 2014 showed that citizens of multiple African countries have negative perceptions about Chinese companies. In all aspects, from product quality to employment practice to social responsibility and economic responsibility, respondents with negative views of Chinese companies outnumbered those who held positive views. In particular, the environmental responsibility of Chinese firms was viewed critically: 66 percent of interviewees made negative comments, and only 12 percent had positive comments.[26] Ballooning complaints among African publics and international society must have attracted the Chinese government's attention. Whether out

[26] Africans' Perception of Chinese Business in Africa: A Survey, Ethics Institute of South Africa, 2014.

of concern for its reputation or with an aim toward securing friendly relationships with African nations, the Chinese government has recently taken a series of steps to more actively address problems with the socioenvironmental practices of Chinese enterprises in Africa.

At the end of 2007, the State-owned Assets Supervision and Administration Commission of the State Council (SASAC), the Chinese government agency that owns and regulates central government-owned enterprises, promulgated "Guidelines to the State-Owned Enterprises Directly under the Central Government on Fulfilling Corporate Social Responsibilities." The document emphasizes the importance of corporate social responsibility for Chinese SOEs and asks them to take measures to "[c]onstantly improve [their] ability to make sustainable profits." It defines social responsibility broadly as product safety, resource conservation, technological innovation, employee rights, and public welfare. SOEs are asked to establish a communication mechanism to disclose CSR activities and engage stakeholders.

In March 2009, MOFCOM and the State Forestry Administration jointly published the "Guide to Sustainable Overseas Forests Management and Utilization by Chinese Enterprises." In February 2013, MOFCOM and MEP also jointly published the "Environmental Protection Guide for Outbound Investment and Cooperation." These documents require Chinese enterprises not only to abide by forestry and environmental protection laws of the country in which they are doing business, but also to conduct environmental assessments and create an environmental management plan. It also encourages Chinese enterprises to engage in green procurement, recycling, and local community activities.

In addition, Chinese business associations of various sectors have issued or are working on CSR guidelines for outbound investments in their sectors. In September 2012, China International Contractors Association released the "Guide to Social Responsibility for Chinese International Contractors" to "establish a benchmark of social responsibility" for construction firms and to encourage them to operate overseas contracting projects in a more responsible way. Regarding environmental protection, the guide gives instructions on four aspects, including environmental management, resource saving, waste and emissions reduction, and ecological protection. In October 2014, the Chinese Chamber of Commerce of Metals, Minerals & Chemicals

Importers and Exporters issued "Guidelines for Social Responsibility in Outbound Mining Investments." It acknowledges that mining may have a significant impact on the environment and requires that Chinese firms develop appropriate plans and conduct regular assessments. In May 2017 a more encompassing "Guidance on Promoting Green Belt and Road" was issued jointly by the National Development and Reform Commission, Ministry of Foreign Affairs, MEP and MOFCOM, highlighting the importance of "ecological civilization and green development" and calling on enterprises to "promote environmental infrastructure construction" as well as "observe ... environmental protection laws, regulations and standards."

Although these documents cover a wide range of CSR topics, it is important to note that these Chinese texts are "Guides" or "Guidelines" rather than laws and regulations. Therefore, they function more as suggestions and lack the binding force that laws have. In their language, these guidelines rarely employ the imperative "shall" and instead often use the term "encourage" with respect to social and environmental protection actions. All the guidelines emphasize that Chinese businesses should respect and abide by local laws in the country of investment. Consequently, they are written rather in general terms, with no specification for types or risk levels of investments. They suppose that companies should find specific regulations in their host countries and decide their behaviors correspondingly.

Yet, this general orientation has proven problematic in the African context. As noted earlier, African countries' environmental regulations are not always well established. Some foreign investors can make use of loopholes in legislation and administration to lower environmental treatment standards "legally." Under such circumstances, the principle of abiding by local regulations may sound like empty words. Furthermore, Chinese firms tend to have limited knowledge of local laws. As a Chinese lawyer in Ghana said, "Chinese companies are not used to looking into laws for standards of behavior. They believe that money is the lubricant which can get everything done."[27] To some extent, this is a continuation of normal private sector behavior in China, where connections with officials are often more important than laws. In the lawyer's opinion, Chinese managers merely knew the regulations vaguely, and few of them had precise understanding

[27] Interview with Chinese lawyer, Accra, Ghana, July 2014.

of the legal system and requirements. This entrepreneurial culture of listening to money rather than laws is an impediment to Chinese investors' careful study and obedience of local regulations.

In spite of the practical difficulty of applying these guidelines to Africa's reality, the promulgation of the guidelines did demonstrate proactive attitudes regarding socioenvironmental issues on the part of the Chinese government and industry. Not only do all the guidelines mention environmental responsibility, but as we described earlier, two major documents are dedicated to environmental protection. As Ciprian Radavoi and Bian Yongmin have observed, the Chinese government is inclined to detach environmental issues from those of workers' or human rights, because transnational regulation of environmental practices is less controversial politically and perceived to be more feasible to implement.[28] The release of six guidelines within ten years was a promising start for China to regulate its extraterritorial corporations. However, the challenges of implementation show that mere guidelines released by the Chinese government are not sufficient. More actions and more stakeholders ought to be included to make effective changes in practice.

In fact, apart from the government, Chinese banks have played and are playing an important role in influencing companies' overseas behaviors. Many Chinese banks now have clear guidance regarding social and environment assessment when they give loans. China Exim Bank and China Development Bank, the two most important Chinese lenders to Africa-destined projects, requires all project developers to complete a social and environmental assessment before they approve any loan. China Exim Bank also hires third-party consultants, often Western companies, to evaluate social and environmental impacts prior to loan approval.[29] China Exim Bank, China Development Bank, China Industrial and Commercial Bank, and Bank of China have adopted the "Equator Principles" on green credit policies, vetoing projects that do not pass environmental

[28] Ciprian N. Radavoi and Yongmin Bian, Enhancing the Accountability of Transnational Corporations: The Case for "Decoupling" Environmental Issues, *Environmental Law Review* (2014) 16, 168–182.

[29] Guiding Opinions on Environmental and Social Evaluation of China Exim Bank's Loan Project (Zhongguo jinchukou yinhang daikuanxiangmu huanjing yu shehuipingjia de zhidaoyijian中国进出口银行贷款项目环境与社会评价的指导意见).

assessments. In 2008, China Exim Bank suspended funding of an iron mining and infrastructure construction project in the Belinga region of Gabon. According to the Gabonese government, China Exim Bank required the constructor of the project, a Chinese state-owned company, to conduct an Environmental Impact Assessment (EIA) following international standards after it received a protest letter from a local nongovernmental organization (NGO).[30] This case shows how banks can be effective in overseeing and monitoring the overseas behaviors of Chinese firms. Consistent with the increasing policy emphasis of environmental consideration, the Green Finance Committee of China Society for Finance and Banking announced "Green Investment Principles for the Belt and Road" jointly with a few international financial institutions in November 2018. These nonbinding principles encourage public and commercial banks to invest in green investments. The document was signed by some thirty organizations, including major Chinese banks and China International Contractors Association, during the Second BRI Forum in Beijing April 2019.

Certification by international standards also contributes to improved environmental practices. More than a hundred thousand Chinese enterprises have obtained ISO 14001 certification, which reflects implementation of an effective environmental management system.[31] This signals that these Chinese companies fulfill international environmental best practices and pay attention to environmental conservation even in their overseas operations. In the words of a former executive of a Chinese SOE, Chinese firms no longer differ fundamentally from Western companies when it comes to recognition of international criteria for environmental sustainability. Currently, the main problem lies in implementation and practice.[32]

30 Oxfam Hong Kong, Understanding China's Overseas Foreign Direct Investment: A Mapping of Chinese Laws and Stakeholders, 2012, p. 32. www.oxfam.org.hk/en/what-we-do-category/advocacy-and-campaign/china-and-the-developing-world/publications/understanding-china-s-overseas-foreign-direct-investment-a-mapping-of-chinese-laws-and-stakeholders (accessed July 18, 2020).

31 Arthur Mol, Environmental Governance Through Information: China and Vietnam, *Singapore Journal of Tropical Geography* (2009) 30.1, 114–129 (p. 121).

32 Arthur Mol, China's Ascent and Africa's Environment, *Global Environmental Change* (2011) 21, 785–794 (p. 791).

8.4 Dilemma Between Environmental Responsibility and Development Responsibility

Despite the recent movement toward convergence with international norms, China still has fundamental differences in how it views environmental issues. This core philosophical position drives part of the reason for environmental disputes about Chinese investments in Africa. These disputes ought to be separated from noncompliance with environmental regulation, for they do not stem out of an agreed criterion, but rather touch on principles that remain controversial.

Many of the controversies concentrate on infrastructure construction. Chinese firms are frequently criticized for helping African countries build dams and highways that may greatly impact African ecosystems. Sudan's Merowe dam on the Nile River is a representative case. Sinohydro and China International Water & Electric Co. were contracted to build the dam in 2003, and China Exim Bank was the main financier for the project. The dam was put into operation in 2010. It was the longest dam in the world at the time of its construction and expected to double Sudan's power capacity once it came online. Although an environmental impact assessment had been conducted and approved by the Sudanese authorities, some international NGOs and institutions, including the United Nations Environmental Program, insisted that the environmental impact assessment was substandard and did not sufficiently consider downstream impacts.[33] Moreover, the Sudanese government's violent resettlement of inhabitants from the dam site attracted local and international attention. In this context, several organizations accused Chinese enterprises of ignoring the socioenvironmental consequences of the project.

Interestingly, the Chinese government and the firms involved also laid emphasis on environmental preservation in their response to this criticism, though with a different emphasis. While international civil society highlighted potential detriments to the environment, and the forced relocation of residents, a spokeswoman for the Chinese Ministry of Foreign Affairs made it clear,

[33] EAWAG, Independent Review of the Environmental Impact Assessment for the Merowe Dam Project (Nile River, Sudan), March 15, 2006, pp. 5, 76; United Nations Environment Programme, Sudan Post-Conflict Environmental Assessment, 2007, p. 228.

Hydraulic and hydropower facilities are infrastructure projects which are of general interest for African countries. They are also critical for the long-term economic development of African countries. In the cooperation of this kind, China attaches great importance to local people's livelihood, to the environmental impact which may be caused by the projects. Strict environmental assessments and environmental standards are implemented. China has always required its companies to comply with local laws and regulations in the course of operation in Africa.[34]

A Chinese project manager said that Chinese contractors and the Sudanese government had made additional investments to carefully treat all possible points of waste discharge so that hazardous materials would not pollute the Nile River. He reported that construction waste, plastic waste, and organic waste were classified and handled separately. To counter criticism from environmental activists, the firms adopted high-level European standards in a country where this was far from the norm.[35]

Here we can see that the builders of the Merowe dam were just as aware of environmental protection as were those opposed to the project. However, the two groups had divergent perspectives and evaluation criteria. One party stressed the importance of the dam for the socioeconomic development of local society and on the basis of belief in the fundamental good of the project; it then tried to limit the pollution caused by construction. The other side wanted to suspend the "mega-project" completely, arguing that it would seriously impact the local ecosystem and the lives of the original inhabitants. In modern times, similar disputes about dam construction have occurred not only in Africa, but all over the world. In the early twentieth century, technological advances for constructing large hydropower plants drove a wave of enthusiasm to build mega-dams in Europe and America. Grande Dixence Dam in Switzerland, the Hoover Dam in the United States, and the Tennessee Valley Authority in the United States were all celebrated as iconic projects in a time of rapid industrialization. They

34 Ministry of Foreign Affairs Opposes Accusation That China Building Dams in Africa Will Threaten the Environment (*Waijiaobu fandui guanyu zhongfang zaifei chengjian daba weixie huanbao dezhize*外交部反对关于中方在非承建大坝威胁环保的指责), *China News Service*, May 15, 2007. http://news.sina.com.cn/c/2007-05-15/195912994680.shtml (accessed July 18, 2020).

35 World's Longest Dam Built by China Hydropower Completed (*Zhongguoshuidian chengjiande shijie zuichang shuiba quanbu jungong*中国水电承建的世界最长水坝全部竣工), China Energy News, April 19, 2010.

provided power that was badly needed, controlled floods, and facilitated irrigation. However, since the 1960s, large-scale dams have faced increasing criticism in the West. The main objections have been as follows: (1) Large construction projects alter natural water flows, affecting the life cycles of fish and other species; (2) dams may increase sediment and accelerate accumulation of toxic materials, thus degrading water quality; (3) large numbers of inhabitants need to be resettled during construction, and the social costs of this may be very high; (4) gigantic scales and complicated processes are accompanied by huge risks, and in retrospect many megaprojects have not realized the predicted benefits.[36]

Thus, in Western countries after the 1970s, construction of large hydropower plants nearly came to a halt. There, the trend shifted toward building small-scale hydraulic projects. Yet interest in mega-dams did not diminish in developing countries in Asia, Africa, and Latin America. China's Three Gorges, Brazil and Paraguay's Itaipu, Ethiopia's Tekeze, Sudan's Merowe, and the proposed Grand Inga on the Congo River all strive to be bigger and taller than what came before. New records in terms of dam size and power generation capacity have been set again and again. Environmental activist groups in the West have expressed concern and criticism toward this phenomenon, pointing out various negative effects of the dams on the environment and society. By contrast, defenders of mega-dams have claimed that large-scale infrastructure facilities are necessary for the development of poorer countries. Asit K. Biswas and Cecilia Tortajada from the Third World Centre for Water Management in Mexico wrote,

> There is no doubt that small dams and water-harvesting techniques will undoubtedly help in rural areas and smaller urban areas … . however, small water structures alone would not be able to resolve the complex water problems of urban areas and major industries where demands for water are extremely high, and are increasing, and where rainfall is scanty and erratic. Large and medium dams will be essential to continue to provide water to meet the escalating needs of a steadily urbanizing world for decades to come. People in the western world will have to realize that …… The

[36] Andrea Kraljevic, Jian-hua Meng, Patricia Schelle, Seven Sins of Dam Building, WWF International. 2013. https://wwf.panda.org/?207987/7-sins-of-dams (accessed July 18, 2020); Dams: The Advantages and Disadvantages, Environment, Health and Safety Online. www.ehso.com/ehshome/energydams.htm (accessed July 18, 2020).

situation was previously no different in their own countries, where large dams had to be built to satisfy their own water needs. Having completed the necessary construction of large dams in their own countries, they are now opposed to the construction of large dams in the developing world, where societal needs are growing exponentially.[37]

China is itself a prominent supporter of large hydropower projects. By 2017, 96 dams had been constructed or were under construction in the world whose height exceeded 200 meters, 32 of which were located in China, accounting for one third of the total number.[38] The government's strategic "Twelfth Five-Year (2011–2015) Plan" and "Thirteenth Five-Year (2016–2020) Plan" both put emphasis on large hydropower projects and further transformation of China's hydropower development. Tian Zhongxing, director of the Hydropower Administration under China's Ministry of Water Resources, acknowledged environmental risk related to hydropower plants, but took the position of "choosing the lesser of two evils."[39] This means not only that hydropower is considered less harmful to the environment in comparison to other forms of energy, but also that underdevelopment is worse than environmental change. The Chinese government views the evil of a nonzero amount of environmental degradation as an evil necessary to industrialization and modernization. Sometimes the environment may even need to be retransformed to counter changes caused by global industrialization. As an official of the National Energy Administration explained, "Because of climate change, the precipitation belt moved north … this requires construction of hydropower plants which have an adjustment function. Large and medium hydropower stations generally have such a function. Therefore, large and medium hydropower plants should be the focus of construction."[40] This points to a core dilemma of structural

37 A. Biswas and C. Tortajada, Development and Large Dams: A Global Perspective, *Water Resources Development* (2001) 17.1, 9–21 (p. 12).

38 China's 200-Meter-High Dam Densely Distributed, Safety Risks Cannot Be Underestimated (Zhongguo 200 mi jigaoba miji, anquanfengxian buke qingshi 中国200米级高坝密集, 安全风险不可轻视, November 10, 2017, *China Energy News*. www.sohu.com/a/203507979_115479 (accessed July 18, 2020).

39 China's Hydropower Development Enters the Fast Lane, with Target of 350 Million Kilowatts (*Woguo shuidian fazhan shiru kuaichedao, mubiao zhizhi 3.5 yi qianwa*我国水电发展驶入快车道, 目标直指3.5亿千瓦), *China Energy News*, September 7, 2011. www.nea.gov.cn/2011-09/07/c_131109599.htm (accessed July 18, 2020).

40 Ibid.

transformation and global modernization today. Even if underdeveloped countries do nothing, they may still suffer from the environmental impact caused by other countries' industrialization. Seen from this viewpoint, they need technology and large-scale action to balance the environmental changes already unleashed by others.

To be sure, the rapid industrial development of China and other developing countries in recent years has contributed to global climate change. However, in terms of per capita energy consumption, China and other developing countries still lag significantly behind developed Western countries. Per capita electricity consumption in China (3298 Kwh) was only a quarter of that in the United States (13,246 Kwh) in 2011, whereas electricity consumption and production for a Sudanese (143 Kwh) is less than 2 percent of that for an American.[41] In France, Germany, Canada, the United States, and other developed countries, approximately 70 percent of hydropower resources have been utilized, but in China only approximately 40 percent of hydropower potential has been developed, and in Africa, less than 14 percent of hydropower potential has been tapped (see Table 8.1). Consequently, developing countries argue that limiting hydropower exploitation will unfairly affect their development opportunities.

China's own development needs and experiences make it sympathetic to the needs of other developing countries. Consequently, megaprojects that have not received funding from Western and multilateral institutions often get approved by Chinese financers. In addition, with the competitive advantage they have gained from participation in thousands of construction projects in China over the past generation, Chinese firms have become the main contractors for dam projects in the developing world. As of November 2014, Chinese firms were involved in the construction or financing of 375 dams in 74 countries.[42]

As we have seen from the Merowe dam case, it is too simple an accusation to say that environmental issues are neglected by

[41] World Bank and CIA Fact Book 2014. I intentionally used the figures between 2008 and 2011 to support the argument. As China grows rapidly, the latest figures have already become similar to those of the industrialized countries, and therefore cannot explain China's argument ten years ago. Correspondingly, China has changed a lot of its environmental policy. However, as Africa's industrialization is still lagging behind, China's attitude toward the environment and development in Africa has not altered much.

[42] China Overseas Dams List, *International Rivers*. www.internationalrivers.org/resources/china-overseas-dams-list-3611 (accessed July 18, 2020).

Table 8.1 *Utilization of hydropower potential, 2008*

Country	Hydropower Generation (GWh/ year)	Economically Feasible Hydropower Potential (GWh/ year)	Utilization Rate (%)
USA	270,000	376,000	71.81
Germany	16,975	20,000	84.88
Canada	372,000	536,000	69.40
France	68,600	98,000	70.00
China	684,000	1,753,000	39.02
Sudan	4,333	19,000	22.81
DRC	7,303	145,000	5.04

Source: Hydropower and Dams, World Atlas, 2009

advocates for large projects. In fact, supporters of such projects demand that the development needs of poorer countries be sufficiently considered along with environmental impacts. As a South African engineer put it:

> We always forget that the Environmental Impact Assessment was originally supposed to be an environmental and social impact assessment. We've seen that the social element has largely been lost. You never hear a substantive argument about the livelihood benefits of a project, you always hear about the environmental benefits and impacts. … … And my concern is that we need to rebalance the discussion to ensure that the loud voices of environmental advocates are heard, but are balanced by equally loud advocates for social equity, which is very important as well for economic growth, which is a critical enabler of social development. And I think we've lost that.[43]

Chinese constructors in Africa represent this kind of balanced viewpoint. Placing emphasis on developmental responsibility, they believe that transformation of the natural environment is an inevitable part of the development process. It is notable that developing countries are willing to pay environmental costs not simply "in pursuit of materialism," but rather to achieve social equity, namely to reach a level of

[43] Olivia Boyd, "China brings dams back to Africa," China Dialogue, July 10, 2012. https://chinadialogue.org.cn/en/energy/5032-china-brings-dams-back-to-africa/ (accessed July 18, 2020).

development similar to that of industrialized Western countries. In fact, these countries have learned from historical experience that if they do not catch up with other countries, they will not be able to manage even their own environment due to the rapidity of global climate change–a problem that paradoxically requires resources that are obtainable only through economic development.

This dispute between development responsibility and environmental preservation may continue over the coming decades. As we can see, consensus has hardly been reached among the various positions, as they are rooted in divergent social, economic, political, and environmental needs. This is not necessarily a bad thing. While emerging countries continue to strive for their development rights, the developmental mindset also needs a balancing voice to moderate the speed and severity of environmental change. Indeed, Chinese government agencies and firms do not always stick to the doctrines of development. They have gradually, but remarkably, increased emphasis on environmental preservation in their domestic and overseas operations. Their attitudes toward socioenvironmental changes in structural transformation are consistent with their characteristic pragmatism. While steadily pursuing economic development through entrepreneurial engagements, the Chinese are open to experiment various measures to make the economic activities more sustainable. They do not view environmental preservation as opposite to industrialization, but respond to environmental challenges in the transformative practices, considering solutions as a part of the dynamic comprehensive transformation.

To summarize, as a large number of Chinese investments have arrived in Africa within a short period of time, they have greatly transformed the continent's natural and social landscape. It is true that more relaxed environmental regulations in Africa have attracted firms from more polluting sectors in China. A few unscrupulous Chinese investors also lower their environmental standards in Africa when they find loopholes in host countries' regulations. Others may cause unexpected socioenvironmental consequences because of lack of local knowledge or experience.

In this context, regulatory systems ought to be enhanced correspondingly. To be sure, improving the capacity of African authorities, which have the appropriate juridical sovereignty, is pivotal for any kind of regulatory enhancement. The environmental problems accompanying

Chinese investments reveal that African authorities have not been entirely prepared for the new trend. These problems are not completely caused by foreigners, but also by obsolete or incomplete regulations unfitting for modern industries and by the inexperience of administration vis-à-vis foreign investors. Improvement of environment-related legislation and administration in African countries will better regulate business activities and serve public interests in these countries' structural transformation.

However, efforts from the Chinese side are likewise important for influencing the behavior of China's multinational companies. To ensure healthy and sustainable collaboration with African partners, the Chinese government, banks and business associations have actually taken steps to raise the environmental awareness of their companies in Africa, provide guidance on environmental best practices, and monitor the environmental impacts of projects. Chinese efforts to improve environmental practices have to a large extent borrowed from international standards. However, in assessing potential avenues for future progress, China has a fundamentally different view on the necessity of environmental change within the process of economic development. Drawing from its own experience, China realizes that rapid industrial development must be accompanied by large-scale socio- and environmental changes. The change is in fact not a choice of one or two countries, but a necessary outcome of industrialization, which has also been seen in developed countries. Nonetheless, today, developed countries place more emphasis on environmental protection, while developing countries stress equal rights to development. The dilemma of economic development and environment in the modern world is that industry and modern society necessarily impact the environment, but in poor countries, environmental conservation also requires commanding resources that are obtained only through productivity elevation. Clearly, a balance between development and environmental preservation is required, but countries often diverge on where they believe this balance point to be. China, being a developing country itself, calls for more space for development. This position will probably remain a starting point for China's environment policy in the coming decades. So, although there has been a convergence of Chinese policy in recent years toward Western norms, the Chinese approach remains an alternative to the West. Still, it is simplistic to make blanket statements about

Chinese behaviors in general in Africa. Chinese actors have diverse environmental practices, depending on the dynamics of industry, company ownership, and country context. Guided by common pursuit of sustainable growth, these engagements converge to explore a new balance between development responsibility and social responsibility.

Conclusion

After reviewing various aspects of Chinese engagements in Africa, we have now better insights into the drive for the growing bilateral ties. I argue that, as an alternative to the Washington Consensus, coevolutionary pragmatism presents a different way of understanding and promoting development: target-oriented instead of model-oriented, nonlinear circular synergism instead of linear causal mechanism, and experiments with large varieties instead of setting universal rules. This manner of thinking goes beyond the dispute of specific political systems, economic policies, or cultural traditions to address a more fundamental drive of comprehensive transformation toward industrial market economy. However, social, political, and cultural specificities are not neglected, but are highly regarded and integrated by this thinking. Setting sustainable productivity growth as the goal, the nonlinear approach stresses working flexibly in diverse contexts and interacting with various existing institutions.

Implications of Coevolutionary Pragmatism in the China-Africa Relationship

With the concrete cases in the development of China-Africa relationship, we can observe how coevolutionary pragmatism functions. As discussed in previous chapters, the long-lasting and comprehensive growth of bilateral ties since the 1980s should be attributed mainly to the adoption of pragmatism in the collaboration. More specifically, the pragmatism of collaboration consists of three interrelated elements: (1) the unwavering target to promote sustainable economic development, (2) corresponding transformation toward market economy and industrialization, and (3) flexible approaches to coordinate multiple aspects and interact with partners during the transformation.

1. The importance of setting the goal in this coevolution process can never be overestimated, as all the scattered ad hoc experiments form a consistent transformation only through the common target. China's

market-oriented reform and the change of China-Africa relationship both started with a shift of focus from political ideology to economic and productivity growth.

The new goal has an ambivalent nature. On one hand, economic growth seems to be a universal demand in today's world, neutral of cultural, religious, or political values. On the other hand, the pursuit of sustainable productivity growth originated from the industrial capitalism. China and other developing countries chose this goal only after a century-long struggle with the Western industrial powers. The target therefore has a political implication of striving for independence and sovereignty. Paradoxically, when China accepts the values of global capitalism, its rapid development gives it the capacity to resist foreign influence. Such an experience adds a political subtext to the goal with a nonpolitical appearance. Thus, the promotion of business and modernization can sometimes be interpreted as a new approach of China's long-time policy to support movements against Western hegemony. Nonetheless, the political implication is covered and largely diluted by the economic interests, which are indispensable from global capitalism. The seemingly straightforward goal of pragmatism in the China-Africa relationship has indeed deep-rooted complexity.

2. The socioeconomic transformation that is required to achieve the goal of continuous productivity growth is even more complex. As traditional, subsistence societies evolve into industrial societies with deepening specialization, extensive division of labor, and massive market distribution, almost all social classes and every aspect of social life are greatly affected. Different stakeholders may have differing views on the benefits and losses. Communal gains may need individual sacrifice. Long-term benefits may require high costs in a short period. The transformation inevitably generates numerous controversies and disputes.

Moreover, the changes are highly interdependent. Without industries and markets in place, the society cannot develop expertise on market regulation, entrepreneurship, infrastructure management, and others. Yet, without these supporting conditions, industries and market can hardly sustain. The chicken–egg dilemmas exist in China's own reform as well as in China-Africa cooperation. The interdependent transformation also means that foreign experience or knowledge cannot be simply transplanted. Every society has its unique manner of coordination.

3. Being aware of the complexity in the structural transformation, Chinese lay emphasis on building synergism instead of using linear mechanism or fixed models. Gradualism and experimentalism allow various parties to mutually influence each other. As the book shows, no matter in trade facilitation, infrastructure construction, agricultural assistance, manufacturing investment, or cooperation zones, Chinese government and enterprises responded to challenges and criticisms in Africa swiftly and demonstrated remarkable flexibility to adjust to different environment. These pragmatic approaches conversely generate incremental impacts on the local societies, too.

Taking the China-Africa economic and trade cooperation zones as an example, the program envisioned by experts and officials in Beijing turned out to have departing growth trajectories and effects. Some zones, such as the Chambishi zone in Zambia, were able to construct largely according to the developer's plan and transform the industrial landscape in the area, whereas other zones, such as the Eastern Industrial Zone in Ethiopia, faced immense challenges to implement their original plans at the beginning. However, the Eastern Zone's experiment and interactions with the local authority gradually changed the policy there. Ethiopia's new effort for industrialization eventually helped the Eastern Zone thrive, albeit in an unexpected manner. The example demonstrates the mechanism of mutual influence: While China-funded projects impact on African countries, the demands and feedback of these countries also reshape Chinese practices. Similarly, interactive synergism can be found between Chinese actors and African workers, business partners, and communities.

Comparison with the Western Approaches

By contrast, the traditional donors and the economists in the West tend to define specific goals, such as output, income distribution, taxation, and governance, as well as the methods to achieve these goals. Yet, the assumed effects of these preset goals and methods are calculated with static models of ideal market economy, insufficiently taking diversity and change in developing countries into account. Hence, the plans often appear as imposed conditionality on the African society and the policy tools seldom function as expected. Sharing memories of struggling with poverty, Chinese actors tend to consider the Africans as team members in the common pursuit of socioeconomic development. China's experience of dynamic synergism enables them to take African initiatives as a part of the open game, in which interaction and coevolution are more important than preset plans. Echoing the metaphor in Chapter 1, Chinese practitioners feel like playing soccer with the Africans, whereas many donors and economists are thinking of constructing machines for Africa. China's stance of nonconditionality not only shows respect for Africa's sovereignty, but also suggests a different way of understanding development. In fact, China has significantly altered many practices in African governments and societies during the collaboration, sometimes through longtime discussion, sometimes through demonstration projects and more frequently through daily interactions, as illustrated in this book. Nonconditionality does not mean indifference but signifies acknowledgment of the African partners' full initiative and their capability of coevolution.

Apart from showing respect to the partners, the Chinese prefer commercial partnerships to one-dimensional aid for the purpose of ensuring the sustainability of growth. Aid programs are principally initiated by foreign actors and given to the recipients in a one-way direction. Without reciprocal rewards, the aid programs often lack a structure to secure a sustainable operation in themselves. China's aid projects in the past, as well as those of other donors, suffered a great deal from the unsustainable mechanism and have to rely on further foreign assistance. Moreover, since these projects and programs are short-term by nature, they are unable to catch up with the transformation of local society in the long run and often become alien, obsolete, and abandoned after a while. By adding commercial interests into aid projects, China-Africa economic ties have improved both sustainability and effectiveness.

Of course, coevolutionary pragmatism does not provide an omnipotent solution to all the problems of underdevelopment. Concrete challenges require specific techniques and tools. The discussion about the Chinese approach and thinking does not deny the values of the experiences and skills obtained by the Western experts. Addressing broad socioeconomic transformation, the coevolutionary pragmatism offers a holistic view of the development process instead of sticking to individual problems. Since Chinese have gone through dramatic socio-economic transformation during a relatively compact period, they are more likely to discern the connections between the numerous changes and grasp them together as a whole. Relatedly, they also tend to link different aspects of the development to tackle the chicken–egg dilemma. For instance, infrastructure construction is planned in coordination with industrial investment and special economic zones, which are further orchestrated with efforts to urbanize, to build clusters, to launch policy reform, and so on.

Indeed, Chinese actors are not as experienced in doing business in Africa or as knowledgeable of African society as many Western peers because of the relatively short history of China-African cooperation. Quite a few operations, when observed separately, may appear clumsy, but the spirit of coevolution tolerates experiments and mistakes. Initial mistakes may even become beneficial for the overall development as the mistakes call for active revision and mutual adaptation. Although there have been frequent controversies about Chinese engagements in Africa, from environmental issues and labor disputes to substandard products and debt burden, none of them stopped the growing trend of bilateral ties. Meantime, we can see from the research in this book that the Chinese reacted to the challenges by adjusting policies or enhancing communication. A swift response to challenges and capability of self-correction belong to the essence of coevolutionary pragmatism, which follows the principle of "crossing river by touching stones" and keeps moving forward through trial-and-error experiments.

Linkage to China's Own Development

In this connection, we can see that coevolutionary pragmatism is a consistent principle guiding both China's own market-oriented reform and China's engagement with Africa. The experience of transformation at home shapes the direction and manners for Chinese engagements in Africa. Chinese enterprises, when facing challenges in Africa, often refer to what happened in China before and are confident that the obstacles may eventually be overcome through transformation. While most Westerners may be frustrated by the lack of market regulation, insufficient facilities, weak supply chain, or unproductive workers, Chinese regard them rather as opportunities. China had similar problems decades ago and managed to solve them eventually. Thus, Chinese players are optimistic about repeating their success in driving development, believing that China's today can become Africa's tomorrow.

However, the optimism based on the experience does not mean that Chinese want to replicate the so-called "China model." The diverse and constantly changing experiments have already rendered it impossible for practitioners to rely on definite models within China, let alone in the different context of Africa. The borrowing of experiences does not mean simple transplantation of models but needs to be analyzed in more depth. First, China's experience provides a different angle to observe the problems in development. As noted, successful examples of transformation lead more people to think about opportunities rather than risks and become more willing to initiate ventures. Although the effect is just psychological, it is critical for solving the chicken–egg dilemmas in the structural transformation, because it can mobilize tens of thousands of Chinese businessmen to operate and invest in Africa. In an underdeveloped market, where economic inactivity coexists with deteriorating regulation, infrastructure, and industrial support as well as unfavorable sociocultural conventions, the arrival of numerous foreign enterprises may turn the trend toward a virtuous circle: growing business activities stimulate amelioration of business environment and supporting services, which in turn attract more investments.

Second, the impacts of Chinese engagements on Africa's structural transformation are closely related to China's current development stage. In comparison with advanced economies in the West, China's level of industrialization makes it more likely to collaborate with African countries. The capital-intensive business models of the developed countries consider the small African market unattractive, whereas Chinese firms can find numerous complementary needs with the African partners. African consumers welcome reasonably priced industrial products. Cost-efficient construction firms are extremely needed to build Africa's infrastructure. China can also supply all kinds of generic machinery for manufacturing investments in Africa. Conversely, Chinese manufacturers require large amounts of raw materials and resources from Africa. Africa's developing market and abundant population provide opportunities for the further expansion and relocation of China's industrial sectors too.

Third, China's development experience opens people's eyes about the possibility of different sociopolitical patterns in the modernization process, superseding the state–market dichotomy. To make business possible in not-fully-functioning market systems in China and Africa, enterprises and government have experimented with various approaches other than those used in the advanced economies, for example, state-funded financing for infrastructure or combining construction contracts with natural resource deals to reduce risks. Special economic zones are created to attract foreign direct investment and facilitate reform, too. In spite of the government's active involvement, none of these measures rejects the principle of market economy. China's experiences exactly proved that distribution and production via market mechanism can effectively elevate productivity. From the narrations in the book, we can see that almost all the Chinese stakeholders in Africa are convinced of the importance of market economy, and most of the projects strive to include market mechanism. They just have to make concrete market activities possible within Africa's diverse and challenging sociopolitical conditions. The assistance of the state, as one of the pragmatic approaches, aims to facilitate the formation of a functioning market mechanism and promote broad sustainable growth. The relationship between the state and the market is not fixed but can be flexibly adjusted according to practical needs of growth.

In summary, what effectively drives China's phenomenal growth and ever-increasing impacts on Africa is not any specific political-economic pattern, since the patterns have been constantly changing. The key to China's success is, paradoxically, the lack of a defined model, as it allows diverse practices and flexible adjustments. The pragmatism opens more possibility for developing countries to transform than the dogmatism. With the consistent goal of development, the pragmatic thinking enables multiple stakeholders to coevolve in diverse contexts through open attitude and real business. This finding also suggests that the pragmatic approach is not limited to China and Africa. Any actors in the structural transformation can think and act alike. Western societies experienced similar transforming synergism in their own history of industrialization too. Yet, people in established industrial societies may overlook the changing dynamism and fall into dogmatism of certain static models. Such mistakes are not limited to Westerners either, but can also be found among Chinese, Africans and any persons who fail to see the whole picture of gradual comprehensive transformation. In this connection, the true implication of this book is to use the ongoing China-Africa engagements to remind readers of a holistic manner of understanding and promoting development that is common to all the transforming societies, but is easily concealed by fragmented observations.

Destination of Development

Finally, the pragmatic coevolution is driven by a supposed common goal: sustainable productivity growth, which primarily refers to modernization and industrialization in the context of developing countries. However, this is by no means a self-evident choice. As noted in Chapter 1, almost all the countries in the world, except those with short histories, have experienced the shift from venerating traditional religious and ethical values to prioritizing productivity growth in the modern era. Corresponding to the value shift, the social organization and living style has dramatically metamorphosed. For most developing countries, such transition of social values and organization did not initiate from the indigenous communities but were compelled by the global trend that originated in western Europe. Industrial capitalism overwhelmed all the other sociocultural forms with its ever-increasing material power and spread the pursuit of productivity growth worldwide.

To be sure, the pursuit of modernization and industrialization has attracted numerous criticisms in almost every society. Some blame capitalism for its exclusive focus on material wealth. Others insist on preserving traditional values and reject market economy as imposed foreign culture. Apart from the value crash, people are also increasingly aware of the troubles within the modernization, from income disparity and voracious consumerism to cultural homogenization and environmental destruction. Concerned with these intrinsic problems of modernization, many critics, in Africa and outside Africa, strongly resist pursuit of industrialization in developing countries. As China and Africa vigorously promote market activities and industrialization in their collaboration, they frequently encounter vehement protests and immense obstacles. A large part of the socioenvironmental disputes or policy swings related to Chinese engagements in Africa are deeply rooted in Africans' skepticism on industrial capitalism and their confusion about the direction of development.

Chinese understand the challenges of transformation and the intrinsic flaws of modernization too well, for they just recently experienced a similar shift at home. However, in spite of the costs and agony, most Chinese, no matter practitioners or theoreticians, firmly believe that market-based industrialization is the necessary path for developing countries. The analysis in this book clearly demonstrates such general consensus among the Chinese actors. This is not a view of developmentalism, as some scholars may label it, but a conviction out of century-long real struggle. China's downfall and renaissance during the modern era have taught everybody in the country vivid lessons that resistance to the global trend only leads to underdevelopment. Sustainable productivity growth is the sole approach to escape further suffering. The pursuit of growth primarily does not look for material enjoyment but seek rational accumulation. Max Weber named the frugal life-style of capitalists "worldly asceticism."[1] Likewise, the Chinese entrepreneurs and workers in Africa are widely depicted as "hard working" and "eating bitterness." For the practitioners, modernization has never meant to be glamourous paradise, but rather a solemn mission full of rough challenges. While religious feelings may have driven early capitalists in the West, the actors in developing countries today are often motivated by the painful memory of being overwhelmed and dominated by foreign powers. Only when a society succeeds in harnessing the power of industrial capitalism through transformation can they truly get rid of the colonialism and take their destiny back into their own hands.

Therefore, the goal of economic growth in the China-Africa collaboration is actually determined by world history. It's by no means a perfect choice, but proves to be a must for all the developing countries within the current international system. The irony is that the "iron cage" of capitalism, as described by Max Weber, cannot be broken when people stand out of the cage to resist the immense power of industrialization. A country first needs to become a part of the "iron cage" and thus reinforce the cage, and then it can reflect on the practices of modernization and realize the predicament of modern society. However, it is still an open question for the whole world, developed and developing countries alike, to explore how human beings can

[1] Max Weber, *The Protestant Ethic and the Spirit of Capitalism, translated by Talcott Parsons* (London: Routledge, 2005), p. 53ff.

eventually escape the fate of "iron cage." This is a much more profound question than what is discussed in this book. Every reader ought to continue thinking about it after finishing this reading. The conclusion on approaches and impacts of modern development is opening the door for further reflection and questioning.

Index

Lightning Source UK Ltd.
Milton Keynes UK
UKHW021812100822
407098UK00020B/373